Negotiating Identities

PRINCETON STUDIES
IN CULTURAL SOCIOLOGY

──────────── EDITORS ────────────

Paul DiMaggio

Michèle Lamont

Robert Wuthnow

Viviana Zelizer

Negotiating Identities

STATES AND IMMIGRANTS
IN FRANCE AND GERMANY

Riva Kastoryano

Translated by Barbara Harshav

PRINCETON UNIVERSITY PRESS
PRINCETON AND OXFORD

Copyright © 2002 by Princeton University Press
Original title: *La France, l'Allemagne & leurs immigrés: négocier l'identité*
© Armand Colin Publisher, 1997
Published by Princeton University Press, 41 William Street,
Princeton, New Jersey 08540
In the United Kingdom: Princeton University Press,
3 Market Place, Woodstock, Oxfordshire OX20 1SY

All Rights Reserved.

Library of Congress Cataloging-in-Publication Data

Kastoryano, Riva.
    [France, l'Allemagne et leurs immigrés. English]
    Negotiating identities : states and immigrants in France
and Germany / Riva Kastoryano ; translated by Barbara
Harshav.
      p. cm. — (Princeton studies in cultural sociology)
    Includes bibliographical references (p.) and index.
    ISBN 0-691-01014-5 (alk. paper) —
    ISBN 0-691-01015-3 (pbk. : alk. paper)
    1. France—Emigration and immigration.
2. Citizenship—France. 3. Identity (Psychology)—
France. 4. Germany—Emigration and immigration.
5. Citizenship—Germany. 6. Identity (Psychology—
Germany. I. Title. II. Series.

  JV7925 .K3713 2002
  305.8'00943'09045—dc21

                        2001050011

British Library Cataloging-in-Publication Data is available

Publication of this book has been aided by the French
Ministry of Culture—Centre National du Livre

This book has been composed in Sabon

Printed on acid-free paper. ∞

www.pup.princeton.edu

Printed in the United States of America

10 9 8 7 6 5 4 3 2 1

10 9 8 7 6 5 4 3 2
(Pbk.)

ISBN-13: 978-0-691-01015-1 (pbk.)

ISBN-10: 0-691-01015-3 (pbk.)

FOR VIKTOR, MY BROTHER

Contents

Acknowledgments

This book draws from a considerable body of individual and collective research principally under the aegis of the Centre d'Études et de Recherches Internationales (CERI), at Sciences-Po, Paris. Research support in France has also come from MIRE (Mission pour la recherche expérimentale, Ministère des Affaires Sociales) for the research on *Attitudes politiques des populations de culture musulmane dans le paysage politique français* (The political attitudes of Muslims in the French political landscape); from MRT (Ministère de la Recherche et de la Technologie) for the project on *Les minorités en Europe* (Minorities in Europe); from the DPM (Direction des Populations et Migrations, Ministère des Affaires Sociales) for *Les associations islamiques en Île-de-France* (Islamic associations in Île de France); from MRT for the research on *Les réseaux de solidarité transnationales en Europe* (Networks of transnational solidarity in Europe). My research in Germany was supported by the CERI and the Franco-German Committee of the CNRS. I thank Hinnerk Bruhns, its director at that time, for his help and recommendations. In the United States I was a visiting fellow at the Center for European Studies (CES) of Harvard University, where I had extensive discussions with Nathan Glazer, Mary Waters, Peter Hall, and Ulf Hedetoft (Alborg University, Denmark), who invited me several times to Alborg to discuss the hypothesis of the book with his colleagues there.

There is not enough space here to mention all the names of friends and colleagues in France, Germany, and the United States who contributed to this work. But I would like especially to thank David Landes for his friendship and intellectual support. I am also grateful to Guy Hermet for all the work he put in the manuscript in French. I am also indebted to Pierre Hassner, Anne-Marie Le Gloannec, Pierre Rolle, Rémy Leveau, Bertrand Guillarme, and Virginie Guiraudon for their comments and to Jean Leca for stimulating discussions. Beate Collet provided linguistic help with the German documentation.

I would also like to thank the political actors involved in the issues of immigration and integration, as well as the representatives of local and national, social and Islamic associations in France and Germany who accepted me, shared their thoughts, and allowed me to participate in various meetings. I hope that the interpretations and analyses in this book do not violate their thought but rather might help advance the discussion.

After this book appeared in French, I spent three months at the Princeton Institute for Advanced Studies in the autumn of 1997. I am grateful to Joan Scott, Michael Walzer, and Clifford Geertz for providing an exceptional framework, where I was able to exchange ideas with them. Thanks are also due to friends and colleagues who organized seminars at various American universities: Laura Frader, Shannon Stimson, Aron Rodrigue, Martin Schain, and Mark Kesselman. These opportunities enabled me to discuss issues of theory and methodology with students and professors. These exchanges provided guidelines for revising certain parts of this work for the American edition.

My work also profited greatly from three months in *Wissenschaftskolleg* in Berlin in 1998. While there I updated material and exchanged ideas in conversations with several colleagues as well as in seminars that they organized for me. I would like to give special thanks to Rainer Münz, Ayse Caglar, Czarina Wilpert, Klaus Bade, and Uli Bielefeld. These exchanges provided guidelines for revising certain parts of this work for the American edition.

Last but not least, I owe a great deal to Michèle Lamont for her stimulating presence at Princeton and afterward, for her encouragement, and for her friendship. I would like to also thank Mitchell Cohen for his valuable editorial suggestions.

Introduction

THIS BOOK ADDRESSES the role of the state in constructing communities and expressing collective identities. It also examines the effect of identity demands on the states, their institutional structure, their historical representations, and their identities. Comparison between France and Germany, with important references to the United States, provides a guide for my analysis. In the three countries I looked at the modes of organization, mobilizations, and identity demands of the descendants of immigrants or minorities on the one hand, and official rhetorics, social policies, and institutional dynamics on the other. By studying these matters, this book also seeks to elucidate the status of the nation-state today: its principles and institutional structures, its capacity to adjust to new realities and new terms of citizenship.

In sum, this book explores the state's capacity to negotiate identities. The "negotiation of identities" provides a model of development common to all democratic countries no matter what their definition of the nation and their principles of citizenship. For democratic states, negotiations are a way to deal with the unexpected consequences of immigration. In Germany the guest workers (*Gastarbeiter*) are now there to stay, and they claim the right of citizenship. In France, although most of the young generation of North African origin do have French citizenship, they now also express their allegiance to a state of origin. This has led Germany to policies of integration (*Integrationspolitik*) rather than policies for foreigners (*Ausländerpolitik*). France has fashioned new targeted measures and a new vocabulary addressing integration rather than assimilation. Therefore, unlike republic, unity, and equality—the ideas that made the European nation-states and engendered the construction of national models—the general tendency now is to maintain identities by managing them: immigrants' identities and national identities. Guided by pragmatism, such an approach helps manage the contradictions between myth and reality, discourse and action, ideas and facts.[1]

The model of negotiations of identities derives from the dynamics of interaction between states and immigrants or minorities. For states, it constitutes a means—perhaps the only one—of integrating into the process of globalization by establishing itself as an actor. In fact, several works on globalization are directing attention to the crisis of the nation-state.[2] Some of them declare the end of the nation-state, others develop scenarios for the "post-nation-state."[3] All of them agree that it is obsolescent and cast doubt on the coincidence between the political structure and the community of belonging, between the state and the nation. Some works emphasize the immigrants' attachment to their home country, the increasing influence of international law, supranational institutions, regional alliances, and the global economy. All of these are beyond the control of the state. Interdependence between internal and external situations, which is now inevitable, challenges the legitimacy and sovereignty of the nation-state, as well as its unity. Its power to define a common identity, a sense of solidarity and loyalty consolidated within a single political community, is at stake. Thus the state's ability to negotiate within its boundaries can reveal that it is still pertinent as a legitimate framework of recognition and citizenship. The question arises more acutely in Europe, where the shaping of a new political space indicates that nation-states have been outmoded.[4]

FRANCE, GERMANY, AND THE UNITED STATES

In this book the analysis of negotiations of identities concerns mainly the attitude of France and Germany toward their "immigrants" or "foreigners," according to the terminology used in each country. I systematically compare them with the United States, not only for the heuristic value of the comparison but also because the United States serves as an example or counterexample to the other two countries for the management of so-called minority identities.

Comparative studies of immigration, integration, and citizenship, as well as of the concept of the nation, rest on ideal-typical dichotomies. According to these "ideal types" or "models," France is the perfect example of a nation-state that sees itself as universalist and egalitarian. The so-called French model, based on republican individualism, implies and entails the assimilation of individuals who have become citizens by choice.[5] By contrast, the United States is designated as an "antimodel," a country that recognizes cultural, ethnic, racial, religious, and sexual communities as groups acting in political life, as opposed to the French model, that is, a "nation divided into nations." In another vein, the French model is also opposed to the so-called German model—the French elective and political conception of the nation versus the primarily ethnic and cultural German attachment to common ancestors.[6] Germany, however, sees France as a republic based on principles of citizenship whose goal is to assimilate all its members above and beyond cultural or religious identity, and it regards the American model as an example of democratic arrangements in which different cultures centered on ethnic communities can organize and express themselves.

The point of departure for my work, however, is the parallel developments between the three countries and the convergences to which they lead. As a matter of fact, all three are countries of immigration, even if official discourse in Germany has denied this reality until recently. A convergence can be detected among the policies of immigration control in these three countries, especially among their policies of integration.[7] This convergence extends to laws about citizenship.[8] In fact, the two European countries are going through the same transition—from an economic and provisional immigration to one of permanent residence and the emergence of new actors (among immigrants and within the established political class) focused on these issues, which give them their political force. At the same time, France and Germany are experiencing the same difficulties as the United States: suburban ghettos (*banlieus*), ethnic enclaves, and inner-city slums—places that combine foreignness and poverty and are seen as sites of conflict between cultures, between the residents and the police, and between communities and the nation.

These parallel facts lead to a similar questioning. France, Germany, and the United States, three republics born in and of different historical contexts, have similar identity problems: of immigrants on one hand and of the nation on the other. The three societies are trying to answer the same question: how to reconcile differences that arise in society and roil its politics while maintaining and affirming the nation's integrity.[9] The political reactions show some similarities as well. All three countries rely on democracy and liberalism to develop special programs for groups that are excluded from the process of assimilation. All such programs are aimed at reducing social inequalities while bearing in mind that these social inequalities relate to cultural differences.

The three countries have also adopted the same tactics. Political action in integrating immigrants and citizenship takes the form of reactions, in which reason and passion, economic interests and national ideologies, democratic morality and the weight of traditions, are blended. All three use the same sort of discourse, the same words and concepts, which travel from one group to another, one political party to another, and one country to another. These words and concepts in the three social and political contexts are used to represent and designate the Other in the same way, thus normalizing the political debate on immigration. Left and Right use the same words but give them a different content and meaning.

NEGOTIATING IDENTITIES

The similarities among the three countries, however, do not erase national and social particularities; each case is specific. This is one of the paradoxes emphasized in this book. The states maintain national models. But these national characters take shape in distinctive ways in reaction to immigration or to the presence of immigrants.

Social reality appears in the interactions between states and immigrants. Through interactions between states and immigrants, policies are deformed in practice and the models derived from the historical sociology of each nation are applied only approximately. France oscillates between a republican ideal of national unity and a pragmatism that takes account of the political motivations of immigrant groups organized in communities. Thus, in the 1980s, "political indifference" toward identities gave way to a policy based on the "right to be different." Germany hesitates between an ethnic conception of the nation and the requirements of a democratic society and hence pays lip service to the idea of a multicultural society. Both countries echo targeted policies applied in the United States in reference to affirmative action.

Thus, relations between states and their immigrants are constantly becoming more complex and more remote from traditional national representations. Even though national models serve as a link to the past in order to justify the present and to reinforce national identity and state sovereignty, a common evolution toward a new stage in the development of nation-states appears to be emerging, the stage of *negotiation of identities*. The issue for states is negotiating the ways and means of including the descendants of immigrants into the political community. The issue for individuals or groups formed into communities is to struggle against every form of exclusion, political, economic, social, and/or cultural.

But identities are not commodities and are therefore difficult to negotiate. Abstract, fluid, and changeable, they reflect and reveal the profound emotions of individuals, peoples, and nations. They are redefined and affirmed in action and interaction and change with the cultural, social, and political environment. In fact, the concept of identity is a dynamic one. Minority groups (whether ethnic or religious) differentiate themselves from the larger society by their language, their culture, their religion, or their history. They are also defined in opposition to other immigrant groups, but above all in opposition to the national community.

Studies on the negotiations of identities refer primarily to the intercultural or intracultural negotiations of groups or minorities that share the same public space.[10] This book, however, deals with the negotiations between states and immigrants. This approach considers the nation as any community, a historical construct based on the idea of a common past and common cultural referents. Its content, called national identity, has to be redefined to take account of the expectations of social groups within the nation and in comparison with surrounding nations. And the state, from this perspective, is not seen simply as an administrative and juridical power whose role in matters of immigration is limited to the control of flows and thus to the protection of national borders. By *state*, I mean an institutional reality that, although influenced by external forces, has its own internal logic, born of history and nourished by ideology, acting directly on civil society and shaping its political life.[11]

Identities that confront each other and affirm themselves are also negotiated, especially as they are expressed in terms of interests and rights and locate themselves against the state. In France and Germany, the proliferation of immigrants' voluntary associations since the 1980s shows that North Africans in France and Turks in Germany are organized mainly around an identity or identities that take shape in their collective action in relation to their respective states. This is one of the consequences of governmental policies that increasingly intrude into the private domain and issues of identity, thus increasing the interactions and reciprocal engagements between states and immigrants in France and Germany, as in the United States, and creating at the same time a space of transaction, a "market," where groups compete for public resources in order to express their cultural and identity differences publicly.

This ethnic market is created by the state in France and Germany. It appears empirically as the logical consequence of the so-called policies of identity instituted to manage integration and leads the descendants of immigrants to form a community. Whether ethnic, religious, or interest based, a community is a form of organization structured around state-recognized associations. Such a structure allows the community to negotiate each of its elements of identity with the public authorities. For activists, guardians of a collective identity created in terms of loyalty and affective symbols in reaction to public discourses and policies, identity becomes the strategy of action, the shaping of a community, the tactic necessary to get declared particularities recognized and to negotiate them with the machinery of the state.

Relations between states, whose substance is the nation, and immigrants organized in a community are an arena where ethnic or religious communities—perceived as "dissident" communities by some elements of public opinion and politicians—compete with the national community. The emergence of these communities in modern societies clearly reveals the contradictions between the social reality and the ideology of the unified nation-state. The concept of community does indicate objective or subjective forms of belonging and the particularistic allegiance of its members. This conflicts with the modern idea of nation, which, according to Max Weber, is the only one born of modernity and has political legitimacy because it is universal. Therefore,

analyses of the shaping of immigrant communities and their politicization raise the question of loyalty: loyalty to the nation and to their
own communities.

States contribute to the formation of communities, which are imagined or shaped in relation to policy in order to gain recognition. They
also contribute to the definition of identities around which a community
might be structured. The hard core that cements a community is elabo-
rated in interaction with the state. In France, for example, mobilizing
the political community around the issue of the veil reinforced an identification with Islam on the part of the descendants of immigrants and
turned religion into a mobilizing force that lends the community its
essence by opposing *laïcité* (secularism). In Germany a national identity
that was defined in ethnic terms (including religion) contrasts with the
collective German identity, which is expressed by a belonging transmitted by one's ancestors. Reunification, the arrival of the *Aussiedler*
(immigrants of German origin), and the influx of asylum seekers in the
last few years have reinforced feelings of belonging to collective identities in German society: the natives and the foreigners. Debates on citizenship and the dual citizenship demanded by immigrants from Turkey
underline the confrontation of two identities whose ethnic boundaries
are confused with national boundaries on both sides. In reality, the
identity demands within them refer the states back to their own contradictions, which originated with the creation of nation-states and which
remain unresolved because they have been blurred ever since. These
contradictions are subject to negotiations today. Thus in France the reli-
gion/laïcité pair is at the heart of the negotiations. In Germany it is the
identity/citizenship duality that is to be negotiated. These dualities at
the basis of the definition of collective identities—both national and
communal—become the most pertinent element of negotiation for both
parties on both sides of the Rhine, for they are also affectively, symbolically, and ideologically charged and hence the hardest to surrender.

So, it is up to the states to accommodate to reality by adjusting policies, restructuring institutions, and redefining the terms of citizenship.
Negotiations of identities thus become a means of establishing a new
balance between social forces and the national interest, between emerging community institutions and public authorities, between the state
and the nation. At the same time, these negotiations appear as a way of
managing the pernicious effects of the applied policies.

THE NATION-STATE IN CRISIS

Negotiations of identities also allow states to remain a structuring force
of a collectivity, defining the limits of recognition and the terms of citi-

zenship. Relations between states and immigrants (even more generally, between states and "minorities") reveal that the reappraisal of the state does not necessarily lead to its erosion. Nation-states are obviously undergoing a reappraisal of the legitimacy of what had been their strength: a nation that is culturally and politically unified, territorially limited, and consolidated by a sovereign state both inside and outside its boundaries.[12] This political structure, invented in eighteenth-century Europe and combining culture, politics, territory, and identity in a unified project,[13] is weakened by internal and external forces. The appearance on the political scene of communities organized around a common experience of immigration or around a common language, religion, or nationality or even around the same territorial reference,[14] each demanding a recognition of declared identities, is perceived as a challenge to its unity. The extension of these identities to transnational solidarities, the political participation they imply, and the increasing influence of supranational institutions, regional alliances, and the global economy are, in fact, beyond the control of states.

Negotiations of identities leads to the reestablishment of the role of the state in the definition of a common identity of citizens and of a feeling of solidarity and loyalty consolidated around a single political community. This constitutes a way of "mending" contradictions, reinventing the bases of the social bond, guaranteeing internal peace, and avoiding violence while complying with the new democratic norms that promote differences and equality.

Such a view contradicts the hypotheses of a postnational affiliation, which rely on the adoption of international laws expressed in terms of human rights and refer to the person or the residence, and not to a legal citizenship defined by criteria established by each of the sovereign nation-states.[15] This argument derives from transnational modes of organization and participation that allow the individual, whether an immigrant or not, to get around national policies—in this case, the demands of citizenship. My research shows that, in fact, the consolidation of transnational solidarities intends to influence states from the outside. Even if, in some respects, the transnational networks contribute to the formation of "separate communities," such communities now appear as indispensable structures for negotiating with the national public authorities the recognition of collective identities constructed in frameworks that are still national. In Europe, for example, the objective of the transboundary structuring of association networks is to reinforce their representation on the European level, but its practical goal is to lead to a recognition at the national level. The militants, even those most active at the European level, represent the states as the only "adversaries" with whom they ultimately have to reckon.

CITIZENSHIP AND MULTICULTURALISM

Obviously, the representation of the nation that justifies the concept of citizenship and its bond with nationality affects the strategies and modes of participation of the politically active descendants of immigrants: a citizen voter in France, a political actor who is trying to find ways to influence political decisions in Germany. My analysis favors a definition of citizenship linked with individual or collective political commitment and participation in the public space.[16] This commitment marks the start of the exercise of citizenship itself, and even more, of the shaping of an *identity of a citizen*. It is also expressed in the cultural community and within national institutions. Multiplicity of identifications and allegiances has become a source of "suspicion" with regard to the immigrant in France and Germany, and has colored all debates of immigration and citizenship.

In the three countries, the discussion thus crystallizes around citizenship and multiculturalism, even "multicultural citizenship."[17] It is linked to status, law, identity, and belonging. Since the 1980s, citizenship has been established as a major issue in the social sciences, at the intersection of law, philosophy, politics, and sociology. Altogether, they raise the fundamental question about the universal ideology represented by the nation-state in contrast to the private, on one hand, and to the definition of a common civic space of political participation, on the other.

The concept of citizenship—as of nationality, since the two are interdependent and "interchangeable"[18] in the framework of the nation-state—is defined above all as the individual's belonging to a political community. This belonging takes shape through the social, political, and cultural rights and the duties that are embodied in the very idea of citizenship. The legal act that concretizes that principle implies the inclusion of "foreigners" in the national community whose moral and political values they are supposed to share. Moreover, they are supposed to adopt and even appropriate historical references as proof of a complete adherence and loyalty to the founding principles of the nation. These, at least, are the expectations, no matter what the legal conditions of access to citizenship, that is, whether the laws favor the right of soil or the right of blood.

As for multiculturalism, it refers to the multiple allegiances of individuals. It is based on the recognition of differences or on what is now called identity politics and consists of promoting cultural specificities within the national community. From the point of view of the states, multiculturalism is presented as a discourse, which they reject or accept, but in any case, a discourse they justify. It also constitutes a political choice through measures applied and methods favoring identity expressions in the public sphere.

In France the term is annoying. It even produces cliques: "republicans vs. democrats,"[19] namely, those who take refuge behind a republican vision of the nation-state, which objects to every communitarian structure, and its recognition, against those who defend a liberal vision granting a place to communities and identity interests in political life. The former are reinforced by the typology developed by R. Brubaker with regard to citizenship in France and Germany.[20] The definition of the nation is linked to the definition of a civic nation and a citizenship that is mainly political in France, and to an ethnic nation and a citizenship that is exclusively cultural in Germany.[21] The normative lesson is inherent in the "community of citizens" that makes the political community the only political membership of the individual.[22] In the same vein, but in terms of an anthropological analysis of family structures in France, Germany, and Great Britain, Emmanuel Todd ends up with a typology categorizing France as universalist because it is assimilationist, Germany as segregationist, and the United States as differentialist.[23] The multiculturalists, by contrast, want to attract attention to the pressures of identity in France, as in all industrial societies, and to analyze them as phenomena that replace the labor movement that produced social conflicts in the past.[24] On the whole, the discussion in France concerns the compatibility between the idea of the republic as one and indivisible and the presence of linguistic, religious, or other communities; between political and cultural belonging within the framework of the nation-state in the search for the "social bond."[25] As for the nature of this discussion, it is located between ideology and the normative in relation to the definition of communities which is now linked to citizenship and multiculturalism, just as much as it refers to a redefinition of justice, democracy, and human rights.

We must refer to works on the city, this time on urban integration, the phenomena of the ghetto, or questions of local democracy, which relate directly or indirectly to the presence of immigrant populations and their spatial and cultural concentration. These studies, along with empirical data, bring a contextual analysis of community construction or multiple identities in a given space.[26] This is reminiscent of the contribution of the Chicago School in the early twentieth century, which concerned the process of the acculturation and assimilation of immigrant populations in the United States. Of course, new research on the city no longer raises the same questions or uses the same methodology, but it does have the same result: a realistic analysis of the modes of social and political organization of the populations living in urban spaces and the modalities of weaving social bonds beyond the space of the neighborhood or even the city.

The discussion in Germany is dominated by the Habermas school of political philosophy and concerns the question of cultural recognition and solidarity in an increasingly differentiated society. Republicanism in this context refers to a social integration and a political inclusion. As a common denominator, the model based on constitutional patriotism proposes a liberal political culture, according to which, whatever the differences in so-called multicultural societies, citizenship is based on the socialization of the actors in the framework of a common political culture.[27] As in the United States, the broader discussion is oriented toward conflicts between liberals and communitarians and raises the question of public order, social peace, and the role of the welfare state in the definition of a new national cohesion. From this perspective, a great deal of empirical research demonstrates the modes of integration of different populations in Germany. As for a comparative approach, the same historical inspiration in the definition of citizenship brings France and Germany together or drives them apart. There, too, we must wait for sociological studies on the integration of the *Aussiedler*, populations naturalized de jure as soon as they arrive in Germany from Central Europe or Russia, to reassess the equation between legal and political citizenship and social integration.[28]

In this book I try to show that, in reality, both in France and in Germany, a rhetoric that rejects multiculturalism is found in contradiction with policies favoring identities in the public space. The expression of multiple allegiances is the result both of the words used in public discussions that locate the Other elsewhere and in social policies targeted toward the descendants of immigrants. The combination reveals an "applied multiculturalism" in both countries, as in the United States. Is this a pragmatic or an ideological response to the management of diversity? It does not matter. In fact, multiculturalism, as concept and as applied policy, is at the core of the interactions between immigrant or minority populations and the states. So is citizenship. Both open the way to identity negotiations between states and immigrants.

Thus, the theoretical question raised by negotiations of identity concerns the redefinition of a balance between the state and the nation. The normative response concerns an institutional assimilation of differences. This consists of integrating differences into the structures of the state. If the policies of so-called (or not) identity seek, paradoxically, a social cohesion in national societies, this can rest only on an institutional basis recognized by the states that define the framework of legitimacy established on equality and justice.

N 3

Works on the incorporation of immigrant populations in Europe show that their mode of organization is integrated into existing institutional structures.[29] Let me add that the power of negotiation of the political activists among the descendants of immigrants is a sign of their commitment in the associations that constitute the framework of socialization and where the rules of the political game and of civic virtue are acquired. Consequently, the organization and functioning of the associations mirror national institutions. Participation in the associations contributes to shaping the "identity of a citizen" for the immigrant and for the whole population. This identity of a citizen, shaped and developed in the associations or in other community structures in relation to the state, constitutes a basis of citizenship that is expressed by attachment both to the national community and to a collective identity that is other than national.[30] Civic virtue acquired in the associations goes beyond the framework of the simple legal definition of citizenship insofar as it is exercised in different areas and on different terms: it is expressed both within a cultural, ethnic, or religious community and within the national community. Such a vision of citizenship contrasts with expectations about the loyalty of the individual with regard to the national community. But, in fact, the actions and strategies of the actors do not contradict their desire for integration into the national community, for a civic participation with equal rights as revealed by discourse and that encourages mobilization. Thus, an *institutional assimilation* arises as the logical consequence of the negotiations that have led the descendants of immigrants to internalize the values of democratic societies. Institutional assimilation results in a restructuring of society in order to avoid the marginalization of a group that does not see itself in the overall institutions or the social and political citizenship, with the ultimate hope of reinforcing identification with the political community.[31]

METHODOLOGY

Every work on comparative politics starts with the question of the state: public policies, political parties, social structure, union organizations—all cases of the organization of political life. Several discussions of the method of comparative politics have contrasted a structuralist approach that favors institutions with a culturalist approach that tries to point out the symbols and values that permit determining the boundaries of a collectivity.[32] The former emphasizes the rationality of institutions, and the latter the importance of interpretation, thus contrasting universalism and particularism, as well as normativity and empiricism.

My approach combines the two. In my research, the issue of the state is essential as a result of the parallel development of immigration in

France and in Germany. Indeed, the first stage of the comparison concerned the modes of organization of the Turkish populations in the two countries, more precisely in Paris and Berlin, where, in 1984, the Turks constituted 47.4 percent of the foreign population, while there were only 18,500 Turks in Paris in 1982.[33] The difference in the modalities of integrating families in the two cities led me to question the role of the state, or more precisely the effect of public policies of immigration on the organization of groups of immigrants and on the formation and expression of their collective identity. Despite the very different policies adopted by France and Germany, despite the quantitative difference of the Turkish population in the two countries, similarities in the modalities of integration were seen: an urban concentration according to the region of origin, the development of the associative movement, and a mobilization around identities. As a result, the comparison between the integration of immigrant families in Paris and Berlin showed the limits of policies concerning immigration, as a flow and as affecting settlement.

I then pursued my study with populations from Turkey in Germany and extended it to the North African population in France: two populations targeted by the media, political discourse, and public opinion in the two countries. This time I concentrated on the associations of immigrants, whether they defined themselves as social, cultural, religious, or national. I carried out in-depth interviews with their leaders and members and observed their meetings, discussions, and mobilizations over a long period. This study was interspersed with interviews with politicians in charge of issues of immigration and integration in the two countries, ministerial departments, union representatives, and those in charge of social services.

Immigrants or the descendants of immigrants, on one hand, and politicians and local and national institutions, on the other, over the long run, did in fact allow me to understand the development of the field of immigration: a development of the issues it poses, the concepts it refers to, and its terminology. Intense interactions between political actors on both sides—representatives of the state (central or federal, the *Länder*, or the local authorities) and individuals chosen to represent the relevant populations according to their nationality or their region of origin or their religion—result in a *process of negotiations in which identities constitute the "good"*; they are expressed in terms of interest and law confronting power on the part of the immigrants and in terms of national interest and social peace on the part of the states. These negotiations of identities also explain the reciprocal influences that produce institutional, discursive, and normative changes. They also affect political norms and values with permanent adjustments. In sum, it is to view "the state as process," as an actor in relation with society.[34]

Negotiations of identity appear in various realms: in rhetoric, actions, and organizations. This results in a methodological diversity that combines the structural analysis of institutions with the cultural data they embody. If the organization and functioning of the associations relate to a structuralist approach, although grasped in its own internal and external dynamic, the norms, values, and cultures invented in their framework necessarily relate to a culturalist approach. This is especially so since the negotiations mainly concern the contradictions between rhetoric and governmental decisions, representations and laws, myths and realities; depend on an overlapping of culture and politics; and relate to a culturalist analysis of the state.[35]

In fact, particularities of the states appear through negotiations. The similarities in the facts and political reactions that led to this comparative study do not prevent the reality unique to each society from appearing through interactions and from making each case specific. Historical continuity competes with social and cultural change to redefine fundamental principles and national symbols. Thus, despite the apparent convergence of political acts, divergences in the representation of the national idea that emerge in discourse tend ultimately to differentiate them. Thus, empirically, interactions between states and immigrants have located religion in France and citizenship in Germany at the core of negotiations in reconsidering laïcité as a non-negotiable value in France and the bond between citizenship and identity in Germany. Religion and citizenship thus constitute fundamental questions that raise a normative challenge to the French and German states in the area of integrating the descendants of immigrants.

These methodological instruments combining theories and facts constitute the fabric of this work. Chapter 1, "The War of Words," is an analysis of words and concepts linked with immigration or the presence of immigrants in France, Germany, and the United States. It underlines the transfer of these words as an indicator of the convergences between these countries not only in their usage but also in their development over time. The words serve in the same way to represent the Other, the immigrant, the foreigner. The historical and ideological weight of the words also locates them with respect to the historical narrative of the national societies.

Chapter 2, on the representation of political traditions, deals with the construction of this national narrative, the artificial and fluid nature of the models, and their limits with regard to reality, political action, and law.

Contradictions between political discourse and social reality create tensions that are crystallized in the territories of identity (chapter 3). In fact, a power relationship is established between the national institutions and the community institutions which make the law in these "territories" consisting of the suburbs in France, the ethnic enclaves in Germany, and the ghettos in the United States.

Chapter 4 shows how, in France and Germany, associations defined as intermediaries of solidarity in the territories of identity *invent a culture* in response to the expectations of individuals who seek an identification there and those of the public powers, in order to achieve recognition.

Although cultures are invented in the framework of the associations, their politicization is carried out in relations with the French and German states (chapters 5 and 6). Since the 1980s, invented, reappropriated, or affirmed cultures have been fueled in large part by public discussions and reinforced by local or national policies, as well as by targeted governmental practices that give them a form and content and in fact locate them in a field of competition for power and thus cause their politicization.

Whenever identities, thus far considered as part of the private sphere, are discussed in the public space, they give rise to negotiations with the states to achieve recognition. Chapter 7, on the negotiation of identities, shows the mechanisms of negotiations and their consequences with regard to relations between citizenship, nationality, and identity and raises the question of representation and recognition and its limits.

Finally, the European Union is a *new space of negotiations of identities*, where all identities are now negotiated, whether national, regional, linguistic, religious, majority, or minority. They are redefined by complex plays of interaction and identification in a new political space that is currently under construction. Nation-states cling to historical achievements and reinforce their particularities by registering them in the models they want to defend. As for the descendants of immigrants, they rely increasingly on the idea of a political Europe to intensify their quest for recognition with the states that constitute the only concrete frameworks of protection.

CHAPTER ONE

The War of Words

> Words are always questioned in terms of their representative
> values as virtual elements of discourse that prescribes the same
> mode of being for all.
>
> —Michel Foucault

THE SCOPE OF THE POLITICAL ISSUE of immigration becomes evident in
the verbal war it produces. Words and concepts concerning immigration
or the presence of immigrants are controversial and loaded with feeling,
sometimes spawning conflicts and sometimes contributing to them.
*Immigrants, foreigners, Islam, Islamism, fundamentalism, ghettos, eth-
nic groups, and communities* are terms and concepts whose meaning
shifts in time and space without regard for "the marks of their ancestral
memory," as Michel Foucault put it.

These words designate the Other and our own perception of the
Other; they conjure up identities and differences and are irrational in
some respects. In short, words, as agents of persuasion and influence,
create public opinion and justify political orientations. Since Michel
Rocard, the French prime minister, announced in 1990 that France
"cannot accept all the poverty of the world," and in Germany public
debate on foreigners has been dominated for thirty years by the theme
Wir sind kein Einwanderungsland (We are not a country of immigration), policies follow and public opinion must choose between national
feeling and political morality, not to mention economic interests.

Headlines are filled with discourse that is often contradictory. The
escalation of "preconceptions" in the Durkheimian sense makes the
subject a commonplace, "allegedly known" (in journalese), where
everyone has something to say. The words come out without thinking.
The vocabulary relating to immigration and the presence of immigrants
thus ends in a linguistic reflex in all three countries and is part of the
conflict.

Thus, beyond simple terminology, words constitute the strategic
weapons taken up by politicians, association activists, social workers,
and intellectuals, who give them a new content according to actions and
reactions. Intellectuals, whose discourse endeavors to be autonomous,
"denounce" or "correct" the increasingly intractable discourse repro-

duced and intensified by the press. Although freedom of speech contradicts the linguistic code of "political correctness" in the United States, in France a juridical limitation does not prevent the politicians from adding their mite and forming public opinion.

A comparison of the terminology in France and Germany concerning immigration or the presence of foreigners shows both a similarity of expression and an evolution of terms. Even if a word or concept developed in a given historical and national context is used for political strategy in another context, we know that it does not transfer so easily. The same word—*histoire, history, Geschichte*—in French, English, and German, wrote Raymond Aron, "applies to historical reality and to our awareness of it."[1] Moreover, since each of those words is loaded with ideology, it raises the question of adaptability to another context. There is also the voyage of words across frontiers between different languages—political language, media language, scientific language—each using the symbolic weight of the words to interpret social reality and to seek legitimacy. The multiple terms connected with immigration and their use with different definitions at different times produce a linguistic chaos that puts the subject of immigration beyond partisan disputes.

This chapter shows how France and Germany, two countries with two different political traditions, are increasingly inspired by the American vocabulary concerning immigration or foreigners and even the representation of their own society. This linguistic contagion demonstrates not only the heuristic status of American social reality and studies but also the acknowledgment of the similarities in all democratic pluralistic societies and the justification of a political convergence among them, even though each country resists giving a different meaning to the same word.

ON THE IMMIGRANT

Twenty years after the decision to stop immigration to France, there was still talk of the immigrant. Article 6 of a law of December 2, 1945, defines an immigrant as "the foreigner who lives in the country for more than three months; he or she then may remain for an indefinite period."[2] This definition does not mention social status, but it tacitly implies that the immigrant is a worker. In Germany the worker is invited. He is a *Gastarbeiter*, a title that grants legal status and underscores not only the limited length of stay but also the reason for the invitation. The term "immigrant," as used in France, tacitly emphasizes the controversial aspect of the presence of foreigners. Its German equivalent, *Einwanderer*, which has recently replaced *Gastarbeiter* in the conventional vocabulary of immigration, looks more like an acceptance of the guests' long stay. One piece of evidence for this is that Marie-Louise Beck, the commissioner of *Bundesausländerbeauftragte*, prefers the terms *Migrantinnen* and *Migranten*, leaving the content as abstract and ambiguous as it is in France.

In France the immigrant no longer seems to have a precise nationality. The term refers primarily to a perception and not necessarily to a reality. It now automatically refers to a person in the highly "visible" group from North Africa—whether the immigrant was born in France or retains citizenship in some North African country. In Germany he or she is a Turk and remains a foreigner—an *Ausländer*—living in Germany. He or she is no longer a Gastarbeiter. In the United States the migrant is someone in the last wave of the many waves that populated the continent over two centuries.

Today politicians and the public often view immigrants in Europe and in the United States as "clandestines," "illegals," or "without papers" (*sans-papiers*). The same applies to refugees, who are increasingly treated as immigrants (legal or illegal). In Europe they have kept coming long after the borders were closed in 1973–74; in the United States they are outside the quota. Politicians define them as "counterfeit immigrants," and the public perceives them as such. They are also regarded as requesting asylum so as to gain access to the high standards of living of industrialized countries. So they are "counterfeit asylum seekers" (*Schien-Asylanten*), and this has created the terms "economic refugees" in the United States and *Wirtschaftsasylanten* in Germany. It is not their number, which is hard to determine, but the perception of them in the collective imagination that has led politicians to blame them for the "problem of immigration," a specifically Turkish problem in Germany: *Türkenproblem*.

Thus, use of the term *immigrant* and its connotations follow from the varied definitions attributed to them in public discourse, revealing the shift from a general discussion toward one aimed at a specific group. That group then becomes the target of the media and public opinion, and immigration becomes a battlefield in which words go to war.

Since the parties of the extreme right in France (the National Front) and the Right in Germany (such as the Christian Democratic Party, or the CDU) have built their campaign on the "problem" of immigration, there has been a war of words. But in France use of those words goes beyond the bounds of the National Front and produces a common arena of discussions and confrontations, first between the opposition and the government. Michel Poniatowski referred to immigration as the "occupation"; for Valéry Giscard d'Estaing, it is the "invasion."[3] Occupation makes the immigrant an "enemy," and invasion makes him or her a "barbarian." By choosing two terms loaded with either recent or remote memories, in time or space, each party tries to attack the current government as being unable to control the borders, the territorial boundary of identity, and to defend national interests; thus they compete with the National Front on the battlefield.

Whereas *occupation* refers to a precise event in French history, an allusion to invasions is broader and has already been used in the past. The word refers to immigration, but in "peaceful" terms, as Jean-Baptiste Duroselle emphasized in his book *L'invasion*[4] and in an article in *L'Aurore* of February 27, 1963: "The Peaceful Invasion: The Arrival of the Blacks." The historian Yves Lequin adopted the term as the title of an article on the various waves of immigrants who settled in France between 1850 and 1930 and their professional and geographical paths.[5] In it, Lequin drew attention to the development of immigration and the atmosphere prevailing in the cities: "More than any other arena, the big city consists essentially of an 'invasion,' which some are beginning to judge as no longer peaceful."

In fact, in the late 1960s, the immigration that shattered this peaceful atmosphere was publicly described as "savage." In an article in the journal *Mots*, Colette Guillaumin raised the question of what meaning could be given to the term "savageimmigration" (in one word). Was it uncontrolled immigration, did the word *savage* refer quite simply to immigration, or was it used in the sense of *exotic*?[6] Under the pressure of public opinion influenced by such discourse, governments today define measures to combat a "savage immigration."

Similar discourse can also be found in the German press even though in relation to a different context. More than regulating the border crossings of "counterfeit workers," after the fall of the Berlin Wall, the Federal Republic is afraid that asylum seekers will abuse the right to stay or that the status of Aussiedler (persons of German origin naturalized de facto) will be counterfeited. "Aussiedler must prove German ancestry"; yet "20% are suspected of not being of German nationality," claimed an article on foreigners in *Der Spiegel* of March 6, 1989.

Meanwhile, "asylum seekers are lightning rods," declared a deputy of the Sozialdemokratische Partei Deutschlands (SPD) in response to the speeches of a CDU deputy, who stated that "90% of the refugees usurp that title." The origin of the asylum seekers does not matter; they merge once again with the Gastarbeiter, for, together, they are seen as foreigners contributing to the *Überfremdung* (foreign overpopulation) of German society. Germany risks being "drowned by external elements." In 1892–93 Max Weber used the terms in his first *Empirical Survey* of the socioeconomic development of Northeast Prussia, referring to the "ethnic" Poles living in eastern Prussia. Today this image, etched in the collective memory, reappears with the massive arrival of asylum seekers

(*Asylanten*). In reaction to the increased number of foreigners (Ausländer), one speaks of a flood: *Ausländersschwemme*. In the 1970s, Germany already was described as a packed ship: *das Boot ist voll* (the boat is full).

In both France and Germany, the immigrant who came or was invited for the economic reconstruction of the country is now seen as troublesome. Since the memory of the economic growth of the Thirty Glorious Years (1948–78) is too recent, imagination seems to draw on resources from a more distant past, particularly from national political crises.

BOUNDARIES OF IDENTITY OR "THRESHOLD OF TOLERANCE"

Metaphors draw the attention of public opinion to the boundaries of acceptability: the frontiers and beyond, a threshold that is not to be crossed, the "threshold of tolerance." That expression appeared in a report on the policy of "relocation" in Nanterre in 1964 and was intended initially as a marker. As a result of a local study on the inhabitants of the shantytowns, the report implied a ratio—the threshold—of foreigners to natives. If that proportion was exceeded, tensions and then conflicts would appear. Once the politicians got hold of the term, its "marking function" yielded to its "polemical function,"[7] which was magnified in the media. A headline in *Le Figaro* of October 21, 1980, reads: "More Than Four Million Immigrants," adding in large letters: "At the Threshold of Intolerance." Thus, the initial empirical aspect has assumed an ideological form that lends itself to political strategies and aims at collective sensibilities. The idea has subsequently been used, often indirectly, in many opinion polls with questions like: "Do you think there are too many foreigners in your neighborhood?"

The "threshold" very quickly stretches from a neighborhood to national borders. The "tolerance" attributed to the inhabitants of the neighborhood is projected onto the politicians, whose discourse anticipates the assumed "frustration" of public opinion about immigration. Both the Left and the Right seem to be unanimous about the need to remove the specter of immigration. François Mitterrand referred to the "threshold of tolerance," and Charles Pasqua announced that "France can no longer be a country of immigration."

Everyone has a threshold. In France the threshold is not a given number, but in Germany, particularly in Berlin, it does correspond to a precise percentage. It even defines a housing policy for foreigners in the city (*Zuzugssperre*) that forbids newcomers to move into neighborhoods that have 12 percent or more of foreigners of the same nationality,[8] and a limit of 20 percent has been set for the children of foreigners in school as part of an integration policy after the 1980s. Thus, the "threshold" in Berlin is closer to the American term "critical threshold," used to evaluate mixed neighborhoods of blacks and whites.[9]

But Germany is also experiencing a shift toward an undefined notion of the threshold of tolerance, working from the local to the national scale, and from one group to another. In fact, the massive arrival of Aussiedler[10] and asylum seekers, whose number has constantly increased since the wall came down, has led to discussions and even a law proposed by the CDU "to limit [requests for asylum] to preserve harmony." Parliamentary extremists are taking advantage of the situation to sound a call to arms on the presence of the Ausländer and to invoke "a bearable limit" of foreigners (*Grenzen der Belastbarkeit*). Senate debates allude to integration and to foreigners' right to vote, which are current topics, as if to emphasize what is both politically (un)acceptable and economically (un)bearable about the presence of the Aussiedler by drawing attention to the social cost of their integration into German society. This logic also led to the asylum compromise (*Asylkompromiss*) of 1992–93, which imposed an annual maximum of 225,000 new Aussiedler.[11]

In the United States, the expression "the tipping point" is equivalent to the threshold of tolerance and indicates the threshold of concentration of blacks among the residents of the same neighborhood beyond which whites begin to desert the neighborhood (white flight); this threshold is at about 20 percent.[12]

Thus, terms transferred from one national context to another still follow their own path according to the empirical data that guide them.

THE BATTLE OF NUMBERS

The war of words continues, and numbers constitute the weapons of the war! As the geographer Pierre George emphasizes, "Two facts intersect in considering immigration: the first is a numerical fact expressed in absolute numbers and as a ratio on the local, regional, and national level; the second is a qualitative fact: the perception of difference. This is what makes immigration in this second half of the century original and gives relations between native and immigrant populations a new echo of incompatibility."[13]

The numbers increase awareness and are provocative. They either make fears concrete or provide relief, depending on the analysis and interpretation of the results. In fact, statistics—by definition a barometer of social reality—lead to polemics, depending on how they are used and by whom. First, concerning the number of foreigners, the controversy implies unlimited entry, hence the "real" number of foreigners is much higher than the official census count. Thus, the statistics of the various ministries, specialized organizations, and the national census intersect and sometimes contradict one another. The media set the tone: "Immigration: The Real Numbers," reads the headline in *Liberation* (September 9, 1983); or "Immigration: An Increase of 20%," announces *Le Figaro* (October 20, 1989), with a subhead emphasizing continuity, "Strong Increase in 1989," and an editorial titled "What a Society!"

Each journal has its own interpretation and sequence of reactions. A discussion followed the publication of statistics on the number of foreigners by *Figaro Magazine* of October 26, 1985. The 1982 official census of the INSEE (French National Institute of Statistics and Economic Studies) listed 54,273,200 inhabitants, 50,600,000 of whom were French (by birth or acquisition), 1,750,000 foreigners of European origin, and 1,950,000 foreigners of non-European origin; but the real statistics provided by the Institute of Political Demography for 1985 showed a French population of 51.4 million and a non-European foreign population of 2.6 million, that is, an increase of 650,000 non-Europeans in three years. Such assertions rallied sociologists and demographers, who cast doubt on the precision of these numbers with articles like the one by Michèle Tribalat, a researcher at the INED (National Institute of Demographic Studies): "The Statistics Are Made to Lie" (*Le Quotidien de Paris* of October 29, 1985). Political personalities with opposite tendencies have questioned the good faith of *Figaro Magazine*. The media of both the Right and the Left have given their results, each denouncing the other. Articles with titles like "Immigration: Those Numbers That Hide the Forest," "Roman Numerals or Arabic Numerals?" "Demography or Demagogy?" and "Statistical Crossbreeding" filled the columns of the national dailies between October 2 and October 15, 1985.

The stakes are high because statistics fuel the discourse of the National Front on the definition of who or what is French. "Will we still be French in thirty years?" shouted Le Pen on October 30, 1985, during the broadcast of *L'heure de vérité* (The Hour of Truth), a prime-time television program, drawing on those numbers. He used the increasing number of foreigners entering the country and their fertility rates to arouse a collective fear. By stressing the difference between the fertility rates of foreign families and those of native families, the statistics highlight the values of society in general defined as values of modernity. In this view, the size of the immigrant family, and in some cases its alleged polygamy, represent values considered "archaic," the statistics on the number of children per immigrant family reinforcing the fear of an "internal invasion." Demographers responded by showing that the length of stay of families is accompanied by a significant convergence of birth rates, and that the process of modernization is at work both in France and in the home country.

Moreover, the polemic about the statistics leads to an examination of the "social cost" of foreigners, a measure of their responsibility in the nation's economic crisis and a favorite argument of the extremist parties. "Foreigners are users," said Le Pen, who in 1985 estimated an outlay of Fr 108 billion in family allowances for foreigners and the education of their children. And we also read "How to Save 150 Billion Francs?" in *Rivarol*, an extreme right-wing newspaper (March 27, 1986), or "Land of Asylum or Milk Cow?" in another extremist newspaper, *Aspects de la France* (December 19, 1985).

The "social cost" of foreigners thus alerts public opinion to the limits of the welfare state and, consequently, to national solidarity, especially at a time of economic slump when austerity is imposed and "national preference" finds a justification. In Germany immigration is perceived as "a burden on the economic and industrial development" of the country (*Das Parlament*, January 18, 1986). Responsibility for the economic depression goes to foreigners, to asylum seekers, and to Aussiedler, even though in extremist rhetoric, aid for them is justified by "national preference": "They are Germans, once and forever!" shouted a CDU deputy during parliamentary discussions, deploring the increased "social cost" of foreigners since the wall came down, from DM 40 million in 1986 to more than 200 million in 1989, particularly in employment and housing.

Against the obvious background of an election issue, the battle of numbers fuels arguments over the meaning of received ideas, which show up in public opinion polls as not always disingenuous questions. Hence Alain Girard's first investigation of the subject: "Do you think there are too many immigrants in France?" Or "Do you find the proportion of foreigners [after indicating a percentage] high in your neighborhood?"[14] More recently, a SOFRES (French National Institute for Market Research and Opinion Polls) poll of August 18–22, 1990, for FR3 (third channel, public television), *La Marche du siècle*, and *Le Nouvel Observateur*, raised the question of the cost of immigrants: "Do you think it is normal for immigrants to receive family allowances or unemployment payments?"

Thus, numbers and even polls about immigration do not simply reflect social reality but also *construct* a reality they present as a problem of society, often for political ends.

Who Is Who?

The battle of numbers is primarily about how to classify statistics that challenge the definition of national and foreign. As Stephen Thernstrom emphasizes, statistics are "an important source of—or at least rationalization for—nativist concerns about the immigration invasion."[15] Thernstrom notes that, in the United States, between 1851 and 1960, different immigrant, ethnic, or racial groups were sometimes categorized by the individual's native country and sometimes by the father's, depending on whether the categories had changed. Thus, the classification of blacks as colored changed, to include mulattos and even varying degrees of mulattos.

In France, the official census classifies the whole population under three categories: French by birth, French by "acquisition" (naturalization), and foreign. Thus, once foreigners are naturalized, they move into the column of French by naturalization; their children born on French soil are declared French by birth. Unlike the American census since 1980, which has tried to highlight ethnic ancestry, in France the national and ethnic origin of citizens does not appear in official documents and consequently has no legal or statistical validity. The Code of Nationality sets up statistical categories that exclude "origin" once French nationality is obtained,[16] leading to a statistical invisibility of any "ethnic ancestry." In the last census of the INSEE (1990), however, a new category of "previous nationality" of naturalized French citizens was introduced into the presentation of statistics on foreigners, broken down by age, sex, work, type of household, and so on. The preface of the census of the foreign population referred directly to the changes in the laws of nationality,[17] justifying questionings about the past and introducing an awareness of the conditions of belonging through the generations.

Situations and discourse converge in France and the United States up to a certain point. In the United States variations in statistical data correspond to political changes concerning ethnic groups. Since the adoption of affirmative action, individuals have been urged to choose their own ethnic affiliation as they wanted it to appear in official statistics, under the rubric of ethnic ancestry. This practice—which became official in the 1980 U.S. census—although officially designating a "minority" category, aimed at working toward the idea of a pluralist democracy that has prevailed there since the 1960s. In France, however, "previous nationality," which appears in the last statistics of the INSEE, seems to indicate rather the influence of the Committee of Experts on the Code of Nationality in 1987, and of the televised debates and public testimonies emphasizing the identification aspect of previous nationality or that of the parents of children of foreigners born on French soil, and thus an awareness and statistics of "origin."

The meaning of "origin" became more explicit in the recent survey of Michèle Tribalat entitled "Geographical Mobility and Social Integration."[18] As a response to the inadequacy of classical censuses to analyze immigration and integration, in the survey, the author calls the children of immigrants "persons of foreign origin" and adds, "If we want to follow the future of immigrants and their children, we should stop referring to nationality."[19] She continues to challenge the official census categories by including the criteria of "ethnic belonging" and "ethnic origin," based on the mother tongue of immigrants and their children in the home country of their parents. By creating these categories, she aims at "freeing" French social sciences from the "taboo of origins."

Such a categorization led Hervé Le Bras, another demographer, to a virulent reaction to the use of "origin," in his book entitled *The Evil of Origins*."[20] Le Bras claims that the use of "origin" in demographic classification is a source of racial discrimination, and he sees this vocabulary and assessment of the population as a "convergence between the new direction that French demography has taken and the ideology of the extreme Right with regard to immigrant populations." Such a categorization of generations of immigrants creates another category, called *"Français de souche"* (French from the French stock), which according to Le Bras becomes a way to "ethnicize French nationalism by transforming the French population into an ethnic group."[21]

The discussions of the Committee of Experts on the Code of Nationality in which the young descendants of immigrants publicly expressed a "pride in their origins" and their "loyalty to republican values" were covered by the media. Were these discussions a trap for scholars who adopted the "lived" vocabulary as a scientific tool? Or is there an unadmitted similarity between French and German reality which had been presented prior to that as a dichotomy?

But German sociologists seem to introduce the same distinction in reference to the Aussiedler and thus to distinguish them from Germans of German stock, *Bundesdeutsche*, and Germans from the territories of Germany (*Einheimische*).[22] As in the French case, the ambiguity is created by the legal status of citizenship, for as far as foreigners are concerned, the statistics seem clearer at first glance. The principles of nationality based on jus sanguinis (right of blood) and naturalization, which, until 2000, was difficult to obtain and rare, helped avoid all ambiguity in the definition of the foreigner. Since the foreigner is defined by article 116 of the Basic Law as "any individual who is not German in terms of the Constitution," statistics categorize him or her by how long he or she has been in Germany and whether the residence permit is limited or not.[23] Thus, official statistics classify by permits of residence or work issued by district administrations and show two categories of foreigners: permanent residents, who have permanent cards of residence and work and thus cannot be deported, and foreigners, listed by nationality, with a limited residence permit.

These statistical categories are added to public discourse to reinforce the identification of the individual, the group, the nation. By relegating individuals to a previous nationality, particularly North Africans, France also relegates them to a religious affiliation (assuming that national and religious affiliation are identical) and thereby creates an ambiguous "category." By all appearances, this affects identification with the "acquired" French nationality, for perception of that identity locates the new French somewhere else, separate from "French stock" in their "origin." The title of an article that appeared in *L'Humanité* on December 9, 1985—"Those Frenchmen Who Are Called Mohamed!"—is quite significant in this respect. Does the inability to grasp the origin of the "evil" attributed to the foreigner lead us to seek the origin of the citizen?

Whether *origin* refers to the previous nationality of a new citizen or to membership in a religious tradition (Protestant, Jewish, or Muslim) of those who have been established for several generations, mention of origin suggests the persistence of an ethnic and/or religious identity separate from that of the majority.

In Germany, by contrast, foreigners, the Ausländer, remain Ausländer. Their legal status is transmitted from one generation to the next, so that their children and grandchildren are foreigners as long as endogamy prevails, and naturalization is possible only after fifteen years of residence and only if they give up their original nationality. As for the generations of immigrants, in Germany *second generation* refers to the second generation of foreigners, whereas in France it is used for the second generation of immigrants, and in the United States children of migrants are Americans of the second generation or define themselves as second-generation Americans. Whereas Germany emphasizes the legal aspect of identity, France designates a social status with the term *second generation*, and since the 1980s, scientific language has replaced *second generation* with *young descendants of immigrants*. The terminology concerning the children of immigrants matters not only when it highlights a continuity or discontinuity in legal status but also, particularly in the French case, because it seems to emphasize the point that even if there is a continuity in social status, that is not inescapable!

Yet another category appeared in Germany in the 1990s: the Aussiedler. This is no longer a legal classification referring to nationality but a social and cultural classification referring to the length of stay on the national territory. Bade formulated this ambiguity when he emphasized that "discourse on the *Aussiedler* is an ethno-national euphemism, beause the *Aussiedler* legally recognized as Germans are both Germans and immigrants at the same time."[24]

Within the same country, vocabulary develops as a result of exchanges based on a two-way identification and perception. Like a ball thrown at random, words borrowed from different contexts are picked up by activists who present themselves as the sole guardians of an identity that is trying to assert itself, and they boost themselves higher and harder to signal their ideology. In his essay on names, Harold R. Isaacs traced the social and political history of Filipinos, Indians, and blacks in the United States and showed that names change not only according to the social and political context of the country but also according to how those groups perceive themselves.[25]

In France, for example, young people started to call themselves Beur in the 1980s, a term that combines both a social identity and an identity of origin ("Arab," in a French version of pig Latin) and youth; it is hard to imagine an elderly Beur! Its popular meaning blends an idea of social class, place of residence, and a certain identity of origin. The media refer to "young people of immigrant origin," regardless of their nationality, and present them as a new "category," one that might influence the outcome of elections. "Beurs: a Generation Marching to the Ballot Box," read a headline in *Libération* (March 15, 1993). The emergence of the term *Beur* in political discourse inspired some activists to reject the name, particularly before the municipal elections of 1989, by giving it a utilitarian political role, as in "token Beur." Like some American blacks who now reject the term *black*, which they had preferred to *Negro*, a common term prior to the 1960s, and now accept an African-American identity, some Beurs reject the term *Beur*, which easily lends itself to puns (like "Petits Beurres"). They prefer "Franco-Maghrebian," a hyphenated identity inspired by the American situation, which appears in the bylaws of several associations. More inclusive and corresponding to a cultural and regional identification, this term avoids the ambiguity of expressions like "French Muslims." And even though public authorities do not consider them the same group, public opinion has found it hard to make the distinction.

Different terms used at different times raise the question of identification, the choice for young people between an attributed identity and an identity constructed in relation to the environment, of course, but primarily an identity whose recognition they now demand—the recognition of difference.

"THE RIGHT OF DIFFERENCE" OR "PRAISE OF INDIFFERENCE"

In France this terminology finds legitimacy in a political discourse that favored "the right of difference" in the early 1980s. French society was defined then as "multiracial," "multicultural," "plural," and "pluricultural," and several articles and books have appeared with these titles. These words and concepts have been developed in the American literature on ethnic groups since the civil rights movement of the 1960s, and they have been used in France, as an acknowledgment of a society where different cultures, different races, and different religions coexist. Activists accept this new tendency and paraphrase American slogans as "Beur is beautiful," adopting them as a new identity, printing them on T-shirts, and painting them on walls. Intending to construct a democratic society ruled by principles of equality, this discourse is designed to make public opinion accept diversity as an inherent characteristic of every modern society.

The idea of a multicultural society is also spreading in Germany, where, especially for opposition activists and spokesmen, it is a way to include foreigners in the political pluralism characterized by the affiliation of individuals to a corporation, thus making both public opinion and politicians in general aware that the "foreigners are here to stay." And new terms arise to designate them. In the late 1970s, in public discussion more than in everyday speech, they changed from *Gastarbeiter* to *ausländische Arbeiter* (foreign workers) or *Einwanderer* (immigrants), and not simple *Gäste* (guests). Must they now be considered immigrants or minorities or both: *Einwanderungsminorität*, "immigrant minority," in the words of Daniel Cohn-Bendit, city councillor of Frankfurt in charge of Multicultural Affairs? At least in discourse, FDP—Frei Demokratische Partei (Liberal Democratic Party)—activists grant them the status of citizens as individuals participating in city life and call them *Ausländische Mitbürger*, foreign fellow citizens, or foreign cocitizens, a term that has entered the official discussion. In short, the evolution of terminology demonstrates that Germany is in fact a country of immigration and de facto a multicultural society and hence proposes to include them in society.

In both France and Germany, reactions are heated. Discussions in all areas (intellectual, political, and in the media) revolve around the concept of a multicultural society, which has been systematically associated with the definition of national identity, seen by some as "threatened." Any public allusion to diversity now seems to lead to a questioning of the unity of the nation, in both European countries as in the United States, even though these three countries do not share the same concept of national unity. America laments the "disuniting" caused by multiculturalism, whereas sociologists analyze German unity in terms of "ethnic nationalism" and French unity in terms of "republican civic nationalism."

That was one of the perverse effects of the discourse and policies advocating multiculturalism. Should the American example have been avoided? Studies on the subject emphasized the fragmentation of American society, where the initial pluralism has now yielded to an ideological discourse by ethnic groups demanding public recognition of their uniqueness. For the last decade, several books and articles have tried to demonstrate how this ideology threatens the national identity as idealized by the melting pot and leads to the "disuniting of America," the title of Arthur M. Schlesinger Jr.'s book, which draws attention to the fragmentation of American society into several separate communities. Despite the much more varied discussion about difference and its recognition, it is in the banality of Schlesinger's reaction that America is decidedly an antimodel for France.

In France the issue is "exclusion," "ghettoization," and "ethnicization." These terms, used liberally by scientists, the media, and politicians, derive directly from the notion of a multicultural and/or multiracial society. In Germany the term "marginalization" is preferred, but some people in a multicultural society might avoid it. In fact, unlike France, militant German Greens, one branch of the SPD, and association activists are trying to persuade politicians that only a multicultural society can grant a place to foreigners. And intellectuals want to alert politicians to the danger of such "humanist" and "romantic" speeches in the German context. Sociologists are trying to show that the logic of a multicultural society would lead various foreign groups to organize around identities that would reinforce their distinctiveness. They are the reverse danger, and many would avoid the terms. This could result in a reaction reinforcing a similar exclusivity of German identity. Do reactions to multiculturalism have any link to Germans' difficulty in asserting a national identity?

That explains "the praise of indifference."[26] The Left and activists in France have also veered toward the principle of the "right to indifference," especially "the right of similarity." This demand crystallized in the municipal elections of 1989 and corresponded to the outbreak of suburban troubles. Inconsistent as it may seem, identities no longer want to be confined in areas. As a result, "the right of similarity" is opposed to two identities: social and ethnic. In fact, "suburban youth" are defined out of hand as "youth from disadvantaged neighborhoods," and disadvantaged neighborhoods are described as neighborhoods "with a strong concentration of immigrants"; consequently, "suburban youth" are "youths of immigrant origin." This is what had to be proved rather than assumed.

This syllogism has produced a flood of scenarios and concepts borrowed from an American vision of social reality. The term *Harlemization*, as used in France, has drawn the attention of the public authorities and public opinion to the poor neighborhoods inhabited by foreigners. The Goutte d'Or district in the eighteenth arrondissement of Paris is compared to the ghetto of the 1960s and to Harlem in the late 1970s. Since the 1980s, studies of these neighborhoods have conjured up depictions of Harlem, that is, places with a high rate of delinquency, drug traffic, and crime, a place where "even the police can't go" (*National Hebdo*, March 4, 1993). All these phenomena are, obviously, linked with immigration and fuel negative images that only increase suspicion of foreigners. These observations provide fodder for the parties of the extreme Right, whose representatives bemoan immigration, condemn policies, and make public opinion aware of the "evil" from the outside. "Suburbs: Pure Product of Immigration," wrote Y. Briant (National Center of the Independents, or CNI); "The Uneasiness of the Suburbs Is the Pure Fruit of Immigration Policies," stated J. Y. Le Gallou of the National Front in *Le Figaro* of June 18, 1991.

Yet, in the late 1980s, journalists tried to allay fears by drawing attention to the positive nature of relations with immigrants: "Sarcelles: A Tower of Babel Doing Well. Skin, Black, Beur" (*Le Matin*, October 10, 1988); "Long Live the Ghetto!" on the first page of an article in *Politis* (February 1990). Others present these neighborhoods as areas of "rites of passage" of a whole foreign population: "the ghetto properly speaking, the *barrio* as the Americans say, a real sieve of integration into French society." *Le Monde* of December 18, 1988, even emphasized a new form of popular culture born in those areas: "Culture *in* the suburb or culture *of* the suburb." Inspired by the culture of the American ghetto, technically as well as in style and performance, this new culture fits with the break dancing or rap that emerged in the "ghetto" and is now part of American life.

Has France lost its uniqueness? This new political issue challenges the French government's handling of immigration and, even worse, insinuates the Americanization of France. To allay unease, a new comparison with the United States has appeared, this time as an aspect of place. City administrators and experts exchange experiences to acquire an "American view of city politics" and to show how "Amazed America Discovers the French Suburb" (*Libération*, December 7, 1992). All this is to prove that "the situation is much less serious in France than in the United States" (*La Croix* and *L'Événement*, March 15–16, 1992).

Yet, in an article published in *Le Figaro* on May 23, 1991, reprinted in *Esprit*, the sociologist Alain Touraine expressed anxiety about the development of French society, which "is moving from a society of discrimination to a society of segregation like that of the United States," and warned politicians of the "threats of the ghetto." Yet French scientific language had previously been wary of words like *ghetto*, attributed to the American model. In the 1970s and even the 1980s, studies of the city tried to show that there was "no ghetto in France," replacing the word with terms like *reserved neighborhoods* or *enclaves*. This is the argument behind the housing policy of regrouping more by social category than by national, racial, or ethnic affiliation. The ghetto can be only American because of the ethnic or racial segregation of cities, based on the model of the Chicago ghetto analyzed by Louis Wirth in the 1920s and masking the isolation of the Jews, in that case. Today the ghetto is seen as racial, even if it no longer refers only to blacks.

In Germany cities and housing were at the height of postwar reconstruction when the Gastarbeiter arrived, and so the press alerted public opinion to squatters and not to foreigners in the city, particularly in Berlin. When the guest workers were first recruited, they were lodged in homes (*Heime*), but in a 1964 article on foreigners *Der Spiegel* called them ghettos. The term appeared in the caption of a photograph showing the similarity between those homes and the "camps," called *Lager*, where guest workers and refugees were housed. Was the memory of the camps too sharp in the early 1960s, or was it the traditional Jewish definition of *ghetto* that subsequently kept the word out of everyday speech? Yet once the Turkish workers were joined by their families, they were concentrated in neighborhoods that the press nicknamed little Istanbul (*Klein Istanbul*). The most famous area was Kreuzberg in Berlin, one of the tourist sights of the city up to the mid-1980s, like Harlem in New York. The word *ghetto* did gain ground, especially in scientific circles that were once again inspired and influenced by the Chicago School, but there were strong objections to it. The term *immigrant colony* (*Einwanderungskolonie*), introduced by the sociologist Friedrich Heckmann, was adopted to describe the concentration of foreigners in the city, with all its social and economic implications.

Between Assimilation and Return

"Assimilation or return?" That is the question. In France assimilation leads to "the disappearance of foreignness," according to Jacqueline Costa-Lascoux.[27] This process, considered natural for previous waves of immigration, is now taboo. It is perceived as antidemocratic, for it is defined as the total disappearance of the culture of "origin" and deprecates cultural pluralism. Philip Gleason claimed that in the United States in the 1920s, *assimilation* was a synonym for *melting pot*, a process that led individuals of different origins, living in a common territory, to create enough solidarity to sustain a common national life.[28] In the 1920s cultural pluralism emerged as closer to reality and ideologically opposed to assimilation. Since cultural differences were preserved from then on, cultural pluralism was only the coexistence of different cultures. A liberal view of the term defines it as a process of Americanization by stressing diversity in the unity that characterizes American society.[29] Now, the issue is "integrating" that diversity into the dominant trend or "incorporating" it into the political and national culture. It is no longer assimilation, defined in the 1960s as "Anglo-Saxon conformity" by Gordon Milton.[30] In 1993 Nathan Glazer raised the question of the concept and process when he wrote "Is Assimilation Dead?"[31] This question has led other sociologists to rethink both the concept and the theory with reference to the new waves of immigration considered "unassimilable" and to conclude that there are several modes of assimilation, and as the most recent groups of immigrants, the issue is a socioeconomic and residential assimilation.[32]

Thus, even the concept of assimilation has been discarded. In France the term has also been replaced by *integration* or *insertion*. Again, according to J. Costa-Lascoux, integration is a "process that expresses a dynamic of exchange," and insertion "introduces a link between the idea of reciprocity and respect for differences."[33] The French political discussion sometimes refers to integration and sometimes to insertion, preserving the ambiguities of both their political and social content and their significance. Insertion is sometimes economic and sometimes social, and integration is sometimes cultural, sometimes social, and sometimes national. In official discourse, "integration is the struggle against exclusion," and the Ministry of the City, created in 1991, is now called the Ministry for Integration and the Struggle Against Exclusion.

Use of the concept, which has been established in the French discussion with great uncertainty, has thus changed with political strategies. As Françoise Gaspard correctly emphasized, with words that shift between the Right and the Left the issue is "naming that operation of recognizing as French those foreigners who have stayed in France long enough to take root there."[34] Does talking about integration distract the opponent by diverting attention to social problems that make assimilation harder? Or is it another way of winning the trust of the new waves of immigrants, by separating culture from politics and economics, cultural integration from structural integration?

In any case, this change of vocabulary is one result of the "right to difference." The question then is whether the right to difference has altered the vocabulary or vice versa, whether it is the perception of a difference between former European waves and the new, North African one that has produced the formulation of a right. If so, integration is a concept reserved for the "unassimilable" North African immigration, whereas assimilation is for European immigrants.

This is confirmed by polls and editorials where immigration and the inability to assimilate go hand in hand and refer automatically to Islam. "Elusive Islam" is the title of an article in *La Croix* (December 1986) reporting on the "immigrant question" as seen by the Saint-Simon Foundation. "Fundamentalism vs. Assimilation?" queried the journalists of *L'Express* in an article on immigration of April 1990. The historian Pierre Chaunu despaired when considering "The Impossible Assimilation," published in *Le Figaro* of October 31, 1985. The special article, "Immigration: The North African Challenge," published by the weekly magazine *Le Point* in February 1986, summarized the general atmosphere confronting immigration generated either by politicians or by public opinion. Books and countless articles have tried to present Islam favorably, and just as many scientific works have attempted to draw attention to the responsibility of society and its advancement. But extremist political discourse has blamed the "immigrants who don't want to be assimilated," according to an editorial by F. Terré (*Le Figaro*, June 16, 1989).

In November 1989 the case of the head scarf and the discussion it sparked on all levels of French society and in all circles added fuel to the flames. Every news article or commentary on the subject appeared under the rubric of immigration, and the head scarf with the adjective "Islamic," associated with the "veil," which was even called *hidjab* or *tchador*, triggered an open war between those who were trying to exploit the situation to increase collective fears and those who wanted to calm public opinion. The second group included activists, heads of public social action organizations, the churches, and some politicians, who tried to reason and calm passions with scientific proofs.

They rallied together to remove the Islamic-fundamentalist amalgam from public opinion. "Fundamentalists, Enemies of Islam," wrote Arezki Dahmani, leader of the France-Plus Association, in *Le Monde* of January 23, 1993. Even Jean-Claude Barrault, former president of INED (National Institute for Demographic Studies) and Social Action Fund (FAS), who later became adviser to Minister of the Interior Charles Pasqua and the author of a polemical work on Islam,[35] declared in an interview in *Le Monde* of March 15, 1991, that "France can promote the birth of a reformed Islam."

The idea was to emphasize Islam's ability to assimilate and its compatibility with French secularism, and more generally, with the West. That meant talking louder and broadcasting farther than the muezzins preaching on the minaret, in order to fight for "integration against fundamentalism" (an article by J.-M. Colombani and J.-Y. Lhomeau in *Le Monde*, November 29, 1989). Thus there would no longer be any point in talking about assimilation.

In Germany a lot has also been written about "Islam as a barrier to integration." Politicians and intellectuals also question the Turks' "capacity to integrate" (*Integrationsfähigkeit*). Assimilation is not the goal and is not desired by either side. The term *Assimilierung* assumes a negative sound and is often used as *Assimilierung als Einheitskultur* (assimilation to a single culture), which would be even counterproductive vis-à-vis integration. When the word is mentioned, it is limited to the cultural level, meaning lifestyle. It does not include the political realm, much less the nation. The desired reaction is only integration.

Since 1979, integration has been promoted as the basis of Ausländerpolitik (policy toward foreigners). Politically, that means measures to avoid "a structural marginalization" of foreigners in German society, affecting families socially and young people professionally. The measures seemed as vague as the concept itself because, paradoxically, in 1985, they resulted in a policy that encouraged the return of the foreign workers to their home country. The upshot was a parliamentary discussion of the concept of integration (*Eingliederung*). In an official statement of 1982, Chancellor Kohl defined integration as "fitting into German society without conflict and without access to the right of citizenship" (*Konfliktfreies Einordnen in die deutsche Gesellschaft ohne Zugang zum Bürgerrecht*), implying that they were not to think of becoming part of the nation. Thus, for German law, integration is "taking part," which means "neither assimilation nor naturalization, but assuming the rights and duties of a German 'citizen' [*Staatsbürger*]"— but without being one. This appears clearly in the statement of a CDU deputy in the parliamentary discussions of January 18, 1986: only the Left thinks that "full integration in the Federal Republic also demands full civic responsibility." As for scientific debate, it contrasts "integration" with rotation return. The concept of a multicultural Germany is being born. This is accompanied by a "linguistic correction" from Marie-Louise Beck, the new commissioner of the *Ausländerbeauftragte*. She herself is a member of the Green Party and prefers to talk of *Migrations-und-Integrationspolitik*, replacing Ausländer once and for all with *Migrantonen* and *Migranten*, since her party considers Germany a *moderne Einwanderungsgesellschaft* (a modern society of immigration).

The term *integration* has been adopted and assimilated by association activists simultaneously in both countries, and it has become the key word of all activities of social, cultural, and religious associations. In Germany associations of foreigners and the churches understand integration as an equality of rights, as in the slogan "Equal rights for cultural differences."[36] In France *intégration* appears in the definition of projected associations (whatever their activities) in the formula: "to facilitate the integration of immigrants and their families." In Germany, in the 1980s, Frankfurt alderman Daniel Cohn-Bendit created the Office of Multicultural Affairs, advocating a "multicultural democracy" inspired by J.-J. Rousseau's social contract.[37] In France, in 1989, Prime

Minister Michel Rocard created the High Committee on Integration (*Haut Conseil à l'Intégration*). Each of these countries is trying in its own way to handle the cultural and identity aspect of both the immigrant and the nation.

THE ERA OF COMMUNITIES

Discourse on multiculturalism introduces democratic societies into the era of ethnic or religious communities recognized as such. In France heated reactions have led to frequent reminders of republican political traditions that take exception to community representation of populations in a state that recognizes only the individual. Thus, integration has been understood in the French fashion, as in the title of the 1993 report of the High Committee on Integration, which repeats that France, heir to the Revolution, does not recognize any ethnic or religious community, that this is the French model. But paradoxically, the very same politicians who preach French uniqueness are increasingly appealing to "communities": "immigrant community," "Algerian community," "Muslim community." Successive governments "thank" or "consult" or "give the floor" to the "representatives of the relevant communities."

The reference to community is neither inherent in the North African immigration nor the simple result of discourse on integration. The historian Yves Lequin has described the clustering of immigrants in big-city neighborhoods since the 1930s, when "space and community merged."[38] In the 1960s the media mentioned the "Asian colonies of the capital" and the "Spaniards who live in a community with their own rituals, their cafés, their newspaper, their cinema, and their priest," adding a captioned photograph of that community: at Porte Maillot is "the Conchita station where all dreams begin and end" (*Le Figaro*, May 7, 1968).

But today the concept of community is no longer limited to that intermediate stage as in the famous monographs of the Chicago School from the 1920s. In the present discussion, it takes on a political representation not only at the local level but also at the national and even international level. So it is not simply a spontaneous organization arising from spatial proximity, but a solidarity based on bonds of identity constructed to gain recognition in the public arena.

Is this the transition from cultural communities to structural communities? Clearly, the term *community*, used to describe immigrant populations in both political and scientific discourse, in France and Germany, increasingly refers to the nation as a community in contrast to a national community and immigrant communities. In 1974 Valéry Giscard d'Estaing asserted that "immigrant workers are part of our productive national community," implicitly limiting the place and function of immigrants in France to the national community as defined in economic terms. But in the 1980s the issue was no longer solely the "productive national community" as limited to the labor market but rather the "national community" and its identity. In 1985 Giscard d'Estaing also declared that "immigration threatens French identity," an idea that is more widespread as a leitmotiv in the statements of Jean-Marie Le Pen and as a query transmuted into many forms in newspapers and magazines, books and broadcasts. In view of the dangers produced by such discourse, public organizations, particularly the Social Action Fund, which finances associations to encourage immigrants to "form communities" (according to its bulletin), have changed their approach and ruled out "recognition of ethnic communities."

In Germany some federations of immigrant associations have incorporated the term *Gemeinde* (community) into their names, like the *türkische Gemeinde zu Berlin*, thus systematically indicating the nationality of its members. At the same time, scientific language, the press, and even the discourse of politicians or activists refer to an ethnic community, as in the "Turkish ethnic community." Since this formulation always defines the ethnic community by nationality, some people prefer the term *minority* (*Minderheit*). This leads activists to claim the status of a "Turkish minority" (*türkische Minderheit*) in Germany. As in the case of the FAS in France, the term *Minderheit* was used in the first draft of the report of the *Ausländerbereauftragte* of Berlin in 1995 and has been ruled out in the final version and replaced by "Turkish nationals." In January 2000 Marie-Louise Beck, the commissioner, wanted an end to talk of the Turkish community, because, she added, that was a self-fulfilling prophecy.

Concepts such as ethnic communities, ethnicity, and minorities continue to be borrowed from Anglo-Saxon literature, but they change their content in French and German contexts. Ethnicity, an ambiguous concept referring to an identity that is sometimes national and sometimes religious or class-linked, was first defined in France as an anthropological term applied to African societies. But the term *ethnic community* is now converging with its rather vague American concept of groups organized around an identity that has become collective and demanding public recognition of that identity—an identity constructed around a presumed or imagined national or religious origin.

In France, according to *Le Robert Historique*, the word *community* indicates "a totality of persons, and abstractly, the condition of what is common to several persons. Applied to persons, it indicates a religious collectivity (1538)." Was this definition followed by the president of the republic in his address to "the Jewish community and the Muslim community" after the Gulf War in 1991? Since the discussion of secularism in France has rallied all antagonists, *community* currently appears as the antithesis of *secularism*. It conveys a reference to religion. In Germany, however, as an indication of nationality, the word *communities* (in the plural) takes on an ethnic definition that contrasts with the collective German identity. Thus, ethnic, religious, or national communities formed by the descendants of immigrants are defined by the criteria attached to national communities.

In both countries, discourse on the national community has led to a discussion of the principles of support and the mechanisms of inclusion, that is, nationality and citizenship. In France the discussion of citizenship appears as a "rational" reaction to the speeches of the extreme Right; in Germany, as an "urgent" measure, in view of racist actions and the arrival of the Aussiedler. The Committee of Experts on the Code of Nationality in France made public opinion aware of "being French." In Germany the law of foreigners, enacted in May 1989, has made access to German nationality easier for young Turks, but the discussion came up again after the spectacular outbursts in 1991, and since January 2000, there has been a historical change in the laws of citizenship with the introduction of the principle of jus solis for foreign-born children. In political circles on both the Right and the Left, among activists, and among intellectuals, the concern now is the pragmatic sense and ideological meaning of *dual citizenship*: dual loyalty or even, as underlined by the CDU conflict of loyalty, *Loyalitätskonflikt zwischen Heimatland und Gastland*. Is it a privilege or a way of maintaining separate identities?

Thus, in France, the foreigner, who until the 1970s was seen as the "immigrant worker" in the "working class," has been recognized by his identity components and his relation with the "national community" since the 1980s. In Germany the foreigner "invited to work" in the 1960s is now seen as a member of a "minority." As Pierre-André Taguieff has emphasized with the word *racism*, the change in vocabulary is "witness and reflection, factor and actor of general ideological change."[39]

As for immigration, the change in the discussion in France and Germany implies a tendency toward a standardization of discourse and how it is conveyed. Is it a coincidence that sometimes different words do not emphasize any substantive difference and that different words become interchangeable or sometimes change in the same direction and other times in the opposite direction in each of the countries? Despite some openness in language that makes the discussion of immigration public in France, and a relative discrepancy between political and scientific discourse in Germany that concentrates it more on the official level, that discussion certainly operates in the same way in everyday political life in both countries.

Whether it is universalization, linguistic contagion, or converging political strategies, by borrowing concepts from other contexts, political discourse creates not only an interest in the subject but also an identification with aspirations or grievances. The comparison with other countries in the same terms alerts public opinion to the resemblance, shows that the "evil" is general, or else illustrates one's own superiority in handling that "evil." As for scientific language, it has developed by relying particularly on American studies of settlement and ways of organization and mobilization of the groups in question. The abundance and heuristic status of Anglo-Saxon literature on the subject, linked to the historical experience of immigration in the United States, has influenced French and German scholarship and the vocabulary it has created. The same theoretical instruments are used and the same concepts are derived from empirical American data, as if to emphasize the resemblances and differences between the American and European contexts.

The transfer of methods and of terminology is justified for the sake of the universalization of concepts. It is, however, important to untangle national characteristics in translations from one language to another, since words are related to national history, and its representations often cannot be translated and refer to the specific political traditions of each country. Even so, the parallel evolution and content of words and concepts developed in different contexts denote an inevitable convergence in political strategies. Such strategies combine the representation of political traditions, which appears through national rhetoric, and the requirements of democratic societies with regard to immigration and differences.

CHAPTER TWO

Representation of Political Traditions

> The past is an essential element, perhaps the essential element
> in ideologies. If there is no suitable past, it can be invented.
> Indeed, in the nature of things, there is usually no suitable
> past, because the phenomenon these ideologies claim is not
> ancient or eternal, but historically novel.
>
> —Eric Hobsbawm

THE DISCUSSION OF IMMIGRATION now relates to the discussion of national identity. The evolution of the vocabulary analyzed in chapter 1 shows that the "individual immigrant" is now perceived as a "foreigner" belonging to an "ethnic community," which is considered opposed to the "national community." The former struggles for state legitimacy, the latter for harmony and political unity. The dynamic in their interaction raises the question of how the state creates an ethnic community with a specific collective identity while at the same time maintaining the integrity and identity of the nation.

The national community, according to Benedict Anderson, is an "imagined political community"; it draws its ideological influence from its cultural, linguistic, and religious features.[1] Like every community, the national community is based on real, or "imagined," cultural bonds in a specific historical framework. The entire emotional charge of communities consists of politicizing new solidarity and identifications. In this sense, the birth of the national community is an "invention" where ideology and institutions, ideas and facts, culture and politics, meet. In this sense the national community is not only bound by its political unit, as Dominique Schnapper argues.[2] Such a limit to the definition of the nation allows it to be distinguished from ethnicity but may omit its cultural component, since the nation also appears in the promotion of a cultural homogeneity that makes each nation-state historically unique, each following its own path to a political unification and national integration.

United by the same project, differentiated by the ways to achieve it, nation-states today establish themselves in comparison with others. Faced with international economic rivalry, states still position themselves in relation to other powers and compete for moral democratic values and economic performance. Universality clashes with particularity, since such a competition is compensated by a verbal promotion of national difference, exclusivity, and uniqueness. Founding myths fuel the discourse that blends history and ideology with reality, and each nation-state defines itself as the most egalitarian, most democratic, and best suited to the idea of modernity, particularly in its relations to the different social and ethnic groups that constitute the national society. It is in terms of these elements that history is interpreted, facts are reconstituted, and discourse is corrected. The function of these myths is to justify political decisions—resistance or change—and to orient the future while remaining loyal to the representation each of the societies, nations, and states has of itself.

France, Germany, and the United States are represented as three types of nation-states. As a matter of fact, each of them has different political traditions and is marked by different histories. Their relations with immigrants have been analyzed as three models of citizenship and nationality conforming to the terms of national identity shaped by the founders of the nation-state. According to these models, France is represented as the prime example of a nation-state: unitarian, universalist, and egalitarian. It sees assimilation as a basis for equality and points to the United States as an "antimodel," represented as practicing racial segregation. The elective and political perception of the French nation also contrasts with Germany's emphasis on common ancestors and membership in the same cultural community. In the United States, as in France, citizenship is placed at the center of the theory and practice shaping the nation-state, but the doctrine of the French model, based on republican individualism, is the assimilation of individuals who have made a political choice to become citizens (as in the United States), whereas the American model is represented by the French view as a model based on the recognition of communities that express their cultural membership in public life. However, neither of these two models refers to origins or ancestors, as in the German model.[3]

Specific models based on contrasts or similarities might be imagined ad infinitum and would produce just as many possible scenarios combining reality and ideology, although there is not always a firm connection between the two. These models find a justification in "remembered history"; they crystallize a self-perception as a nation-state, its construction, its values, its founding principles, in short, its ideology. They constitute an anchor that allows the development of a coherent discourse connecting a representation of political traditions with the treatment of current reality. They establish the role of national institutions in the maintenance and perpetuation of these principles and indirectly define the place granted newcomers.

For all studies on immigration, integration, and citizenship in France, Germany, and the United States, these ideal-typical contrasts have become inevitable references. Thought on the subject has become almost inseparable from the "nationalization of thought." In France, for example, "clans" have appeared to defend "radical republicanism" as loyalty to the republican view of the nation, as opposed to the "ethnist" view attributed to Germany. Others move toward international experiences and fluctuate between a republican idea of unity and "multiculturalism" as a basis of national unity. These studies are guided more by ideological reconstructions than by present realities, more by concepts that have made the history of ideas than by facts that have shaped history.

Because, in fact, social reality is more complex. Relations between individuals, groups, and states are more fluid, and the models in question are increasingly interchangeable. A representation stuck in the past allows the justification of political decisions, but it clashes with reality and experiences that contradict principles, and it generates tensions, even conflicts, in modern democratic societies. This chapter raises the conceptual question of the link between a representation based on rhetoric and the definition of laws as a crystallization of reality, and of the link between legal and institutional structures and mental structures.

On the Nature of Representation: An "Ideal Nation"

In theory, representation is based on the interpretation of a historical reality that intends to be objective. Yet, especially during the political drafting of a projected nation or state, that representation is transmitted in a form that serves its founders' purpose and desire for perpetuation.

Integration "à la française"

L'Integration à la française is the title of the report of the High Committee on Integration, published in the spring of 1993. In big black letters on a white cover, this title seems to be an appeal to collective memory, evoking French uniqueness and its importance in the assimilation of foreigners. The authors of the report claim that the French model of integration, "based on a principle of equality, contrasts with the 'logic of minorities' that confers a specific status on national or ethnic minorities." The report emphasizes "the profound calling of our country, which, inspired by the principles of the Declaration of the Rights of Man, asserts the equality of men across the diversity of their cultures."

That is how the legacy of the French Revolution is expressed. It is related to the end of monarchy and to the birth of the modern nation-state, seen both as territorial unity and as collective consciousness, as well as a common identification among its members who share the same rights and the same privileges. It marks the end of local and regional allegiances and the beginning of identification with a central state uniting the various provinces of the kingdom of the ancien régime, the "different Frances," into a single nation. The kings of France also wanted to transcend divisions and create unity, but that was not realized until the founding of the republic, "one and indivisible." It is the birth of a national civil society where individuals had to fight for equality as individuals within the framework of national institutions, a civil society taken over by the state, which guaranteed the unity of the new nation it created, even *invented*. State and nation merged to unite the anthropological diversity of the French nation around the same political plan.

This is the idea that Ernest Renan developed in *Qu-est-ce qu'une nation?* (What is a nation?), an excerpt from a lecture he delivered at the Sorbonne on March 11, 1882. Renan defined the nation as a "soul" composed of common memories and plans expressing the desire to live together. He referred to a collective will shared among individuals and groups speaking different languages or belonging to different religions; in short, to groups with different cultural references but united by a single political reference concerning the general will of individuals, beyond cultural, linguistic, or religious affiliations. According to Renan, "To base politics on ethnographic analysis is to turn it into a chimera." He thus rejected any political representation resting on the separate identities of minorities; he saw this as a threat to the integrity of the nation. Community bonds and regional or local allegiances were likewise repudiated on behalf of the republican state. Maintaining the integrity of the nation was inherent in its elective conception, formulated as an "everyday plebiscite." These were the principles that *invented* the nation of France.

French reference to Renan's speech has become systematic since the 1980s. This is not accidental. It is a sign of a crisis atmosphere that affects the idea of a national unity directly or indirectly and affirms the need to recall traditions and "memories." Renan's political and legal concept of the nation was a reaction to Germany's arguments of organic bonds to justify the annexation of Alsace and Lorraine. History seems to have proved him right. In 1918, after the defeat of the Germans, the region returned to France. It was not language, hence not a common culture with the people across the Rhine, that was decisive, but the political experience of the Revolution that presumably moved the Alsatians closer to France. So national consciousness originates in a (subjective) political identification, and not in a linguistic identity (which claims to be objective).

The appeal to Renan today is obviously not a reaction to Germany—now an ally in constructing the European Union. Nor is it any longer the territorial definition of the country that is at issue, but rather its identity. Renan's lecture has recently been reintroduced into French public and scientific discussion as a reaction to expressions of ethnic or religious identities expressed by migrants who are mostly from North Africa and therefore Muslims. One partial explanation for this is the feeling that the political nation has been neglected and the idea of state sovereignty weakened for the sake of economic interests that favored immigration. Their settlement and claim for cultural rights are perceived as a challenge to the national community—the only community that counts—and its unity.

Thus, Renan's talk responds to or alleviates the situation and justifies the "French exception." The French nation as an ideal nation nourishes republican ideology and vice versa. Ideologies as basic components of a social and political order obviously produce meaning in times of crisis. France has always claimed to be an example of a united nation, at least externally, and has been at the vanguard of the universality embodied in the Declaration of the Rights of Man. In *Les lieux de mémoire* (Realms of Memory), Pierre Nora argued that the universal values that characterize France "turned a specific national adventure into the emancipating vanguard of humanity and introduced the criterion of progress to realize an essential stage in and through the History constituted by the Republic."[4]

The political plan accompanying these ideas consists of homogenizing the nation. The populations that constituted "nations" on French territory before the Revolution, isolated from the nation of France, were henceforth, by right and duty, to identify with the new nation, the only community granted political legitimacy. The phrase that best illustrates this ideology was delivered by the count of Clermont-Tonnerre: "For the Jews as individuals everything, and nothing as a nation." The very idea of imagining the "one and indivisible" nation split into ethnic groups, into religious and even regional communities—"embryonic nations," as it were—defied the long historical process of forming the nation-state. Citizenship, political identity, became inseparable from nationality.

This plan began to bear fruit under the Third Republic. The army, the schools, and the development of networks of roads, facilitating geographic mobility inside the territory, particularly from the country to the city, helped transform not only "the peasant" but also the foreigner, or the immigrant, "into Frenchmen."[5] Compulsory education and instruction in French (the abandonment of local jargon or regional languages) for everyone (immigrants from a region or foreigners), based on equal opportunity, naturally spread a national ideology but also created a sense of belonging to republican France. Moreover, shaping the nation-state entailed the creation of collective memory and consciousness aiming at the ideal of cultural homogeneity.[6] "Political integration" became synonymous with "cultural integration," even "assimilation" of the individual through the national institutions. This effort at standardization is what characterizes "integration à la française," which, again according to Schnapper, constitutes the "process of national integration."[7]

Dream of German Unity

Such an inclusive perception of citizenship in France contrasts with the representation of an exclusive citizenship based on ethnic identity in Germany. This contrast leads to another national model: the nation defined as an "ethnic nation." The interpretation of *das deutsche Volk* emphasizes an ethnic affiliation that excludes all cultural differences: the cultural unity and organic character of the national community are thus included in the definition of the nation. Whereas the French nation is *invented* in terms of a historic process deriving from the will of the kings and from an emotional bond, the German nation is *imagined* in terms of organic bonds between individuals sharing the same origins, in terms of membership in the German people, even though that people was geographically scattered in two kingdoms with no communication network between them. The two approaches are quite similar in their overlap of culture and politics; a political identity is considered the basis of a cultural identity in France, and a cultural identity constitutes the basis of a political identity in Germany.

The dream of national unity is closely bound to German romanticism. Johann Gottlieb Fichte, in his *Speech to the German Nation*, insisted on the idea of the cultural unity of the German nation. Cultural unity and unity of language (promoted by Johann Gottfried Herder) fueled the German dream of national unity, limiting collective identity to all who shared the same ancestors, the same language, and the same culture. Inspired by Fichte, German nationalism was also promoted via a passionate resistance to foreign "domination." Unity, law, and freedom (*Einigkeit und Recht und Freiheit*) became the decisive values of the German nation. They appear in the "Song of Germany" (*Deutschlandlied*) by the poet A. H. Hoffmann von Fallersleben and reappear in 1952 in the national anthem of the Federal Republic.

The French Revolution, which transformed social and political values in France and elsewhere, led to a negative reaction in Germany, which marked the beginning of the Romantic movement. German Romanticism emerged in the early nineteenth century in reaction to France. Promoting membership in a culture and a people, it rejected the rationality the Revolution inspired and its universal values. Fichte saw rational Enlightenment religion as the cause of the defeat of Prussia, and Romanticism countered that rationality by revising the religious element of social cohesion. While the Prussian reformers, inspired by the French Revolution, were launching the first drafts of the state of law, the Romantics were referring nostalgically to the Christianity that had united the peoples of Europe in the Middle Ages, "the only time in German history in which this nation is famous and brilliant and holds the rank to which, as the parent stock, it is entitled."[8]

The idea of nation was assimilated to a "collective soul." The expression came from French Romantics such as Joseph de Maistre who also reacted to the ideas of the French Revolution and the political nation. De Maistre emphasized "the idea of the encompassing totality" of the nation, in contrast to "the idea of free association" implied by "the nation-contract." Thus, the soul of the nation is its cultural uniqueness, whereas Renan's reference to the nation as a "soul" composed of memories is the reverse approach, assembling the differences to build the nation—hence its universality. For German Romantics, the notion of *Volksgeist* (spirit of the people) expressed distance from the Enlightenment and became the constituent element of the German nation.[9] Thus, the idea of the *Volksnation*, "nation of the people," developed in contrast to the *Staats(bürger)nation*, "nation of citizens," as defined in Revolutionary France.

Such a concept of the German nation stoked the fear of a loss of identity and expressed a retreat into time, as long as it was rooted in the past. The past was the Holy Roman Empire, the ancestors, the sense of belonging to an "imagined" community of origin; the Revolution was the future, the hope of a new society, the inauguration of new institutions designed to create a new consciousness as well as uncertainty about the future.

The movement of nationalist ideas dates from the Revolutionary period, the German state from 1871. The idea of nation, which initially was cultural, preceded the birth of the state. Its creation was aimed mainly at defining a territory. Thus, national consciousness predated political organization. Territorial instability led to a redefinition of political borders and national borders. Moreover, the absence of a center, produced by weak institutions, did not lead to a political identification. German identity that went beyond the borders of the Reich had no political meaning recognized in the new state, yet nationality was defined as a combination of ancestors and territory (the past), so that Germans outside the borders of the state would at least preserve their German nationality. In principle, Germanness (*Deutschtum*) also applied to Germans living in neighboring states because they belonged to the German people as so defined. This principle has been applied to Aussiedler, coming from the territories of the old empire and German citizens de jure because of their German ancestry.

"E Pluribus Unum"

The national unity of the United States is based on cultural diversity. The phrase *e pluribus unum* expresses the conviction that history would bring unity from diversity to the new American land. The United States is characterized not only by a multiethnic and multicultural nation composed of various waves of immigrants from Western Europe, but also by the fact that all populations of various origins have been seen as belonging to a single nation. The opening words of the Preamble to the Constitution, "We, the people of the United States of America," clearly attribute a political character to the "people," consider all the cultural diversity of the individuals who make up the nation, and do not assume an ethnic character as in Germany.

Jean de Crèvecoeur, a Frenchman who emigrated to the United States in the 1760s and took the name of J. Hector Saint-John, defined the American as the new man. In his *Letters from an American Farmer*, published during the American Revolution, he wrote: "Here individuals of all nations are melted into a new race of men." The term *melting pot*, the title of a 1908 play by Israel Zangwill, came to symbolize that mixture of languages, cultures, and religions in the New World and even served as a national ideology. Jane Addams stated that Zangwill "had performed a great service to America by reminding us of the high hopes of the founders of the Republic."[10]

The new man in a new nation, "the first new nation," as Seymour Martin Lipset called it. Born in 1776 with the Declaration of Independence and later the Articles of Confederation, that new nation marked a territorial break and a new national representation, separate from Great Britain, the colonists' country of origin, and shaped by geographical and political distance. The American Revolution, predating the French Revolution, introduced a unique historical discontinuity in comparison with France, where the Revolution did not eliminate anything from the national feeling. France remained "one of the most precocious and most solidly united nations of the west," where, for Colette Beaune, "French national feeling has been constructed throughout its history since the

Middle Ages."[11] The French Revolution redefined the national ideology with new central institutions that structured and neutralized social relations and relations to power, which was now central, whereas the American Revolution was to define a new identity on a new territory. *Immigration* and *freedom* became the key words in shaping that new nation.

In the United States national ideology derived from the same principles as in France. Citizenship there also corresponded primarily to a political choice and included the individual in a political and territorial set. This choice formed the basis of the allegiance of the citizen of a (federated) state and an (American) nation. But the United States, a nation of immigrants, is distinguished from European nations by its cultural pluralism, which "was a fact before it became a theory . . . with explicit references for the nation as a whole."[12] The perception of the Anglo-Saxon or American model is based on the presence of groups and communities that are distinguished from one another by national origin, race, and religion and who participate in political life to defend their group interests, defined as such. This approach is described as "differentialist" by E. Todd and is opposed to the "uniformative" approach of the French model, a contrast often mentioned in discussions of the presence or absence of communities formed by the descendants of immigrants in France. The American liberal tradition is now associated with the weakness of the state and its institutions and its limited intervention in society and economics.[13]

Although the immigrants who settled in the New World did not share the same past and the same references at first, they did identify with the same myths as expressed in the Constitution. According to Élise Marienstras, when "the Constitution laid the foundations of the nation state, the inhabitants of the United States could permanently feel that 'common interest' that raised them above their locality."[14]

THE SEARCH FOR SOCIAL COHESION

Whatever the historical path followed by nation-states, the national idea rests on the expression of a common will. The nation, the "invented" political community, as in France and the United States, or the "imagined" one, as in Germany, is characterized by its references to the past. It is also defined by its attitude toward the present, which is manifested both by an attachment to a collective identity and by the desire to share the same future. At least ideally or by resolution, this promoted a united community tending toward cultural homogeneity and political unity. New ideologies are to be devised to deal with the shift to modernity established by the nation-state. The state now nourishes the sense of belonging to the nation and guards its integrity; it invents "new traditions,"[15] creates new solidarities that lead to social cohesion and to the general integration of society. Despite the differences among nation-states, the path to modernity has been accompanied by the secularization of the state; therefore, new "religions" are to be conceived only to reestablish a political morality and social cohesion: civil or civic religion, religion as culture or identity, as belief or practice, as many combinations as possible questioning the establishment of a new political and cultural balance.

Religions and Social Cohesion

The French nation-state born of the Revolution embodied modernity and promoted the values of equality among individuals and of freedom. *Emancipation*, a key word in the modern state, is simply the individual's release from communal primary relations, guaranteed and supported by the church, and consequently reflects the individual's attachment to new founding values of secondary relations guaranteed by the state and its institutions. The individualism reactivated by the Revolution rested on those impersonal relations that characterize societal relations in opposition to communal relations and have become the only mode of participation in the historical-political community that characterizes the nation.

These changes require what may be defined as new social bonds. The transition of religious minorities (Jews and Protestants) to the status of citizens, which came with emancipation, made laïcité the "ideological cement" that replaced the "spiritual cement" of the ancien régime.[16] Laïcité, secularism, resulting from a struggle of the republicans against church control over the state, has been presented as a value linked to science, progress, and reason, and the idea of secularism resulted in the neutrality of the state with regard to religion. Neutrality has become synonymous with tolerance, because it presupposes freedom of conscience in private and personal life. Laïcité was then defined as the principal element of social cohesion, the pillar of republican France.

By contrast, German nationalism, stoked by antirevolutionary sentiments, rejected the very idea of secularism. The *Aufklärung* (Enlightenment philosophy) was not really against religion, just as rationality was not against Protestant piety. The concern for equality it embodied consisted mainly of destroying the barriers between the clergy, the nobility, the middle class, and the peasantry, and, in this sense, *Aufklärung* means both secularization and modernization.[17] After the formation of the federal state, the *Kulturkampf*, as in France, was characterized by an effort to guarantee social cohesion by minimizing the role of the Catholic Church while limiting Protestant influence on politics as well.

The individualism of the German Romantics merged with the sense of being part of a comprehensive cultural community, a sense resulting from long education (*Bildung*) and participation in the creation of a common culture and identity. The individualism of the Romantics was thus expressed by devotion to the collective German identity and the fear of losing it.[18] Linking the individual to the community contrasted with favoring French individualism in the sociopolitical arena.

This expression of a special collective identity was manifested in the national consciousness by *Kultur*, as contrasted with the *civilisation* that referred to "a Court society," described and analyzed by Norbert Elias in *The Civilization of Manners*. According to Ellias, *Kultur* is German, whereas *civilisation* is more suited to French identity as part of a worldwide reference and to France defined as the bearer of *civilisation*. Further, for France, colonization, "a human duty," parallel to the English slogan of the White Man's Burden, constituted a first stage in the assimilation of other cultures into French *civilisation* and the universal values it embodied, even if the civilizing mission was often attributed to the church, which was considered universal. Nevertheless, modernization for colonized countries meant accepting the Western values of the French nation-state. *Kultur*, however, is particularist by definition, and the German Reich did not take on the civilizing mission of France. Rudolf von Thadden reminds us that the German Reich "didn't try to 'Germanize' the local population in its colonies."[19]

Religion is inseparable from *Kultur* and from the German national feeling. Both took shape during the battles against Napoleon, the Revolution, and French secularism, in brief, against "anti-Christianity." The historian Thomas Nipperdey demonstrated the Christian character of German nationalism in the construction of the Cologne cathedral. This cathedral, planned by Ernst Moritz to commemorate the battle of Leipzig that united all the Germans, was seen as a "monument to the nation" in the discussions it produced. Its opening was celebrated "as a festival of hope of the 'German renaissance' and of unity for the liberals," a unity based on "the German people and not only on princes and states," a unity that included "the Constitution, participation of the citizens, constructing the state from the bottom up."[20] Note that the preamble of the fundamental law of 1949 begins with: "Aware of its responsibility before God and men."

The construction of the cathedral is significant because it emphasizes the link between nationalism and Christianity. Beyond nationalism, religion plays an important role in the search for social cohesion, mainly in the definition of solidarities. After the state was created, churches organized into associations, and pressure groups influenced the establishment of the welfare state.

Secularism was not the central issue in the New World. The Founding Fathers thought in terms of administrative creation of a federal union as the basis of a nation-state. The ideological cement was supplied by the civic culture, the only one that could create an identification with the new nation among the various religious, national, and linguistic communities.

This civic culture, the product of a political education aimed at making every individual or group embrace the republican values of the "first new nation," has been turned into a component of social cohesion and unity. Optimistic observers see it as promoting pluralism, since it allows groups freedom, first to exist as such, and then to express their own economic and political interests. Following this logic, community solidarities among individuals of the same origin overlap with patriotism or rather reinforce it, prompting Tocqueville to express amazement at the speed with which newcomers accepted republican values and symbols.

Yet, even if states have managed to break with religious tradition, language often refers to religion. In the United States historians have shown how support for civic culture is accompanied by the adoption of a religious vocabulary that reinforces the republicanism of Americans. These symbols combine attachment to republican values and to the authority of God to define the "good American," in which all citizens recognize themselves. They swear loyalty to the Constitution when they are naturalized, swear on the Bible in court, and celebrate Thanksgiving, the expression of gratitude to God (even if all Americans—both old and new immigrants—consider it the perfect secular holiday because it transcends and accommodates all religious beliefs); the president blesses his people and his country at the end of every official speech and publicly goes to church every week once he is elected.

Inspired by the *Social Contract*, academics have developed the notion of civic religion to express the combination of the American attachment to God and the republic. But unlike Rousseau's negative definition of "Roman Christianity," American civic religion reconciles individual freedom and the authority of God, belief in republican values and commitment to religion as an expression of individual freedom.[21] Thus, Marienstras argues that the American nation "combines reason and religion in a synthesis that allows the body politic to be cemented and glorified."

In France the republic, called the "oldest daughter of *the church*" has taken on a holy character. Claude Nicolet pointed to the religious metaphors used in the establishment of moral rules; if the republic is to be fully realized, "suffrage must be universal, free, and (mainly) enlightened, like the church."[22] Even Renan, in his lecture on the nation, referred to the Jacobin Church and defined it as a secular religion. When secularism, or laïcité, became a new doctrine, any public display of religion was rejected. The vocabulary was secularized by using the adjective *civil*, which expressed fundamental bonds in society in the nineteenth century: "civil order," civil state," "civil right," "civil marriage," "civil burial." Thus, "civil" replaced "divine."[23] From a legal standpoint, the constitution of 1795 had already introduced a partial secularization in marriage, health, and education, but the legal separation of church and state dates from 1905, after the Dreyfus affair. The flagrant conflict between (secular) republicans and antirepublicans (defenders of religion in public life) in the affair illustrates the importance (and/or rejection) of religion. The republicans won the battle, from then on representatives of the church were mere civil servants, and all references to religion disappeared from the public arena; its symbols, for example, were removed from the walls of public welfare hospitals. Belief in God was now only a private matter. But not until the constitution of October 27, 1946, did secularism become law, and that was reiterated in the constitution of 1958.

Nevertheless, secularism, or laïcité, is ambiguous about the boundary between culture and religion. Culture refers to religious identity and religion to belief or practice. Research on French religious expression shows a constant decline of practice, which is easily measured, unlike the cultural reference, which remains abstract and hard to measure but which appears whenever it confronts another religion, for instance, Islam today.

Yet the idea of laïcité is inseparable from the "indoctrination" implemented by the public schools under the Third Republic. It is not surprising that its contemporary challenge arose when some young Muslim girls wore their head scarves in school.[24] Jules Ferry introduced a radical change in 1882 by making public, secular, and free primary school compulsory for everyone, including girls. The school then became the instrument for propagating secularism. The centralization of instruction and the creation of secular teachers' training schools entrusted the school with the role of unifying the nation. Of course, seeking national unity and social order in the republican school amounts to obscuring the educational wars that preceded the law of 1882, which consisted of "getting God out of the school."[25] The moral vacuum produced by the abolition of religious instruction in curriculums was filled by civic instruction. The school became the bearer of new moral values, which, Mona Ozouf maintained, were "the virtues of order and obedience [that] make up the portrait of the French as economical, hard-working,

honest, and disciplined."[26] With the creation of the public school, relations between it and the private school, understood to a large extent as
a denominational establishment, were defined by the Debré Law of
December 31, 1959, ruling on the private school of general instruction,
under a contract with the state, either individually or in an association.[27]
But it was in the republican school instituted by Jules Ferry that the
question of national unity and social order arose, which led François
Bayrou, minister of national education, to say in the parliamentary
debates of October 1994 that "French national identity is inseparable
from its school." However, the tensions between private instruction (in
religious establishments) and public instruction are felt even today
whenever the educational system in France is called into question.

Defining New Solidarities

Nevertheless, if religion is not at the core of social cohesion anymore,
new solidarities are to be imagined in order to give a content to a unified nation. In France the state has become the main agent to unite the
nation, "the authority of social production," according to Pierre Rosanvallon. Moreover, the state in France is also the agent of cultural production. In Germany the community reference of the nation is the
product of an elite, educated middle class familiar with public duty.
Hence, social cohesion resulting from the cultural community consisted
of abolishing class and cultural—religious—divisions. In both countries, the army was an authority of socialization that originally promoted national unity along with intense national identification. It was
the only institution to unite all citizens, no matter what their social or
even "ethnic" origin. In France the army served the republic; in Germany, as Norbert Élias indicated, it also provided "codes to the middle
class." The system of recruitment included Prussians in the army along
with other groups not necessarily of German descent (*deutscher Ab-
stammung*). Thus it transcended distinctions of class and origin, which
explains the importance of the military in unifying the nation. The citizen volunteered to become a soldier during the war of liberation against
Napoleon at the beginning of the nineteenth century. Community bonds
were consolidated and patriotic sentiment increased in the mobilizations
of 1848, during the war against France in 1870, in the creation of the
state in 1871, and finally in the Great War of 1914–18.

Yet economic progress intervened in shaping national unity in Germany, as ideas did in France. It is interesting to note that a work by
Ferdinand Tönnies, *Gemeinschaft und Gesellschaft* (Community and
Society), began to permeate public opinion twenty-five years after its
publication in 1887, just as Germany was feeling the consequences of

economic progress as a threat, seeing the shift from an agrarian society to an industrial one as a shift from "community" to "society." But at the same time the basis for an economic argument in consolidating the nation rests on the idea that Germany was an economic nation before it became a politically unified one,[28] hence the *Zollverein* (the customs union) established in the 1830s between the various German states. Rising wages and a rising standard of living led to a considerable slowdown of German immigration to America at the end of the nineteenth century, when economic expansion reduced departures from two hundred thousand in 1881–82 to twenty thousand in 1895.[29]

The notion of progress, connected with the Enlightenment and rationality in France, yielded concrete social measures in Germany. The authorities encouraged social progress along with economic progress. Many social protection measures, such as old-age insurance and disability payments, were introduced between 1883 and 1891, and then until the turn of the century, as a means of "domesticating" the working class. The aim was to redefine national solidarity by redistributing resources. In this context the economic and intellectual middle class brought a new dimension to the nation, defined as a social nation. This goal was still alive after 1949 and influenced the political reconstruction of Germany.

But a social and economic nation does not have the emotional, even passionate, charge produced by the imagined cultural nation in Germany or the invented nation in France. Its political expression makes all the difference. That is what led Helmut Plessner to define Germany as a "delayed nation" (*verspätete Nation*), delayed in its political construction. Plessner attributed this delay to the role of the middle class in its formation and the absence of the state in the formation of the nation as a political unity. In France, in contrast, Pierre Rosanvallon has argued that the social nation lagged behind Germany and the United States in the introduction of social policies because of an overly "philosophical" and "abstract" notion of progress that limited state action in the social realm. The establishment of social hygiene dates from 1905 and the Ministry of Health from 1920. In fact, it was mainly the demographic loss caused by the Great War that led to measures to fight the "internal enemies" of syphilis, tuberculosis, and so on.[30]

In the United States, however, individualism limits the social action of the state. Social action is then assumed by voluntary associations or mutual aid organizations for members of the religious community or the neighborhood. The liberal tradition refers many social problems to private institutions. This communal solidarity and this dependence on private institutions can be sources of inequality, given the variations in the internal organization of communities, in the meaning of solidarity, and in the financial resources available. The combination of these mechanisms challenges the universalism of the American state in the establishment of the social bond.

Revolution, reform, or counterrevolution—all shape the definition of the nation and its ideology. After all, ideas create history, or at least its representation. Periods of ideological movement and ferment mark the history of mentalities and political decisions. They shape public opinion, reassure citizens, especially in time of crisis when basic principles confront realities that follow their own path and elude the control of states. Recall the long road traveled by nation-states to devise a national unity. They do this to define the political and cultural borders while adapting to the surrounding realities, for the national sentiment is also forged in relation to others; but now it is a matter of immigrants, foreigners inside the national borders.

LIMITS OF REPRESENTATION

The founding principles, which seem immutable, since they are representative of the dominant ideology, thus on one hand clash with new experiences and on the other with the law, which sometimes justifies them and sometimes contradicts them. Their content changes to adapt to situations that are always dominated by a concern with maintaining a representation of integrity, of unity, and to some extent of homogeneity within each nation-state.

The Category of Experience

If ideas create history, experiences shape it. Relations between society and national institutions whose task of cultural homogenization is inherent in the construction of a nation-state fall within the category of experience, the context where migrations, the arrival of new groups with their own cultural baggage, challenge European states. Unlike the United States, a nation made up of successive waves of migrants mainly from Europe, European states do not see immigration from neighboring countries (as in France) or the presence of foreigners owing to changes in territorial boundaries (as in Germany) as contributing to shaping the nation. National fusion, as it has long been represented in the United States, corresponds to a process of absorption and assimilation in European countries.

Immigrants who move into a new country adopt its norms, values, and national codes as part of the process of assimilation. Assimilation corresponds with the process of modernization embodied in the project of emigration. As for the countries of immigration, the absorption of cultural contributions shows their openness to integrating newcomers into the nation-state and consequently into the modern world. For the last ten years, historical studies in France and Germany have increasingly tried to demonstrate that despite differences in ideology, both countries have experienced important waves of immigration since the mid-nineteenth century and are in fact countries of immigration. France is currently aware that one-fifth of its population has one ancestor from abroad, and Germany knows that its industrial development owes a great deal to foreign manpower.[31]

Yet there are nuances and variations. Of all European countries, France has the most experience with immigration and the settlement of foreign groups, whereas Germany has long been a country of emigration. Even when departures for the United States slowed down at the end of the nineteenth century, foreigners on German soil were mainly "internal foreigners," that is, non-German groups in territories annexed at different periods of unification, hence of German nationality.[32] France experienced an influx of foreigners from outside the national boundaries, although mainly from neighboring countries, and Germany found itself with "foreigners" from within the Reich, mainly Poles. Of course, French colonial history differs from German annexation. Masses of North Africans came to France after decolonization as economic immigrants, even though other waves of Algerians who sided with France during the war were settled before 1962.

In France historical studies have shown that immigration always appeared primarily as a response to a demographic problem. Even during the ancien régime, a low birth rate plus an infant mortality of 50–60 percent, epidemics, and departures, particularly of Protestants, resulted in an anxiety about depopulation. As a result of this demographic weakness, Colbert worried about tax receipts, and in the seventeenth century the comptroller-general of finances introduced measures to increase fertility by encouraging marriage, limiting departures, prosecuting deserters, and welcoming migrants from neighboring countries.

In the mid-nineteenth century, however, immigration in France had become above all a demand of the labor market and of economic expansion, as in Germany, and was still manifested by the spontaneous influx from neighboring countries for a season, a year, or an unlimited period. All the Italians had to do was cross the border to southeast France, like the Belgians in the north and the Spaniards in the southeast, even if they then scattered throughout the country. By the end of the nineteenth century, foreigners represented 3 percent of the total population, a proportion that doubled in twenty-five years. However, on the eve of the Great War, new waves of immigrants from more distant countries changed the composition of the foreign population: North

Africans, particularly Kabyles, and Poles fleeing the slump in the mining industry in the Ruhr, found refuge primarily in France. The massive arrival of Italians between the two wars was followed by an influx from the Iberian Peninsula starting in the 1950s and from North Africa in the 1960s. Thus, France today is certainly defined in retrospect as a country of immigration.

Immigration in Germany is mainly the result of an employment policy. "We are not a country of immigration" (*Wir sind kein Einwanderungsland*), declared the authorities. Even if demographic reasons appear as an argument, the main issue is shortages in the labor market.[33] Industrialization, or rather the shift "from an agrarian state with a strong industry to an industrial state with an important agrarian base" at the end of the nineteenth century, triggered an internal migration from east to west, mostly of German Poles.[34] But by the end of the century, foreign Poles from Russia or Austria far outnumbered German Poles in agriculture in the east. Although Silesia and eastern Prussia lacked manpower, the authorities began to be concerned about the "Polonization" of the west, namely, the contact of German Poles who worked there with foreign Poles. Seasonal work then appeared as the only possibility of combining economic interests with protection against the invasion of the foreign Poles (*Überfremdung*). Thus, a system of rotation (*Karenzzeit*) was determined, based on rationing the period of work of the foreign Poles in the west. At the same time, the permanent need for cheap manpower created by industrialization produced a recourse to the so-called industrial reserve army of Dutch, Austrians, and especially Italians, which changed the composition of the foreign population. After World War II, the appeal to the foreign manpower essential to economic reconstruction was directed at the eastern Mediterranean, Greece, the former Yugoslavia, and Turkey.

The nature of immigration in the United States has also changed since the beginning of the twentieth century. The open-door policy that had led to free immigration, largely from Europe, came to an end in the early 1920s, when national quotas were instituted. Yet immigration resumed after World War II, returning to the rates of the nineteenth century. But in the 1970s Asian and Mexican immigrants changed the ehtnic mix of the influx.

The conditions of absorption and acceptance of foreigners or migrants point up the limits of universality in the French and American republican ideals, whereas German particularism remains compatible with its exclusivist principles. As for France, in the 1930s Georges Mauco outlined an immigration policy based on the candidate group's capacity to "assimilate," establishing a hierarchy among ethnicities according to language (the resemblance between the foreigner's mother tongue and French), physical appearance, and moral values, thus a selective immigration. In the United States, in the 1920s, entrance quotas based on national origin were merely "ethnic favoritism" for immigrants from the British Isles, Germany, and Scandinavia as a way of preventing a change in the national mix. In the 1950s the quota system was no longer applied to the country of origin but to the hemisphere; but not until 1965, under the influence of the civil rights movement, did a new immigration law drop all discrimination and adopt a policy of first-come first-admitted.

As for the presence of foreigners in the country, the view of the foreigner or immigrant as a scapegoat is classic, recurring in times of economic depression. Depressions and migrations come in waves, each with its own rhythm, and refer to identities revealed by the presence of foreigners. In France, Gérard Noiriel noted in *Le creuset français*,[35] hatred of the foreigner, which appeared three times during the last hundred years, corresponds to "periods of economic depression and intense social upheavals."

Yet it is hard to define foreigners as a separate legal category once they have become French.[36] To be sure, statistical invisibility seems to suit only Europeans, despite the hostility and rejection they confronted initially.[37] Xenophobic acts seemed to focus on religious differences, recalling the pre-Revolutionary attitude that designated such differences as a permanent otherness. Hence a revival of suspicion of Jews and Protestants. Today it is Islam that marks the boundary of what is foreign, which means that to ensure social cohesion and the identification of every individual who demonstrates support of the political nation to which he or she is attached, the so-called civil religion has gotten away from *civil* and became an instrument of exclusion during times of economic depression, even if that religion is meant as culture and not necessarily faith.

However, there was never a question of universality in Germany. A policy of forced assimilation, "Germanization" (*Germanisierung*), of the Poles of the Ruhr was carried out in the nineteenth century, compelling the Poles of the Reich who had German citizenship but another language and culture to assume German family names and to speak German. At the beginning of the twentieth century, the Center for the Supervision of the Poles was created to prevent the Poles from forming associations, maintaining their identity, and participating in nationalist movements in Poland. The aim was to consolidate the collective expression of their loyalty to the German nation through indivisibility. Cultural particularism gave way to racial exclusivity during World War II. By defining Germans as belonging to the "Aryan race" and Jews to a "Jewish race," the latter were targeted for death. This is not a question of indivisibility.

But in the United States, as in France, the universality of the nation is not devoid of ambiguity. The Declaration of Independence, "the expression of the American spirit, the genuine effusion of the soul of the country,"[38] expressing the hope of national unity, bears the stamp of the colonists. It is peculiar to a nation they were about to shape as they liked, giving the tone to a national identity in the making. Thus they excluded Indians (considered foreigners, members of another nation, and treated as property) and black slaves. This "American dilemma," to use Gunnar Myrdal's term, generated the present gap between the principles of equality and universality in building a nation.[39] Even if the Declaration of Independence marks the citizen's membership in a state and a nation, the contradictions arising from real restrictions increase tensions between groups who demonstrate their right to a "piece of the pie."[40] These principles were used by the Indians and black slaves, who were excluded from an American identity in the making, to question the Revolution.

In *Le destin des immigrés* (The fate of the Immigrants), Emmanuel Todd claimed that American universalism refers to the assimilation of whites, since differentialism is based on skin color. But racial segregation does not prevent whites—although divided into national/religious communities—from xenophobia against them. It did not spare whites themselves, who were divided into religious communities. In the nineteenth and early twentieth centuries, economic slumps gave rise to prejudice and xenophobia. Labor movements hostile to foreign competition, particularly to Catholic immigrants from southern and eastern Europe, attempted to limit immigration mainly to Anglo-Saxons from countries corresponding to their proportion in the American population prior to 1882.[41] On the local level, the chaotic handling of municipal governments created political cleavages between various religious and national groups. The Irish, for example, rallied to defend themselves initially against the anti-Catholicism of American nationalism, in which religion was also used to exclude those who did not conform to a WASP identity, which was defined as dominant and legitimate.

Thus actions developed and groups formed. Immigrants at first, natives through their children, yet separated by religion, race, or national origin, the newcomers formed ethnic communities that sought political representation to defend their own interests and those of their native land. Under those conditions, the search for political representation of so-called ethnic groups appears as a defense of equal rights and then of equal opportunity. For blacks, the collective memory of slavery has resulted in a division between immigrant blacks and American blacks, which would not have had an impact if a racial differentiation were not at the base of the American model. But it is an important distinction for the self-perception of these groups, for their demands, and for their place in the present multiculturalism.

Thus, empirical examples show that experiences do not always follow the representations advanced in the idea of a nation. Although institutions try to maintain and transmit a rational idea of nation as part of the creation of the nation-state, practices create feelings and emotions, even an irrationality fueled by a primarily cultural definition of the nation.

Representation Stops at the Law

The limits of representation of the past appear clearly when ideas encounter rights, when rhetoric meets laws, when principles confront reality. In all three countries, defined as states of rights, the right of access to nationality and citizenship refers directly to this confrontation between principles and identities.

In France the right of nationality is granted to anyone who expresses the wish to live there; hence, naturalization is seen as a way to assimilate foreigners. An exception was the Vichy government and its attitude toward foreign Jews.[42] Under the ancien régime, the foreigner born outside the kingdom, declared to be of good moral character and expressing the wish to spend the rest of his days there, could obtain the status of naturalized citizen. Merchants justifying their stay and promising to end their days there received a letter of nationality from the sovereign giving them the right to bequeath property and exempting their heirs from the right of escheat (*droit d'aubaine*). This social category was decisive, as Rogers W. Brubaker noted.[43]

There was one major constraint, that of religion. In his book *Les étrangers sous l'Ancien Régime*,[44] J. Mathorez argued that "to acquire the status of Frenchman, the foreigner generally had to be a Catholic; but in the sixteenth century, at the height of the wars between the Catholics and the Protestants, the latter received letters of naturalization; except during the years preceding or following the revocation of the Edict of Nantes, the letter was frequently contravened. Only Muslims were made to abjure their faith before being admitted as nationals."

Under the republic, the right to nationality, now linked to citizenship, was awarded to anyone who moved onto French soil, without distinction of class, race, or religion. Access to citizenship and nationality was based on the ideology of universalism and the principle of a voluntary and individual act in accordance with the right awarded since the Revolution. This is the logic of civilization, which today seems to be replaced by the logic of citizenship, and the *mission civilisatrice*" of France is now addressed to those who live within the national territories.

But economic and demographic necessities have qualified those principles. In 1804 the principle that every child born on French soil is French (jus soli) was rejected by the court, and the Civil Code introduced blood relationships (jus sanguinis) as a criterion of nationality. From then on, a child born of a French parent was French.

Subsequent periods saw the development of a combination of jus soli and jus sanguinis, depending on the situation. In the nineteenth century, military preoccupations led the government to require the grandchildren of immigrants (by the law of double jus soli in 1851) and then the children of immigrants (by the law of jus soli in 1889) to serve France. After World War I, the demographic shortage had to be filled by easing the naturalization of foreigners (law of August 10, 1927), who represented 7 percent of the total population in 1918. The ministerial orders of August 13, 1927, noted that "if yesterday's law implied that the *de jure* assimilation preceded *de facto* assimilation, all that remains now is to pursue the *de jure* and *de facto* assimilation of immigrant foreigners simultaneously."[45] At present, the right to nationality combines jus sanguinis and jus soli and adds the wish for naturalization. This law dates from the ruling of 1945 on the Code of Nationality and is no longer part of the Civil Code.

Naturalization has changed owing to the policy of integrating foreigners, with marriage or the length of stay as its conditions. The criteria of naturalization are the candidate's "good morals" and knowledge of the French language and "culture." The emphasis is on socialization. The criterion of choice for young people born in France of foreign parents was made explicit during the public debates on the reform of the Code of Nationality, when it was determined that they must now take steps to obtain French nationality. This criterion that was implemented in 1993 when Charles Pasqua (Rassemblement pour la République, or RPR) became minister of the interior. Being born on French territory and socialization in the school system of the republic no longer constitute sufficient criteria for being French. The jus sanguinis introduced in 1804 expressed the legislature's "distrust of foreigners . . . in a country at war." Today, "distrust," at least in discourse, concerns the use of nationality. Requiring a deliberate choice also seemed to be a response to the apprehensions of politicians and public opinion who see nationality "desecrated" by a "paper citizenship." Even if the ways to acquire nationality remain unchanged in practice, expressing the "wish to live together" symbolically announces the individual's allegiance to the country of choice and the desire to share "its fate." Statistics show that nationalization doubled between 1973 and 1993 (33,616 in 1973, 73,154 in 1993). And since the procedure was implemented in 1993 until its repeal on August 31, 1998, the demonstration of will by young people represents an average of 20 to 30 percent of naturalizations.[46]

In January 1998, based on Patrick Weil's report on citizenship and nationality, Jean-Pierre Chevènement (Parti socialiste, or PS) instituted a new law rescinding the need to express "one's will" in order to become a citizen, substituting merely a permanent stay on French territory for at least five years.[47] According to estimates, more than 120,000 persons acquired French nationality in 1998.

Even more interesting is the granting of a title of republican identity to a child born of foreign parents holding a right to stay. This right, which is valid until the child's acquisition of French nationality, exempts the latter from a visa and allows the child to move freely in the Schengen zone.[48] Despite its purely functional use, such a right seems extremely symbolic as a preparation for a republican identity as a fundamental value of French nationality, and it demonstrates once again the link between rhetoric and law on the subject of citizenship.

In Germany public debates focus on the "importation of workers" rather than on immigration. Transforming a country of emigration into a country of immigration, which produces a statistical change, does not involve any legal modification. The presence of foreigners has not changed anything in the laws on "Germanness" and German nationality.

Although German nationality has been challenged as an impediment to democratic principles, it seems consistent with its own definition of the German nation. If the German nation is defined by a common culture, the basic principle of nationality remains sharing common ancestors (jus sanguinis). Such a definition of nationality posed a conceptual and practical problem when the unified state was created in 1871, since the new boundaries of the Reich produced an overlap of the concepts of people and territory. Smaller Germany excluded foreigners from neighboring states and included, in principle, ethnic Germans who lived outside its territory. As Rogers Brubaker noted, this produced two forms of citizenship: a political one, corresponding to territory; and a spiritual and ethnic one, based on common ancestors. But a new law of 1913, "on belonging to the state and the Reich," reinforced the ethnic aspect of citizenship by permitting Germans living outside the boundaries to keep German nationality and by rejecting the possibility of granting German nationality to foreigners born inside those boundaries.

In 1949 the Basic Law confirmed the principle of citizenship by descent. Article 116 of the law considers as German any person of German ancestry living within the borders of the Reich, and hence, since the collapse of the Soviet bloc, individuals who can prove their German ancestry (Aussiedler) are citizens by right. Since the 1950s, several waves of Aussiedler have settled on the territory of the Federal Republic. But statistics indicate that in 1990, after the collapse of the Soviet Union, a peak was reached, with 397,000 persons entering Germany. By

1988, 30,000 were granted that status, and more than 100,000 in 1991. Their "immigration" is now part of the absorption of political refugees. As the result of a quota established in 1992, an average of 220,000 ethnic Germans have immigrated to Germany.

As for foreigners, they become permanent residents but legally remain foreigners. German naturalization is conditional on giving up one's original nationality. The idea itself discourages some candidates, and the right of blood thus perpetuates the status of foreigner from one generation to the next. A Turkish child born in Germany of Turkish parents, who were themselves born in Germany, remains a Turk both de jure and de facto. Yet in 1990 the law on foreigners (*Ausländergesetz*) introduced a criterion of socialization allowing sixteen-year-olds to acquire naturalization if they were born and educated in Germany and had lived there for the five years prior to their application for naturalization. The number of naturalized foreigners, which varied between 20,000 and 30,000 a year from 1973 to 1989, rose to 44,950 in 1993.[49] This is because of the new law of July 1993 making the naturalization of foreign populations easier, along with a significant decrease in the cost of naturalization, but dual nationality is still rejected. In 1995 the new government coalition put the issue of dual nationality of foreigners back on the agenda, proposing a new law to grant dual nationality at the age of eighteen to a Turkish child born in Germany of Turkish parents who were themselves born in Germany. At that age, however, the individual must choose between the two nationalities. Politicians refer to that principle, which is similar to that of the double jus soli, as "a test" to gauge the young person's allegiance and extent of identification with the German nation, while the actual dual nationality of the Aussiedler does not raise a question of either principle or identification. Finally, after passionate debates on dual citizenship, in 1999, with SPD at the head of the government, a new citizenship law changed the current of German history on the issue. As of January 1, 2000, every foreign child born in Germany whose parents either were born or have been in the country for the last eight years is automatically German at birth. With a radical switch from jus sanguinis to jus solis, Germany stands today as one of the most liberal states in Europe with regard to citizenship.

In the United States ambiguities in the concept of citizenship corroborate the "American dilemma" and contradict universalist thought. In fact, the urgent need for population has put naturalization at the core of the theory and practice of citizenship, which is based on the right to citizenship by birth and makes nationality automatic, thus reinforcing the inclusive nature of the American nation. Yet the history of American citizenship shows the contradictions about a universalism marked by exclusions and inclusions stemming from racism, xenophobia, and religious sectarianism. Both free blacks and slaves were excluded from American citizenship until the Civil War, even if they were citizens of a specific state; Indians were not granted American citizenship until 1924; the Chinese were categorized as "aliens ineligible for citizenship" in 1882, and that lasted until 1952.[50]

But today the greatest division remains the racial one between blacks and whites: the "two nations," as Andrew Hacker put it, separate, hostile, and unequal. To be black in the United States still amounts to bearing the brand of slavery. In fact, not until a century after the Declaration of Independence was slavery abolished with the Thirteenth Amendment in 1865. Based on the principle of equal protection before the law, it was the Fourteenth Amendment in particular that made blacks citizens in 1868. And finally, only with the Fifteenth Amendment in 1870 was the right to vote granted to them, and they became voters.[51] But they had to wait nearly another century for civil rights and affirmative action, a policy of compensation in effect since 1965, to enforce equal rights in government, schools, and businesses.

The shaping of the nation-state is a process of assimilation. It consists of defining norms to make cultural and identity boundaries coincide with territorial and political ones. The nation, that imagined or invented community, defines its modes of inclusion and exclusion according to its representation. From this point of view, the past serves to legitimate the present. The models make each national experience specific by fixing the past. When the past confronts the present, characterized by a rush to catch up with social and economic transformations, the past, which claims to be enduring, freezes what is perceived as distinct for each national society. The same applies to the way the three countries now relate to immigrants as determined by a continuum in the process of national integration. The new waves of immigrants come up against a mirror reflecting the boundaries of the models and the representations they produce. But at the same time, the settlement of immigrants creates questions about their validity when confronting new realities and their adaptability to new situations, as well as their capacity to establish new arrangements.

At the same time, economic rationality tends to do away with national specificities, for the universality of values is now also based on economic interests. Models serve as a recourse to redefine particularities and reconstruct identity affinities. The social development and transformations they produce generate new connections of individuals and groups to their environment. As Hobsbawm and Ranger have emphasized, it is necessary to work for "new devices to ensure or express social cohesion and identity and to structure social relations."[52] New models are fitted into the development specific to each of the countries. New relations between states and society, states and immigrants, states and identities, are woven into the connections between representations of political traditions and the assertions of new identity constructs.

CHAPTER THREE

The Territories of Identity

> Space is where power is asserted and exercised, and certainly in the subtlest form, that of symbolic violence as unseen violence.
>
> —Pierre Bourdieu

ALL INDUSTRIAL SOCIETIES TODAY are experiencing the same unrest and blaming it on immigrants, either those defined legally or those perceived as such. Suburbs (*banlieues*) in France, slums, ethnic enclaves, ghettos, all those places where otherness and poverty go together, where unemployment among youth is far above the national average, are presented as conflict zones between civil society and the forces of order, between generations and cultures and between national, local, and community institutions. The United States and France (which define themselves as countries of immigration) and Germany (which does not) have developed similar relations with the most recent waves of immigrants. Therefore models based on the representation of political traditions and principles of citizenship, developed in the previous chapter, no longer hold. Reality clearly shows a single model based on interactions between states and immigrants. Relationships are characterized by tensions and clashes, inducing both sides to negotiate identities.

In France suburban housing projects have become the locus of unrest. Tensions have appeared between the school—the main institution embodying the principles of the "one and indivisible" republic—and the students who flaunt their "differences" as members of a specific "community" in neighborhoods with high concentrations of immigrants, particularly Muslims. In Germany racist attacks have led Turks to form a "minority community," felt as a means to demand rights, as in the United States.

The formation of a community in order to legitimate any claim from the state is perceived as the formation of a "dissident community"; public demands for the recognition of cultural differences are a source of tension because they are perceived as a challenge to political traditions. In both France and Germany, as in the United States, membership in ethnic communities generates distrust of society and its institutions, and vice versa. Politicians view this as a problem of loyalty; individuals view it as difference transformed into an instrument of resistance.

This situation triggers other tensions because the Other is perceived as unassimilable. In France the Other is the Muslim, in Germany the foreigner. In France he or she is described as not following the rules of laïcité; and in Germany, the foreigner is not part of the German "we." In both countries, Muslim and *foreigner* are synonymous. In the United States, the most recent waves of immigrants from Latin America (called Hispanics or Latinos) have seriously generated a redefinition of the concepts of American assimilation or pluralism. Their insistence on their language as a strong identity marker not diluted in the melting pot justifies arguments like those about religion in France and nationality in Germany. But it is a temporary split, because the real gap, as several studies and testimonies have emphasized, is inherent in the more permanent and structural difference of race or color, terms that are never used in the French and German contexts.

The combination results in mutual rejections, especially since, in Europe, public opinion and politicians have realized that immigrants have not simply moved in but have struck root in their new society. Neighborhoods where identities established themselves have become areas of tension, even conflict, leading to policies that are increasingly targeted to specific populations. Paradoxically, discourse on the inability of these groups to assimilate is accompanied by a search for increasingly differentiated solutions, as if to compensate for the political indifference of the early stages, as shown by the increasing intervention of the state to regulate social relations in those areas. The founding principles of the state now yield to a political pragmatism guided by experience, and discourse takes refuge in political traditions.

INCOMPATIBLE EQUATIONS

In France historical studies of the various waves of immigrants from eastern or southern Europe between the nineteenth century and the middle of the twentieth century have drawn attention to their assimilation into the nation. The cult of assimilation, the basis of national unity, produced indifference toward linguistic or religious origins, which were obscured or suppressed in private life once they passed through the mill of institutions. Gérard Noirel even argued that immigration was not part of French national history. In time, public opinion, initially always hostile to the foreigner, seems to end in an indifference that makes assimilation easier, or assimilation simply creates indifference. In Germany, in the early twentieth century, the Poles experienced "Germanization," that is, forced assimilation.

Forced or not, these processes of assimilation have now been shunted off to oblivion. In France new concerns came with the most recent migrations from the southern and eastern Mediterranean. The nature of relations between North Africa and France changed, and France's "civilizing mission" in its former colonies continues in another form on its own territory. After an initial restrained welcome in the workplace, then in the city and the schools, proximity unites equals under the same social and legal rules in a liberal democratic society. The same is true in Germany, where economic interests between Germany and Turkey have produced what can be called a marriage of convenience of Turks and Germans. But that bond has lasted for some time now and includes a demand for rights, thus infusing the relationship with passion. This development recalls Tocqueville's observation that, in the United States, "the prejudice rejecting the Negroes seems to increase in proportion to their emancipation, and inequality cuts deep into mores as it is effaced from the laws."[1]

In France and Germany, at any rate, beyond discourse, public opinion does not seem prepared to accept foreigners as an integral part of society. A 1953 book on immigrants by Alain Girard and Jean Stoetzel showed that North Africans had much "less opportunity to adapt to French life" and consequently evoked "less sympathy among the French public." At that time, the book found that North Africans were just above Germans in attitudes rated, since the Germans were still considered enemies and were in last place.[2] In 1966 the "ten negative characteristics" were attributed mainly to Algerians, who were mentioned 129 times, as opposed to 39 times for Africans and 13 times for Portuguese.[3]

In Germany, in 1971, "Gastarbeiter" came after "drug addicts" and blacks in a ranking of "people you would not like as neighbors";[4] but in 1981, 36 percent of those questioned would have accepted Gastarbeiter into their circle of friends as against 26 percent who were opposed. But the fact remains that, within the category of Gastarbeiter, those questioned saw the behavior of the Turks as most different from that of the Germans (69 percent), more than the Greeks (47 percent) and the Italians (42 percent). Even more than their behavior, however, it is their mere presence that concerns the Germans, who in 1982 thought there were too many foreigners in their country and wanted to pay them a bonus to go back to their own country or to fire them from their jobs to encourage them to leave. That may be a premature reaction to an a priori long-term settlement challenging the official discourse, which still considers Germany "not a country of immigration" and is designed to appease public opinion.

France, however, is realizing, in retrospect, that it is a country of immigration, or at least that is what historians and demographers have been demonstrating since the mid-1980s.[5] This means that the Muslims, like preceding waves of immigrants, might follow the same path of assimilation, that traditional mechanisms would reduce or destroy the "cultural distance"—in the terminology of that time—expressed in the polls. But then, in November 1989, the issue of the Muslim head scarf ignited hostilities, and public opinion saw it as proof of the "incompatibility" of Islam and the West, the inability of the Muslims to assimilate universal values and integrate into French society. The polls also consistently emphasized the feelings of the French, not about immigrants but about Islam. In 1985, 42 percent of those questioned thought that most immigrants (synonymous with North Africans) "will not be able to integrate into French society because they are very different," but in 1989 the percentage had risen to 51 percent.[6]

The mirror effect of immigration or the presence of foreigners focuses the discussion on values acquired in the process of modernization, which are considered essential: first, the role of the school and then the status of women, since the two are now linked. The school, perceived as the major institution of the republic, always guaranteed national unity and thus far has assimilated the children of foreigners, just as it made Frenchmen in the various regions of the country. Education was discussed at length in public sessions on nationality held by the Committee of Experts from September 15 to October 21, 1987, because of its function of socialization and "the preeminent importance of schooling in the process of integration."[7]

Two years later, with the introduction of a religious garment into that "sacred" institution, politicians and the public saw a serious threat to the republican school, its ideology, and its principle of laïcité equality and unity. Society and the public authorities were assigned the urgent task of saving the school. As for the status of women, the IFOP poll (French Institute for Opinion Polls) of November 1989 showed that 76 percent of those questioned in the total French population thought that Islam implied the "submission of women," which certainly constituted an obstacle to their emancipation, freedom, and modernity from a universalist point of view. The head scarf presented an image of girls who were "victims of religion," wrenched from all those values that only education could guarantee. Jules Ferry had made school compulsory, for girls as well, in order to guarantee equality of opportunity for children of different social classes and sexes in the long run.

In Germany pervasive racism and the politicians' inability to mitigate "hatred of the foreigner" shifted the discussion of immigration from economics to society and politics, accompanied by a questioning of citizenship and the social, legal, and, of course, ideological aspect of it.

When German reunification occurred, the perceived and experienced cultural difference between West Germans and East Germans—called pejoratively *Wessis* and *Ossis*—had already cast doubt on the validity

of the notion of the German folk (*das deutsche Volk*). The proposed
new law of foreigners, in effect since 1991, is even more integral to that
discussion. As if to underline the resemblance between the young Turks
who were born and educated in Germany and the young West Germans, as well as the difference between the West Germans and the East
Germans, this law introduced the idea of socialization into the concept
of citizenship for the first time. The new criteria for acquiring nationality consider schooling in Germany of the children of foreigners, their
knowledge of the German language, and their progress toward assimilation. The declared intention is to "facilitate" the naturalization of the
young Turks who have been socialized in German institutions. The tex-
tual change is significant, but it is doubtful whether mentalities and
ideologies can follow it, especially in light of the slogan of the East
Germans: "*Wir sind ein Volk*" (We are one people). Three days after the
fall of the Berlin Wall, at spontaneous rallies as the wall was being
dismantled, the crowds had shouted "*Wir sind das Volk* (We are the
people), meaning "We represent democracy." This change is a clear
indication that the reunited German people is defining itself once again
by its ethnic affiliation.

THE ETHNICIZATION OF TERRITORY

Since the 1980s, the press increasingly has been reporting riots in the
French suburbs, the best-known being Minguettes in 1981 and 1983
and Vaux-en-Velin (suburb of Lyons) in 1991. These reports are accompanied by photographs of burned cars, looted display windows, riot
police, and young people throwing stones. Editorials begin with
"youths from the suburbs or young descendants of Algerian immigrants." Yet, until recently, French public opinion attributed such scenes
to the black "ghettos" of big American cities, even though the nature
and extent of the riots in ghettos are altogether different in the two
countries. In Germany the most spectacular images were those of burn-
ing buildings inhabited by Turkish families on almost every floor. The
ones most notorious in international opinion were the fires set in Mölln
in November 1992 and in Solingen in January 1993, which cost the
lives of two Turkish families. This violence expresses hatred of the foreigner (Ausländer) by the youth of the extreme Right, who see the
young descendants of the immigrants as a threat to their own economic
and social integration, as in France. In both countries, the social questions raised by immigration crystallize in the urban setting, which
becomes the space where tension and violence prevail as modes of collective expression.

Suburbs in France: Places Managed by Tension

The French suburbs are places where affiliations are juxtaposed, fragmented, and united, fighting with one another and then marking off territories. Identities began to be juxtaposed there in the 1960s, when families of all regional and national backgrounds were "saved" from shantytowns and "rehoused" in low-income housing, those impersonal complexes—which were modern when they were built—on the outskirts of big metropolitan areas. Experts talked of a rehousing policy and not of housing, to emphasize a fact inherent in industrialization and its effects on urban policy. In the 1970s many working families, both French and foreign, particularly Portuguese, thus proved their access to modernity by moving to the suburban housing projects. Even now, policies of renovating old and unhealthy neighborhoods are accompanied by a policy of rehousing their inhabitants in project houses in HLM, translated as low-rent apartments. But the residents of the HLM, which is currently the main image of the suburbs, as François Dubet has emphasized, "seem to get away from traditional representations of the working class on the one hand, and of poverty on the other."[8]

The ethnic composition of the population of the suburbs has been drawn clearly over time. The first families who moved there, whether or not they were French, saw themselves as members of the working class and then embarked on upward mobility by moving into houses and making room for newcomers. In the second phase, families were necessarily foreigners and newly gathered in France, but the areas were still nationally heterogeneous and included North Africans, Turks, and Senegalese. Thus, in Mantes-la-Jolie, for example, "We saw those blue-collar and white-collar families arrive, dreaming of a house, working close to Paris, but forced to come to Mantes to find prices suitable to their financial means. Others came to occupy the apartments of Val-Fourré for want of anything else. Their integration into society has never assumed the forms of those who came ten years earlier. So the neighborhood has gradually been transformed, become proletarian, and received more and more immigrants."[9] The departure of the former, the immigrants and individual networks to settle the new ones meant that North African, Turkish, or African families were concentrated in certain housing projects in the suburbs: Saint-Denis, La Courneuve, Mantes-la-Jolie in Île de France, Minguettes in the Lyons suburb, Marseille-north, Lille-south, Cité-Montclair near Avignon, to cite some of the best-known ones. The composition of this immigrant population means that Islam has become the trademark of the suburbs. Are these neighborhoods tantamount to "Muslim ghettos"?

The very idea of a ghetto is rejected in France. Discussion has focused mainly on the criterion of nationality and not religion. Specialists in urban policy point to the national heterogeneity of the immigrant and Muslim population to report that there is no ghetto in France, especially in comparison with the United States, where race is the decisive factor.

Indeed, no building and certainly not a whole housing project in France is inhabited a priori by families of a homogeneous nationality. Yet it is hard to deny the predominance of one national group, which looks like a certain homogeneity. In Borny-Metz, in 1990, in Descartes School, only 29.13 percent of the students were French, 25.24 percent North Africans, 35.60 percent Turkish, and 7.7 percent Southeast Asians. In the housing projects across from the school, the Turks are the most visible group, and most of them come from the same region of central Anatolia. Does this result from the practices of public offices of development and construction that assigned families low-rent apartments?[10] Or is it because families prefer to stay with their own people? The question is moot. But clearly there is a concentration of population, if not of the same national origin at least of the same religion, Islam.

Yet the heterogeneity of the Muslim population in the suburbs does lead to a fragmentation of identities resulting from an overcrowding that juxtaposes families from "the same area" with families from "somewhere else." In the long run, distinct concentrations of populations of the same linguistic, ethnic, and racial background appear. United initially by their social status and income level, families of the housing projects are now separated by their national and religious affiliation. And social relations are often limited to fellow countrymen living close by.

Each of the microenvironments thus formed corresponds to what Max Weber called a neighborhood community. But unlike Weber's definition of a group of individuals joined together to defend their interests, particularly in negotiations with local authorities, as in the United States, these various neighborhood communities of the suburbs are distinct from one another by their nationality or "ethnicity." Other criteria then intervene, such as the percentage of "foreigners" in a building, that is, its representation. Families thus redefine behavioral norms, imposing social control based on a hierarchy of values designed to prove their own moral superiority over their neighbor, thus defining the boundaries of a micromilieu and strengthening the identity fragmentation of the territory.

These so-called neighborhood communities are also characterized by their resistance to the proximate or distant environment. Hence the maintenance, even reinforcement, of a culture expressed as a culture "of origin," dissociating members from one another and creating new divisions. But at the same time, this resistance to the environment unites families on a religious basis, particularly when there is a collective request for permission to build a mosque or to assemble in a room in city hall on Muslim holidays, for example. But by and large, families of different national or ethnic backgrounds are isolated from one another within the housing projects, which themselves are isolated from the larger society.

"Colonies" of Turks in Germany

In Germany, as in the United States, "outsiders" live in inner cities. Frederick Heckmann calls their concentration colonies, or ethnic colonies (*ethnische Kolonie*), a term indicating both the nationality and the social situation of the inhabitants. So whereas in the French suburbs identities are juxtaposed and fragmented yet under the common Islamic denominator, in German cities there is a show of unity where families of the same nationality (e.g., Turkish) meet; in American ghettos there is an impression of color homogeneity to the foreign observer. Reflections on the French suburb are initially social but are actually ethnic. This is also valid for German discourse, although with a logic that appears just the opposite. As in France, urban planners primarily advance social criteria to explain the concentration, but the network of relations regulating the housing market puts the ethnic criterion at the top. In any case, these neighborhoods combine class and ethnicity in the same way, although with a rhetoric of denial in France.

Studies on the housing of Gastarbeiter show that 50 percent of families from Turkey are concentrated in only 4 percent of German territory,[11] obviously in industrial regions such as the states of North Rhineland, Westphalia, and Bade-Würtenberg[12] and the working neighborhoods of cities like Cologne, Düsseldorf, Frankfurt, Munich, and Stuttgart. In these cities, Turkish families represent more than 35 percent of the foreign population—except for Frankfurt, where they constitute 19.5 percent of the foreign population in 1991, outnumbered by former Yugoslavians, who made up 20.4 percent of that population. In other industrial cities, they live mainly in old neighborhoods, often near railroad stations: thus, in Frankfurt, where the concentration is not as high as elsewhere, 75 percent of the foreigners live around the railroad station. In these inner-city neighborhoods, populations of the same national origin gather (Turks, including Kurds, or former Yugoslavians). Other neighborhoods of the city and other cities present the same picture.

Kreuzberg in Berlin is an extreme example of concentration. Families who in the 1960s came from Turkey and gathered in that old part of the city, later nicknamed *Klein Istanbul*, have lived there for almost three generations. In 1975 the Turks represented 67.8 percent of the foreign population in Kreuzberg and 16.8 percent of the total population of that quarter. The Berlin senate then implemented a policy of dispersion (*Zuzugsperre*) that forbade Turkish nationals to move into concentrated areas and expressed the ban concretely with a stamp on the last page of their passports. The policy of dispersion aimed at limiting the percentage of foreigners of the same nationality in a neighborhood to 12 percent, since the authorities were afraid of the "ghetto."

Despite that restriction, the proportion of Turks in Kreuzberg kept increasing: in 1983 they represented 19.3 percent of its inhabitants, and the most recent statistics of the Berlin senate indicate that they constituted 63 percent of the foreign population in that neighborhood in 1992, that is, 20 percent of its total population.[13] For the sake of comparison, the Turks constitute 48.1 percent of the foreign population in all of Germany.

Settling Turkish nationals began with family groups. The working-class neighborhood of Kreuzberg, which had been neglected after World War II, initially attracted heads of families who had been living in homes (*Heime*) where their employers had placed them. The choice was imposed on them by the rent, which was certainly proportional to the quality of housing and how the neighborhood was perceived. Moreover, Kreuzberg was more open to foreigners, since landlords preferred them to the squatters who were widespread in the neighborhood. Even today, the renovation that began in the 1980s has not driven the Turkish families out of Kreuzberg, which has become a leading neighborhood. Similarly, after the unification of Germany in 1989, the fact that Kreuzberg was literally at the center of unified Berlin and the target of investors changed neither the composition nor the reputation of the neighborhood. Kreuzberg remains Little Istanbul. Nevertheless, like its inhabitants, it has followed a social development that elicits a better response to the needs of its clients, who are now seen as Berliners of Kreuzberg.

AREA AND ERA OF TENSIONS

Such spaces indicate the failure of the migratory plan and spark frustrations that erupt in violence. Violence becomes the expression of the rage of youth.[14]

Social Immobility and "Ghettos"

Concentrations in suburban France or in inner-city Germany show that the situation of immigrant or foreign families, twenty or thirty years after they arrive, is fairly similar to what it was at the start. In fact, several French and American monographs emphasize their concentration in a new space as a natural fact, which allows them, as Yves Lequin claimed, "not to break completely with the native country that is forgotten and a host country that looks foreign." Spatial proximity and the sense of sharing the same past are both objective and subjective elements that consolidate bonds within the flexible boundaries of the group formed by the immigrant experience. At first, housing conditions and the image of the neighborhood hardly matter: Italian families in Boston's North End,[15] like those in Marseille[16] or Lorraine, tried to revive the lost "paradise" in the new local communities.

At least that is true for a certain time: the time of upward mobility, the key to integration into the larger society. In fact, upward mobility has often been cited as the factor that dissolves these "neighborhood communities" built on a common language, a common religion, and common interests. Voluntary concentration at the start of the immigrant experience was seen as transitory and temporary; in most cases, it formed an intermediate stage that facilitated the transition from community to society, the process desired by all migrants. If immigration was part of the progress toward modernization through social success, it had to end in integration into the economic and cultural institutions of society, hence assimilation, following the laws of the market. That was also what the larger society desired. National institutions, professional associations, labor unions, and churches were there to help newcomers realize their original plan while trying to maintain social cohesion.

But now, in France, the permanent grouping in the suburbs no longer seems to result from an individual choice but is perceived, rather, as the failure of the project of immigration. A long-term ethnic grouping linked to poverty reflects the negative identity of the community and refers to the idea of concentration, which has become synonymous with segregation. Its inhabitants, the members of the community, are called "excluded" in the official language in France. Actually, they are "excluded from assimilation" as well as "excluded from social integration" and are grouped together. Is this the result of "rehousing" policies or of the situation, or of de facto discrimination in the housing and labor market? In any case, closing the labor market in a society that, paradoxically, looks more open, if only because of the development of communication networks and the sudden emergence of the media, is not a sufficient answer to these questions.

Alain Touraine has argued that European societies are shifting from a vertical society, characterized by a class hierarchy, to a horizontal society, "where the important thing is to know if one is in the center or at the periphery."[17] He referred to the youth of the suburbs on the out-skirts of the big cities who use collective action to express their desire to move "to the center." The term "social void" expresses the hopelessness of people younger than twenty, who represent 40 percent of the popula-tion from Val-Fourré to Mantes-la-Jolie and 45 percent in north Mar-seille. In these zones, foreigners and the foreign-born constitute 49 percent and 55 percent, respectively, of the total population, and unem-ployment reaches a high of 20 percent and obviously affects mainly young people. In other suburbs, the rate goes beyond 50 percent and affects Algerian youth especially. The phenomenon is classic in the United States, where, according to William Julius Wilson, the ghetto is now linked to a new social category he calls the underclass.[18] Unem-ployment, poverty, and dependence on the state are the lifestyles of the ghetto residents, those who remained behind after upwardly mobile blacks left to engage in other work and scattered throughout the city.

In Germany, by contrast, social mobility does not seem to be a reason to leave the neighborhood. Particularly in Berlin, upward mobility is manifested by opening businesses in other areas of the city, and not by leaving the residential area. Thus, as I have mentioned, Kreuzberg was not drained of its Turkish population when the area was renovated; indeed, its improvement reinforced the inhabitants' identification with the space they have appropriated. Renovation meant an increase in rents, in the standard of living, and in upward mobility. Precisely because of renovation, Turkish families thought they could finally "get rid" of the squatters, the punks, those neighbors "who make the area look bad." But they also thought "it was better to have the punks in view as a bad example of modernism and the dangers of assimilation" for their own children. At least this is the way families from Turkey express their resistance: the ethnicization of the territory helps to main-tain group boundaries.

Violence, Rage, and Fears

Rage has settled in those spaces. It is expressed through violence. In France, in October 1990, the riots of Vaux-en-Velin reminded people of those areas abandoned by some and inhabited by others and that have been taken over by those who were born or grew up there and are now labeled "excluded." Thus, one characteristic of the suburb is the *perma-nence* of settlement in those "impersonal places" that have become the mainstays of *nonintegration*, commonly defined as places of exclusion.

In Germany the rage of the young foreigners is combined with a fear of racist attacks, the humiliation of skinhead atrocities, and anger at police indifference toward brutality. Youth gangs have strengthened their organizations and declared open war to defend their territory. "No Skin [a synonym for neo-Nazi] can get into Kreuzberg, and those who try to attack us in the U-Bahn [the subway line to Kreuzberg] had better watch out," they say. Thus, areas of mutual segregation are drawn: "*No skin, keine Ausländer.*"[19] Some of these youths seem to want to fight with equal weapons, call themselves Turkish Skins, and use the same violence as the German Skins, sometimes offensively and sometimes defensively. The Black Panthers, Street Fighters, Anti-Fa(scists), and Ghetto Girls are other gangs with whom they collaborate and socialize. Their idols are the American street gangs, as indicated by the gang names they choose, their language, and the way they dress. Some have long hair like the hippies of the 1960s (Anti-Fa), others wear baseball caps backward, like the young blacks or Puerto Ricans of the American ghettos.

Although young people in France are less organized than those in Germany, they also identify with the same American idols and their problems: racism, exclusion, and failure. Verbal and sometimes physical violence guides their interpersonal relations in public; it has its own rules and is part of the "street code," in the words of Elijah Anderson.[20] Violence gives them a territorial and ethnic collective expression, a means of ruling by provocation. But in the French suburbs, as in the special neighborhoods in Germany, these acts are localized. The solidarities they create are made, unmade, and remade. The combination produces a fragile and incidental structure that appears mainly as a challenge to the law.

Tensions and violence are thus linked to immigration, stoking xenophobia, a major theme of the National Front campaign in the municipal elections of 1983, when that party won 17 percent of the vote in Dreux.

IN SEARCH OF THE SOCIAL BOND

All the tension and violence that occurs almost every day threatens social peace and political order. As Georges Balandier has emphasized, tension and violence indicate "the inability of societies to define and convey their meaning clearly, to impose their norms, their codes, their rules, to handle their ordeals, to win the support of the majority of men who constitute them."[21] From this perspective, countries that confront questions of immigration take measures to "revitalize" the neighborhoods and guarantee their integration as well as that of their inhabitants into the overall society, for tensions express the distrust or the mutual lack of confidence between the larger society and the immigrants. The issue for society and its institutions is their adaptation to prevailing norms; for individuals, identity becomes both a refuge and an instrument of resistance.

The measures vary from one country to another. According to a report of the Organization of Economic Cooperation and Development (OCDE) on territorial development, some countries limit their action experimentally to specific neighborhoods, and others "are part of the general strategy of the public powers to combat the concentration of urban deprivation and exclusion."[22] For the most part, politicians combine a rhetoric that evokes fundamental principles and gives them their symbolic weight with a functional approach that responds both to the demands of the populations and to the concern of the states to maintain public order.[23]

In France the problem is posed in terms of the "social bond" (*lien social*), a term inspired by a sociological or political tradition that refers to the idea of national solidarity, cohesion, and integration. In Germany the official reference to the social bond applies mainly to the labor market. The "pact of solidarity," introduced by Chancellor Adenauer just after World War II, was based on able-bodied young people taking care of the elderly for the sake of solidarity between generations. Therefore, public authorities insist on social peace and the economic integration of the young Turks. Violence and political disruption are interpreted as reflections of economic problems, particularly those affecting the skills of the youth and the difficulties of integrating them into the labor market. The same is true in France, but there the unemployment of youth of North African origin is part of an economic situation affecting all of French society, whereas in Germany the problem assumes an ethnic character. Since German reunification, the competition that has erupted between the newcomers from the east, or the Aussiedler, and the young foreigners who were already living there has been expressed in tensions that stem from turning social problems into ethnic ones.

Universality and Ethnicity

This situation poses a challenge to democracy. The intervention of the French and German governments fluctuates between concern for maintaining political traditions and a pragmatism that emphasizes a "political apprenticeship" in dealing with the presence and settlement of immigrants or foreigners in democratic terms.

In France the state, "schoolmaster of society," in Pierre Rosanvallon's words, uses its administrative and ideological influence to secure social cohesion. The motto is "social integration." It is defined as the basis of the social bond and thus opposed to "exclusion." In Germany the state operates through the intermediary of semipublic institutions that function like large associations and form pressure groups, the only organizations that can negotiate the interests of individuals, in this case foreigners, with government agencies.

The existing structures reflect the ideologies of the institutions that form society. In France official discourse based on the principle of universality denies any "special treatment" of the foreign population or immigrants. Yet the influence of colonial history in relations with North Africans cannot be ignored. Considering the years of the Algerian war of independence, Yves Lequin emphasized that the acts carried out against the North Africans were "marked by the spirit of 'native affairs' strongly tinted with paternalism."[24]

Today, even if France and Algeria interact within the sphere of international relations, it would be wrong to ignore the influence of the colonial past on relations with Algerians living in France. The logic of intervention is general, "color-blind," but specific reasons influence its application.

In Germany the Gastarbeiter's generic status as workers allows them to benefit from existing organizations and receive the same social allowances as the Germans, at least as long as they have a job. Their interests as workers are also defended by the Federation of German Labor Unions, which includes representatives for each nationality in every trade.

Yet there is a shift toward functioning in terms of the national community, which is becoming even clearer in the social arena. Caring for the Gastarbeiter recruited by the Federal Employment Office has now assumed an ethnic character through the special treatment of foreigners by nationality. The important influence of charitable organizations on the welfare state in general and the absorption of guest workers in particular also introduce the religious element into their special treatment. The division of labor between them is done according to nationality, but in reality, it is by religion that foreign workers are welcomed by a charitable organization. In fact, they are cared for by Caritas (a Catholic organization) if they are Spanish, Italian, Portuguese, Polish, or Croatian (the former Yugoslavian nationality is divided by the faith of the various ethnic groups—now nationalities), by the Diakonishches Werk (Protestant organization) if they are Greek and Orthodox, and by the Arbeiterwohlfahrt (a labor union affiliated with the SPD, created after the mass arrival of the Turks) if they are Turks or Bosnian Muslims. Thus, the institution of absorbing foreign workers is determined in principle by nationality, but in reality by religion.[25]

In France, in the cultural arena, a universalist ideology still explains the tendency of national institutions to homogenize differences, even if the Algerian case appears ambiguous, since Algeria also intervenes in decisions affecting its nationals, as Turkey does for Turks in Germany. But in Germany cultural action was explicitly and automatically delegated to the native country, refers to bilateral agreements between governments, and is part of the legal status of Gastarbeiter. Otherwise, the strictly "organizational" care for foreigners is limited to informing them of their rights as guest workers. The main reason is clearly to keep them "ready to go back." But the same motivation guides government measures in France too, although this is not acknowledged. In both cases, teachers from the country of origin are responsible for teaching the language and culture of that country. In France this operation is the new program specified in 1973, and in Germany it has been part of the agreement made with Turkey from the beginning. Similarly, in 1977, the French state, worried about its relations with North Africa, adopted measures to facilitate Islamic religious observance. These operations are obviously surprising in an ideological framework that advocates assimilation.

Redefining Solidarities in France

The permanence of the subject of suburbs and exclusion in public discussion, its appearance in the media, and its effects on public opinion, which are used by extreme right-wing parties in their speeches and campaigns, have led politicians to seek ways to include the "migrants" in the urban fabric. A redefinition of solidarities has been obvious on the local level, coinciding with the implementation of a policy of decentralization since the 1980s. In fact, the policy of decentralization affects all areas of social life: the neighborhood, education, the professional training of young people, and even the cultural expression of immigrants.

Local officials, teachers, and social workers have joined forces to improve educational conditions, since local tensions crystallize in the schools. How is it possible to deal with a class of thirty-six different nationalities, who are below the national average in educational achievement? This is why schools located mainly in neighborhoods defined as high-priority urban zones (Zones Urbaines Prioritaires [ZUP]) are the focus of specific measures stipulating that "more must be done where there is less." This is the concept of educational policies accompanied by specific programs introduced into those establishments since 1982 by Alain Savary, the minister of education.

This situation can be compared with the American policy of affirmative action for groups defined as oppressed minorities, which is designed to "compensate" for past discrimination and inequalities in education or hiring, to fill that gap, particularly between blacks and whites, which

Andrew Hacker called the "two nations." Its pernicious effects are now attracting the most attention and have produced terms like "positive discrimination" and "affirmative discrimination."[26]

But in France no measure is specifically oriented toward immigrants, their descendants, or foreigners, at least not officially. In discourse, "less" is determined economically, like social handicaps. The state does not take account a priori of the national or religious origin of families but refers to all economically disadvantaged families. Local actions are undertaken to improve neighborhoods and their image, using various means: if possible, by dispersing the group that "lowers values" or by encouraging the residents to participate in the neighborhood's social life. To calm fears and antagonisms, the less must be integrated into the more.

Seeking the source of unrest in social problems and not in cultural differences is part of the universalist concept of social relations. In *The New Social Question*, published in 1994, Rosanvallon emphasized that universality is based on opacity and that "information promotes differentiation."[27] "As society gains more knowledge of its differences, a considerable change in the perception of fairness tends to be produced," he wrote. This logic might include the circular letter concerning the high-priority zones of education (Zones d'Education Prioritaires—[ZEP]), which enumerated problem "zones," where 28.9 percent of the students are children of foreigners, as opposed to 10.8 percent on the national level.[28] "The project of the high-priority zone of education, from its preparation and development to its implementation, must emphasize concerns about foreign children and children of foreign origin and must integrate suitable educational and pedagogical answers," wrote Hubert Prévot, secretary of state for integration in a document on social policies of integration presented to the OCDE in March 1991.

However, how can the incidents of Minguettes during the summer of 1981 be ignored, along with the media attention they received with the March of the Beurs, or the "Convergence" movement of suburban youth who attracted the attention of the public authorities and defined their modes of intervention? Did that not prove that more must be done in all areas of social life for sixteen- to eighteen-year-olds, predominantly those of North African origin? In fact, following the 1981 incidents of Minguettes and their recurrence in 1983, the testimonies of the magistrate, the police chief, and the director of the Health Department are significant for their evaluation of conditions there: "No traditional local institution now plays the social role assigned to it."[29] Is this the chronicle of a failure announced in order to develop intermediaries who know that they are now aimed at the immigrants? Exclusion is not simply geographically peripheral; it also refers especially to institutions and the labor market, to educational failure, to unemployment. In discourse, the evil is primarily social and must be corrected by society; in reality, however, the social element is closely linked to the cultural.

Yet the authorities responded with the law of associations for foreigners in October 1981 and even mobilized resources to encourage immigrants to organize into associations. Parliamentary debates on the law clarified the politicians' intentions that the creation of associations for and by foreigners was considered "a particularly effective channel because of its flexibility to initiate social action in the framework of the policy defined by the public authorities."[30] Moreover, the law specifies that these associations are meant to be "the expression of national, cultural, and social solidarities, and thus they constitute a means of breaking the isolation that transplanted persons may suffer."

The associations are part of the development systems of urban society (Développement Social Urbain, DSU) launched by the policy of decentralization. They are now religious, social, and cultural, representing the mosaic of differentiated groups that form local communities. Some are specifically defined as neighborhood associations. They unite young people no matter what their religion or national origin, organize fairs and concerts, and demand the participation of all the young people in the housing project. The idea is to enhance neighborhood relations and ensure a social solidarity based on the interests of the neighborhood and its inhabitants, thus weakening ethnic solidarities as sources of tension between various groups and local authorities.

The Fund of Social Action, the main source of money for the association's social and cultural activities, doubled its allocations between 1980 and 1983, financing 2,300 organizations in 1983 instead of 500 three years earlier.[31] This organization, created in 1958, originally aimed "at promoting a general social initiative on behalf of wage earners working in metropolitan France in professions targeted by the Algerian regime for family grants and whose children reside in Algeria."[32] But after its activities were decentralized and dispatched in different regions with appropriate structures in 1982, the FAS reoriented its initiative toward "the specific representation of immigrant communities." The declared objective was to "create intermediaries" in order to facilitate the integration of immigrants. In the integration of immigrants, "the FAS is the state," affirmed its director, Michel Yahiel, in 1988.

The FAS started to decentralize its activities and representative structures in 1985. The declared objective was to help associations to form on the local level, orient their future activities toward neighborhood life, create neighborhood solidarities, in short, reestablish the social bond. In September 1990 the government released Fr 100 million to sixty pilot sites for integration through the intermediary of the FAS.

Following the 1981 events of Minguettes, several reports on the condition of the city were written, several committees were created, and projects were carried out. In July 1988 Prime Minister Michel Rocard appointed an interdepartmental delegate to the city, and in December 1990 a state minister for the city was named—Michel Delebarre, who presented an "antighetto" project at the first session of parliament. Since the summer of 1991, what Jean-Louis Bianco, minister of social affairs and integration, and Kofi Yamgnane, secretary of state, have really pursued is integration through an urban policy.

These appointments and the haste to define measures indicate the urgency of the situation. Moreover, the government immediately released Fr 300 million for suburban neighborhoods and the struggle against exclusion. Grants have increased every year; in 1993 the plan to boost the city established a budget of Fr 5 billion for neighborhoods and cities in trouble to distribute to various agents in the field, associations, and programs of urban solidarity.

In this new context, private organizations like CIMADE (an association of Protestant mutual aid), the churches, and associations of solidarity with immigrants contacted the militant faction of the target groups, which often consisted of labor union activists, students involved in youth movements, or refugees with enough political experience to "formalize their assembly." The city council grants them rooms to hold discussions on the right of residence, various categories of residence cards, housing policies, and ways of fighting racism. The cultural centers join the associations in celebrating the national holidays of the various groups in the neighborhoods. Schools also organize cultural exchange days when children trade culinary specialties or crafts, and prevention centers work with the associations to find internships for young people in businesses, aimed at promoting professional advancement.

Social services use the term "networking" or "knitting" to describe these networks of associations intersecting with those of organizations specializing in immigration, or of the many diverse centers working with the local authorities. These networks are based mainly on personal relations between those in charge of urban social services, elected officials, association activists, and some of the migrants who are designated as representatives of an implicit community because of their economical or social status.

The territorialization of identities and the conflicts it engenders still require other approaches. Intercultural mediators and neighborhood mediators appear as new agents who regulate conflicts in zones with a high foreign concentration. A report on mediations in the city emphasized the weakening of associative, labor, political, and religious organizations: "Two decades ago, there were natural intermediaries, places of dialogue between various social groups, between citizens and institutions, instruments of social cohesion."[33] In another sense, the appeal to mediators resembles a return to the neglected individual.

A "Multicultural" Germany

In Germany, too, in the late 1970s, several reports on the "guest workers," contradictory as they may seem, agreed on one fact: the foreigners "are here to stay." Even if Germany was still "not a country of immigration," measures had to be taken to insure the social and economic integration of the foreigners. The welfare state extended to professional training for youth. In each *Land*, political parties, educators, and associations of parents discussed the role of the school and what measures to take to educate the young Turks. Autonomous in their decisions about the terms of integrating Turkish families, the *Länder's* defininition of their own model varied according to the government in power, its concept of immigrants, and its attitude toward their settlement. Hamburg, whose state and municipal government is social-democratic (SPD), even granted foreigners the right to vote, although it was subsequently annulled; and Daniel Cohn-Bendit (Green Party), the municipal councillor of Frankfurt, tried to prepare public opinion to accept the idea of the multicultural society.

In 1981 the Committee of Foreigners (Ausländerbeauftragte der Bundesregierung) was created in Berlin. This federal institution enjoyed freedom of action in all local decisions, principally to help foreigners create their own organizations (*Selbshilfe*). The equivalent of the FAS in France, this committee finances association projects judged to be of "social benefit," that is, designed to unite young foreigners of every nationality and Germans in common activities. Social benefit also means salvaging deviants, the unemployed, delinquents, and young members of violent gangs. The idea is akin to community organizations in the United States that unite migrants by national or religious origin (or both) for an integrated community structure.

In Germany, because of the federal structure of the state, the networks among various organizations are woven within regions that handle foreigners autonomously or within a national group living in a *Land*. Since the 1980s, foreigners have created study and work groups to channel the discussion of immigration, conditions of residence, and naturalization laws. In 1981 Turkish students, including activists of the alternative Berlin slate (the Greens), and others affiliated with the SPD set up a study group called Initiativkreis Gleichberechtigung "Integration" (the Integration Equality Initiative Group, or IGI) to promote a new phase in the organization of the Turks from the perspective of settling in West Germany. At least formally, this ended the groups representing Turkish political parties, even the smallest extremist factions, which were sources of sometimes bloody conflict with the Kurds and even among the Turks themselves. This new phase was characterized by efforts to rally German politicians and make them aware of the changing reality of immigration and the need to alter their discourse and even legislation. It also tended to move public opinion to accept and encourage relations between Turks and Germans. After unification in 1989, the city of Berlin was assigned the role of mediator, but that had more to do with the development of the former East Berlin than with the integration of the foreign population in the city.[34]

The major task is still up to the Committee of Foreigners and the local municipal governments, which have worked with the IGI to help young people stage shows, perform break dancing, or organize sports events. In Berlin the senate granted them whole buildings, called neighborhood houses for multicultural encounter, where each association has a floor. In the middle of Kreuzberg, the ORA34 association (named for the address of the house, Oranienstrasse[35] 34) houses at least five associations, united by a tea house, the Family Garden, in the courtyard. The stated objective is to promote "intercultural" relations, not only to avoid the withdrawal of families or young people, but also to channel their activities. It is also primarily to hold on to young people who have nothing to do with the small political groups that are always present and active on German soil and to try to bring them together. In sum, the goal is to allow the Turks to open outward and to reinforce their internal solidarity with the hope of introducing the foreigners to general society. Acceptance by public opinion and even politicians depends in large part on community integration, and not on national integration as it would be defined in France. The objective is to fashion an image of an integrated community, guided and managed by bonds of solidarity between its members.

Besides, as in France, all these organizations stress that their activities are primarily social. But "networking" or "knitting" is done within a national group and not between different organizations and populations. Interestingly, such a political strategy validates the technical term that designates the integration of foreigners as a "policy of foreigners" (Ausländerpolitik) and not as a "policy of integration," as in France.

In short, to adopt Pierre Bourdieu's expression, the territories of identity in France and Germany correspond to "spatial structures and mental structures." In both countries, immigrant or foreign families are integrated perfectly into spatial structures but are excluded from mental structures. Each country defines its own form of exclusion: social in

France, ethnic in Germany. Yet each appears a priori as the consequences of the same logic of the liberal market that has created them, thus the convergence in the search for solutions in the two countries.

As a matter of fact, both are forced to adapt their structures to present-day reality, but these structures themselves convey the inescapable ideology and traditions inherited from national histories. Nevertheless, systems adopted for immigrants or foreigners in France and Germany evoke the way each society represents itself, the so-called model it wants to embody and expose. Relations between the states and the groups in question demonstrate a single "model" or method of development. France wavers between principles of universalism and a pragmatic particularism. Germany tries to appease international public opinion by adopting solutions to "protect" the foreigners it has segregated. The results are the same. Both countries implement protectionist operations for foreigners and converge in a sort of "applied multiculturalism." Social integration expressed in terms of national solidarity in France, and social integration conceived and channeled toward foreigners in Germany: both reflect the same phenomenon with regard to immigrants, to foreigners, or simply to a foreign body in mental structures.

CHAPTER FOUR

The Invention of the Cultural

> Believing, with Max Weber, that man is an animal suspended
> in a web of significance he himself has spun, I take culture to
> be those webs, and the analysis of it to be therefore not an
> experimental science of law but an interpretative one in search
> of meaning.
>
> —Clifford Geertz

IN WESTERN DEMOCRACIES, government measures promoting social integration are now joined with a discourse on cultural recognition. This also provides a way to justify the word *integration*, which has replaced *assimilation* in France. American scientific and political discussions have adopted the allegedly neutral term *incorporation*, which seems to consider a structural presence and an institutional recognition of differences in civil society and to refer to a "structural assimilation"[1] different from Anglo-Saxon conformity as defined by M. Gordon.

In France as in Germany, associations are intermediaries of solidarity in the territories of identity, they seek recognition of cultural identity. In France, that is within the framework of the "right to be different," a concept introduced by the Socialist Party, in power in 1981, whereas the Right has found a hard core in the association of foreigners because of the liberalization of the law in October 1981, allowing foreigners to create their own organization. Spontaneous gathering based on interpersonal relations in concentrated areas therefore found an institutional and formal structure through associations. These associations of formalized and institutionalized de facto communities needed a cultural content. In Germany, during the 1980s, as a result of synchronized imitation or political contagion, Turkish associations appeared on the public stage. These associations, regulated by a 1964 law stipulating that "any group, even of foreigners, can associate legally on condition of not disturbing the public order or the economic interests of the Federal Republic," aspire, as in France, to define an identity that was intended to be collective, to draw their boundaries, and to create new solidarities.

Henceforth, culture became the constituent element of the new solidarities to be constructed. Its definition is nevertheless ambiguous, as shown by the speeches of the association activists. Whether these leaders assign priority to specifically social or exclusively religious issues, or whether the associations are mainly national or regional, the term *cultural* appears in the name or at least in the bylaws: Socio-*cultural* Association of North Africans and Turkish Islamic *Cultural* Association. The name of the association seems to reaffirm a collective identity as the leaders want it to be perceived or interpreted. Culture then becomes a fact reconstructed by the organization according to the expectations of the individuals who seek to identify with it. Hence its invention. This approach allows the justification of differences with a discourse on history, the past, and roots.

In reality, the term *cultural* in association bylaws conceals social and political divisions. All the diversity of complex societies appears within boundaries that are initially national, drawn by the associations: social diversity (class, sex, age) and cultural diversity, which is sometimes linguistic (Turkish/Kurdish, Kabyl/Berber/Arab), sometimes ethnic, and often regional. This is the case with associations formed by Kurds of Turkish nationality, associations that refer to North African culture and whose chairmen and members specify their Kabyl identity, and a Moroccan association created, managed, and run by migrants from Er Rif. All the anthropological diversity that had been eclipsed by a concern for cultural homogeneity in the formation of the native nation-state seems to have reappeared in some form, as if it were liberated in the country of immigration, where each specific feature constitutes an element of distinction. Ideological divisions affecting some of the Islamic religious associations also come into play, along with positions for or against the government in power in the homeland and positions about policies in the country of immigration. There, too, the battle against racism unites young people, but at the same time, the "sexism of the leaders and activists" alienates the women, who would like "to have their say as women."[2] In short, the creation of associations resulted in a fragmentation based on what Freud called "the narcissism of minor differences."

Discourse alternates with acts designed to shape the cultural. In this sense, identity organizations appear as a refuge, sometimes even a sanctuary, where culture, religion, ethnicity, and nation (of origin) are interpreted, materialize, and take root. Each of these concepts intervenes to transform an informal local community, constituted de facto by spatial proximity, into a cultural one, from a local community to a transnational one, imagined in terms of common identifications.

THE REAPPROPRIATION OF A CULTURAL IDENTITY IN FRANCE

The expression of these differences through fragments of identity draws its legitimacy from history as recalled or from history that has been forgotten and repressed. Each group reinvents its history in terms of a real or imagined past, but one whose content is a product of relations reconstructed at the time of immigration and in contact with another culture. Thus the foreign space sends everyone back to his or her own image; this includes cases in which historical traumas are sublimated in compensation, as, for example, for the Jews or the Armenians.

In any case, in the United States the fever of multiculturalism has now led to a veritable rewriting of history. Excluded from assimilation, blacks invest themselves in an "ethnic" or even racial reinterpretation of the origin of civilization. Martin Bernal's *Black Athena: The Afroasiatic Roots of Classical Civilization* clearly conveys the desire of American blacks to express their ethnic and racial pride.

In France this glorification of origins is nourished by colonial history. Quite evident even in the discourse of young people of Algerian origin, the memory of that past is charged with passion and emotion. The children seem to recall what the parents have tried to forget or suppress, preoccupied as they were by the work that motivated their emigration and caught up in a process of acculturation that "prevented them from transmitting what had been inculcated into them," as one young association chairwoman put it.

Calling on the past, the present thus results in an invention of cultural identity that is trying to find a concrete form in the framework of the associations. During the vote on the law of October 9, 1981, which liberalized the law allowing foreigners to create their associations, parliamentary debate justified this phenomenon: "The association is the expression of national, cultural, and social solidarities and the instrument of their improvement. In that capacity, they constitute a means of breaking the isolation transplanted persons may suffer, of renewing the bonds with the homeland, and of reappropriating a cultural identity." The leader of an association of North African women spoke in similar terms: "If I use the term *reappropriation*, it is because I am convinced that it is full of completely different things from the French. We must not deny those aspects; we must bring them to light but empty them at the same time." She went on: "Reappropriation means that I try to improve the little bit my parents transmitted to me and that makes me aware that the talk about 'we are all the same' is really not true."

Is this the reappropriation of a culture that was already tampered with during colonization, a precolonial culture that is to be reinvented, or a culture that has suffered the erosion of a natural acculturation linked to immigration? The question remains open with regard to the confusion of the concrete acts of associations that are trying to answer it with courses in languages, folklore, and culinary days.

These are not new phenomena. In November 1962 the political office of the FLN (Front de Libération Nationale) in Algeria dissolved its federation with France. From that moment on, FLN's support committees, created during the summer of 1962, were transformed into the Federation of Algerians in France and Europe, thus turning a political organization into a cultural one for the defense of immigrants. Regulated by the law of 1901, the federation channeled its activities to the needs of Algerian immigrants by guaranteeing them language courses and literacy training and by taking care of their housing or employment problems. Other groups emerged from the federations of Algerians, Moroccans, and Tunisians, to "give moral support to immigrants here, but also political and financial support to nationalist movements in Algeria or Morocco." Other, "counterfederations," were formed in the 1970s by students or intellectuals who followed a Third World and internationalist ideology relying on CGT (French Trade Union, related to the French Communist Party) activists, and they assumed the role of the defenders of immigrant industrial workers while trying to make public opinion aware of the reestablishment of democracy in their homelands.

Yet a shift occurred in the 1980s when the associations demonstrated the desire to break with the institutions run by the homelands. From that moment on, the cultural expression of the associations was emptied of its class content. "There is no continuity with the original activities, there is a change," stated the representative of the Association of Moroccan Workers in France. "Our goal was to provide them with moral support at the beginning, but also to show in time a will to take care of problems of housing, childhood, culture, health, education, and so on." Thus, collective memory as support for an identity became the object of autonomous management by the associations, with the past guiding an orientation toward a future free of the guardianship of the host state.

A cultural identity corresponding to the process of permanent settlement must now be defined. That requires getting away from the influence of teachers and imams (Muslim religious leaders) sent by the homeland and taking charge of instruction in the language and the culture imagined as that of origin, regardless of bilateral agreements the homeland has made with the host country. In sum, it is necessary to mark the autonomy of the immigrant group and perhaps even to break with colonial history, aiming primarily at "changing the image of immigration in France," as one interviewee said, even at constructing a new identity by rewriting history. The first step in this process is to change the image of the homeland by integrating the history of immigration into it, in short, to develop a pride that is both national and immigrant.

On this level, Algerian immigration is the most complex. Even if, in principle, it refers to the massive arrival of workers beginning in 1960, it also includes the *harkis*, Algerian soldiers who fought on the French side in the Algerian war of independence, whom Michel Roux calls the "forgotten people of History." They exist in total ambiguity, with regard both to their homeland and to France. Considered traitors by the Algerians, they denounce their treatment by French politicians, an attitude "stamped with neo-colonialism and contempt."[3] But as Muslim French citizens and therefore voters, they have made some peace with Algeria under the protective cover of Algerian immigrants, of the defense of Islam, and of the struggle against racism. Now their children and grandchildren have merged with the Beurs, not only in public opinion, but also because of the social problems or racist prejudice they encounter.

Turks and Turkish Kurds represent another case. Even if Turks might now also express a reappropriation of their identity through a desire for autonomy from institutions linked with their homeland, from the teachers or imams sent by the Turkish government, and from activists defined by their political ideology for or against Ankara, the absence of a colonial past fuels their "ethnic pride," to use Max Weber's term. This allows them to express a difference that claims to be objective compared with other immigrant groups in France, even if its representation is merely subjective: the prestige of a glorious empire that declined but that quickly turned into a republic modeled on a Western nation-state, which then created the image of an independent people and nation.

This applies to both France and Germany, where the discourse on Turkish identity emphasizes these aspects. For example, racist acts led one immigrant Turkish woman to say that "they won't have the same fate as the Jews in Germany; the Turk is a conqueror, doesn't let himself be taken, and he has a state."

As for the Kurds, they draw their pride from an ethnic identity that has persisted despite the assimilationist policy of the Turkish Republic. Nationalist movements that developed in Europe, where Kurds compose almost 30 percent of the immigrants from Turkey, present demands generated not only in an immigrant situation but also by the Turkish Kurds' status as a double minority, both in their homeland and in Europe.

THE ASSERTION OF CULTURAL IDENTITY IN GERMANY

The wish to change the image of North African immigrants in France through the reappropriation of a cultural identity has been confined to discourse and explains the weakness of the ethnic demands of the young people of Algerian origin. In fact, their discourse is devoted to the experience of a "common life" between French and Algerians and the closeness produced by colonial history, as demonstrated by their mastery of the French language and "familiarity with the civil service," as some people are fond of pointing out. Although the Arabic language as an element of cultural identity is at the core of the activities of most associations, it operates mainly as a way to be free of control by the home government. "Arabic courses are held for children on Wednesday, Saturday, and sometimes Sunday," declared one association leader. "This is one of our battles against the agreements with the home country, which sends instructors who have a funny notion of immigrants. They are traditionalists and the children differentiate between French schools and Arab schools. This is the battle for modernity."

But the Turks, both in France and in Germany, regard their identification as primarily national and ethnic, and thus language is a demand and not simply a reaction. In France all their activities are included in the activities of associations as a whole (adult education, training, language courses, sports, folklore, and so on); but in Germany these activities are strictly part of an assertion of collective identity expressed in language. Some secular or religious Turkish associations (the latter preaching in Turkish) do not hesitate, if necessary, to combine language or religion courses with official ones of the Turkish government, even if ideological differences introduce political divisions into the discussion. In Berlin, for example, the Association of Parents of Students encourages an official bilingual education in the city's public schools, but not modeled on the bilingual classes (*Zweisprachige Klassen*) developed in Bavaria when the Turks first settled there. That policy applied in schools with heavy concentrations of foreigners, mainly Turkish nationals, separated into classes taught in Turkish by teachers from Turkey, and it resulted in the segregation of Turkish youth from German youth: for a separate class of twenty-five students, they simply had to be brought from other neighborhoods of the city.

This sort of segregation was the opposite of busing in the United States, where ethnic concentration in big cities was broken up and children were taken out of the "ghettos" to other neighborhoods in order to promote ethnic and racial equality in the school. As a component of affirmative action, the effects of busing have received a great deal of attention; these include the abandonment of public schools, the promotion of private schools, and a heavier concentration of children from disadvantaged ethnic groups. But note that, in its Bavarian version, it is intended instead to maintain difference and not to integrate, to maintain an inequality between Germans and foreigners later on and not to destroy it. The goal was "keeping them ready to go back."

The bilingual education that the Berlin Association of Parents of Students demanded means not separate classes but integrating the Turkish language into the German curriculum. The argument is based on the de facto linguistic separation between the world of the Turks and the world of the Germans; moving from one to the other does not do away with that distinction. "The children in fact live in two languages," said the director of the association. In Berlin (where Turkish-instruction posters in public places like telephone booths, for example, were deemed useless after Turks had been in the city for thirty years) it might seem paradoxical that mastery of the German language by Turks, including women, sometimes first-generation immigrants, is accompanied by a demand for instruction in their own language in the public school. Nevertheless, the intentions seem clear, at least in the discourse that makes language the essential cultural element in maintaining an idea of Turkish national identity. The Kurdish language, however, which is seen as the main element in a Kurdish ethnic identity in Turkey, gains legitimacy in immigration but is not integrated into the bilingual programs demanded by association activists. It seeks recognition mainly in Turkey.

Debates over bilingualism in Berlin, which have now spread into almost all the *Länder*, are similar to arguments about Hispanics in the United States, which were based on the educational failure of the children. The explanation for their low scholastic achievement was found in their limited knowledge of English and in the time spent outside of school. Hence, in 1973, a new law on bilingual education was passed, which revised the Bilingual Education Act of 1968 and allowed the children of newcomers to the country to continue some instruction in their mother tongue while they learned English as a second language.

The demands of the Hispanics in the United States and of the Turks in Germany are based on equal opportunity, claiming compensation for educational failure as the cause of segregation or nonintegration. But unlike the demands of the Hispanics in the United States, where bilingual instruction is justified for primary education, Turkish nationals in Germany have turned their language into a permanent and fundamental demand for a distinct collective identity.

Such an assertion leads to expressing membership in a group whose boundaries are narrowed to preserve an influence it is losing, because it is the influence of the country where the identity was established, and thus external. Hence, the assertion of an identity that is primarily national and Turkish constantly emerges in Germany in discussions of conditions of access to German citizenship. The German nation makes immigrant foreigners define themselves based on the same foundations. Citizenship does require renouncing the citizenship of origin, and refusing dual citizenship does reinforce a primarily national identification. Such an imperative makes all associations, whatever their ideological or

cultural penchants, demand that the right to dual citizenship be introduced into the German constitution. Here too, Turkish citizenship, like
language, creates a desire to maintain a separate identity, the basis of an
ethnic community defined by Turkish citizenship and recognized as such
in the Federal Republic.

Racist violence in the early 1990s, aimed at foreigners, particularly
Turks, turned the ethnic group thus defined into a refuge. Symbolic
images sublimated the diversity of identifications under one national
sign. The most spectacular protest image of Turkish nationals confronting atrocities that cost five lives in Solingen in the spring of 1993 was
the one broadcast by all European television networks: a crowd gathered behind the Turkish flag. The same kind of scene appears in France
too, although in different circumstances, such as the celebration of
national holidays introduced by Mustafa Kemal, in which children
parade in the streets holding paper flags with a portrait of Atatürk,
founder of modern Turkey. But in Germany the concept of the foreigner,
based on a citizenship and nationality defined by culture and ancestors
as well as by territory, makes the flag the symbol of national belonging,
of its independence as a nation. It also marks a structural presence on
German soil and in the public space of an ethnic minority whose identification is to be negotiated.

"ISLAM IS EVERYWHERE!"

The reappropriation of cultural identity and the assertion of a collective
identity linked to the national past justifies the present and prepares the
future for coming generations. Obviously, for them, the issues are no
longer moving from one country to another or defining themselves in
relation to one nationality or another (at least for France and soon for
Germany) but finding their bearings in one or several identities constructed from a situation of a de facto "minority" around a "permanent
difference." In both countries, this permanent difference refers to the
religious difference of Islam in a Christian land. "The Germans are
going to make us German; it will take another few years and they will
assimilate us, but religion will persist," said the head of a family who
grew up in Germany, where he owns a factory for mechanical instruments and is chairman of the association of Turkish businessmen in
Berlin. He thus expresses the "hard core" of identity.

At the junction of memory and identity, religion links not only the
past and the future but also the generations between them, and it
"implies a specific mobilization of collective memory."[4] In a new society, it appears as a response to the loss of references and establishes the
social bond. As Georges Balandier has correctly emphasized, "It is in

religion, especially its cultural or ecclesiastical institution, that tradition finds its most solid anchor."[5] Out of a frustrated traditionalism, immigrants, especially those from rural areas, in the early days of immigration, tried to maintain close relations with the homeland and extended family for as long as possible to ensure respect for their cultural traditions, structured in religious terms. When they first arrived, they tried to establish a social control whose components were drawn from religion, the source of moral and social order, which could be reinforced only by neighborhood relations.

This is true not only for the Muslims. Referring to Polish immigration in France, Janine Ponty has shown that among the Poles, too, the church constituted "the soul of resistance." The merging of national sentiment and religious sentiment made Polish immigrant families in Pas-de-Calais bring a priest from Poland to organize the local community.[6] Several studies of various newly arrived immigrant groups in the United States indicate the same phenomenon of religion as a basis for shaping a community. Often divided by nationalities, the churches and synagogues made up the center of the reconstituted community, and religious leaders were considered the only patriarchs able to maintain bonds between families and help them transmit the traditional values of the old country, expressed in religious terms.

Similarly, in the early 1970s, North African and Turkish families in France and Turkish families in Germany brought imams from their homeland to manage the prayer halls vis-à-vis municipal authorities. These imams were to help them transmit memory, teaching extracurricular courses on the Koran for the children, usually on a Saturday afternoon or Sunday. Moreover, the imams stayed long enough to become central figures in the community, particularly when it was necessary to pray for the death of a relative, prepare the coffin, and return the body to the homeland.

With the proliferation of associations in the 1980s, Islam moved into the discourse of the agents as a source of action or reaction. Even so-called secular associations integrated Islam into the framework of holidays to celebrate, like Ramadan or the sacrifice of the lamb. In general, once rituals become part of the collective memory, they become both religious and national and appear in what Danièle Hervieu-Léger has called "folklorized" religion.[7] "The association is secular, but religion is integrated," stated the chairwoman of the Association of North African Women.

Religious associations have also benefited from the liberalization of the law of associations in 1981. Thus, they were created on the basis of cultural and social associations.[8] Now they refer to the law of 1905, which affects them directly.[9] They also obviously generate action in which "cultural values lead to religious values; they are inseparable," as stated by Yousouf Roty, founder of the association Living Islam in the West, whose activities include publishing studies on "Islamic literature in French, on ritual, in the moral, spiritual, and practical realm of Islam." From one component of a culture for the first secular associations, Islam has become culture in its entirety for the religious ones, as stated by the leader of the Turkish association Islamic Union: "The association is not a religious association, but a cultural, social, and educational association, that is, Islam encompasses all the activities of our everyday life."

Thus, religion becomes another way of reappropriating identity. Its introduction, according to Roty, responds to "a supreme urgency to give the children at least an awareness of Islamic values, and elementary ritual principles that they haven't developed here. And it is from these points of anchor . . . that moral values, social involvement, and so on can be developed." The idea is that a positive image of Islam in French society can make young people identify more closely with their religion and "their origin." Young people "now have to be awakened to this culture, helped to discover it and tell it."[10] An imam in Marseille asserts that "Islam is a religion that manages all society, even brings remedies to it; it is not there to destroy but to build and improve human relations, and you can find that in all the verses of the Koran." So he relies on Islamic associations, he adds, "to inform the residents of the city so that Muslims are better understood in their spiritual life and other areas, for Islam is everywhere."

Ultimately, Islam appears as self-promoting and as a discourse of reaction to an environment that associates it with an image of "violence," "regression," "the submission of women," or "fanaticism." These terms and their opposites were proposed by a 1989 IFOP poll asking a Muslim and a French sample to indicate whether Islam corresponds to peace or violence, to progress or regression, to the protection of women or their submission, to tolerance or fanaticism.[11]

The advocates of Islam as a source of "ethnic pride" marked their arena by opposing secular associations and vice versa. Activists on both sides have developed discourses of mutual exclusion. Leaders of sociocultural associations reinforce their folkloric activities as a way of "offering the children a view of their culture that is not deprecating so that young people see something besides Islamism." For leaders of religious associations, however, identity discourse is fed by the "moral sense" contributed by Islam. "Better a mosque than an Arab bar," said an imam, rejecting the practices of the young "who call themselves Muslims and don't obey the laws of Islam." The bar may have been a reference to the sociocultural associations that define themselves as secular but compete with religious organizations by holding celebrations "where alcoholic beverages are served . . . and where those who want to can drink." This secular view obviously clashes head-on with that of the imams who request prayer halls from the municipal authorities so that they can organize community prayers on the same occasions.

Although the speeches and practices focused on Islam vary, they all aim at combining individual pride and moral training. Religious practice, instruction in traditions, and their system of belief are seen as supports for a lifestyle, a totality of values that can compensate for the sense of "social deprecation" among Muslims in France and Germany. They are also seen as ways of compensating for the shortcomings of faltering national institutions. Islamic associations justify their presence and importance in the French suburbs with their struggle against the delinquency, drugs, and violence of the young.

In Germany Islamic associations claim the same function of social control and salvaging of the young "victims" of immigration, and especially of Western society, which is presented as impersonal and cold. The chairman of the Islamic Federation of Berlin thus indicates on the first page of a brochure that the federation "opens its wings of love and affection to all its brothers" and "is ready to melt all bitterness and coldness [of the environment] in the warmth of Islam."

In Germany more than 90 percent of the Muslims are of Turkish nationality, and 99.9 percent of the Turkish nationals are Muslims.[12] Turkish Islam derives its specific character from belonging to a state whose constitution is secular but to a nation that is profoundly identified with the Muslim religion. The transition from the Ottoman Empire, ruled by the law of the Shar'ia, to a republic that was proclaimed by an urban elite removed the religious content from the official expression of Turkish national identity. Thus, religious instruction was excluded from the bilateral accords between European countries and Turkey. All the same, being Turkish and being Muslim are as inseparable as "flesh and bone."[13] "Our body is Turkish and our soul is Muslim," said one association leader, emphasizing that even though Turkey is a secular state in the Western image, Islam retains its eminently dogmatic nature there. In Turkey, even though Islam is not recognized as a state religion, it remains "the faith of the nation."[14] A study conducted in 1959 corroborated this statement by comparing Turkey with eleven other nations and showing that Turkish children were second—after Lebanese children—in defining themselves by religion.[15] Since the 1980s, the path of the religious party—initially called the Party of National Salvation, then the Party of Prosperity (or Well-Being), and now the Party of Virtue—indicates the power and even strengthening of a religious identity when faced with an ideology defined as secular by its constitution.

Immigration has increased the importance of religion in Turkish identity and has led families to send for imams from the homeland to ensure their children's education. In France their minority status in relation to the North Africans has made them support the North Africans when they want to display Islam in neighborhoods with a heavy Muslim concentration. Even in those cases, however, national assertion leads them to identify themselves with a Turkish Islam, embodied in a Turkish imam who teaches the Koran in his own language; in short, to form a Turkish community as opposed to other Muslim populations.[16]

An Imagined Transnational Cultural Community

Islam binds the identity image of groups from North Africa in France and from Turkey in Germany. It also serves as a bridge between the countries of origin and Europe, between East and West. Islamic organizations stretching from the local level to the international one or vice versa, international Islamic organizations that have gained a following in places with a heavy concentration of Muslim families, are trying by and large to create a transnational Islam, an *umma* (a community of believers), in Europe to identify with the "Muslim people" in general and with immigrants in particular. But even if Islam seems to link many national, regional, ethnic, and linguistic identities, it nevertheless divides them with regard to the political and ideological conflicts that split each of the Muslim countries and to the new divisions inspired by international Islamic politics.

While public authorities in France attempt to recognize an official Islam represented by the imam of the Mosque of Paris, which is affiliated with the Algerian government, Islamic groups hostile to the current government seek followers in the suburbs. In Germany Turkish officials try to emphasize the unique aspects of Turkish Islam and avoid any mixing of "cultural" Islam (as represented by official Turkey) and political Islam preached by the Party of Well-Being, or the Party of Virtue. Nevertheless, the civil organization of that party, called National Vision, still competes with them, in Germany and elsewhere in Europe. In 1990 its secretary-general, Ali Yüksel, a forty-five-year-old engineer with a degree in theology who looks "modern," as the media put it, proclaimed himself the religious leader of all Muslims, the *Sheyhulislam*. Revealing that ambition in Cologne, which houses the headquarters of the European Organization of National Vision, he declared that city the hub of Turkish Islam in Europe because in 1985 a disciple of Khomeini, Cemalettin Kaplan, nicknamed Kara Ses (the Black Voice), created an association titled the Anatolian Federated Islamic State. In

1992 Kaplan proclaimed himself caliph of the believers, "after waiting 70 years,"[17] that is, after the Turkish Republic abolished the caliphate. At his death on May 17, 1995, his followers, arguing "that Muslims cannot remain for one hour without a Caliph," appointed his son to succeed him. In the case of the *Sheyhulislam*, the ideological split between the two Turkish religious leaders in Germany refers to a Muslim Turkish identification, for his status in this particular instance is limited to National Vision; whereas the caliph promotes an Islamic republic modeled on Iran and with an international Muslim identity.

The personal and institutional relations of these two figures with the German and Turkish public authorities and the degree to which they represent the Turkish immigrants will be discussed later. But what is immediately striking in their self-designation is their common reference to the Ottoman Empire, a nostalgic reference signaling a desire to recover a history that regards immigration as liberating Islam from the Kemalist ideology and its secularism. Hence, it expresses an identification that is national in spite of everything, defining the nation ideologically and territorially through the movement of National Vision or obliquely through a reference to Anatolia. But with a reappropriation of roots or with a return to sources, such references become the very expression of an ethnic identity currently connected to the emergence of Islam as a political force in the Muslim world and among immigrants. An ethnicity must be invented to develop the past in terms of present preoccupations in order to increase the influence of those components among the immigrants.

Whereas the identification of the Turks in Germany in extreme cases uses Ottoman points of reference and more generally the national and ethnic framework, among North Africans in France it is expressed by "Arabness." The sense of belonging to the Arab-Muslim world is reinforced by international conflicts that overlap with national and international references beyond territorial boundaries. Thus a geographic area takes shape that not only produces variations in the definition of Arabness and Islam but also establishes bonds of solidarity by a global "victimization" of Muslims. The *Intifada* and the Gulf War are elements outside the context of immigration that become factors of identification for the Muslims of France.

However, among immigrants from Turkey, these international issues seem to be limited to an identification that is more political than religious or ethnic, except in the case of Bosnia. The Bosnians converted to Islam during the three centuries of the Ottoman presence, and in the imaginary collective of the Turks, they represent the modern, European part of Islam, as a self-projection. In this case, the tragic fate of these "blond brothers with blue eyes," who are persecuted for their religion, reinforces the Islamic dimension of an ethnic identity experienced as a solidarity across borders.

The American sociologist Herbert Gans has analyzed the international dimension of the ethnoreligious identification in general as a component of what he calls "symbolic ethnicity," defined as an ethnicity of last resort.[18] In politics, it is expressed through strictly international preoccupations, especially those concerning the country of origin. This is true, for example, among the Catholics of the United States, who consider Ireland an identity symbol, just as Israel is for the Jews. In American political life, lobbying in Congress makes these symbols the justification of the pressure groups that influence international decisions-making. In France and Germany, although reference to an international Islam has assumed an important place in discourse, it is much less involved in shaping a political identity that was developed primarily in specific relations with each of the two states.

Language, nationality of origin, religion, culture—terms and concepts that are sometimes mingled and sometimes separated by artificial or circumstantial boundaries—emerge in the expression of a collective identity imagined in terms of a real or mythical past. They present a repertoire of identity with a whole gamut of options in terms of which individuals or groups can express or manifest a common identification.

The invention of a culture that claims to be collective constitutes a step toward the construction of an ethnic group that asserts itself in the present through claims on the public authorities. The search for recognition imposes the adoption of new identity traits perceived as more relevant to the situation of immigration with regard both to individuals and to French or German institutions. The search for legitimacy reinforces their inventive character and revitalizes an awareness of belonging to an ethnic group that emphasizes its difference with regard to its cultural, social, and political environment.

CHAPTER FIVE

The Politicization of Identities in France

> The French conception of integration must obey a logic of
> equality and not a logic of minorities.
> —*Pour un modèle français d'intégration*, first annual
> report of the Haut Conseil à l'Intégration, 1991

IN FRANCE AND GERMANY, cultures that have been invented, reappropriated, or asserted since the 1980s are also nourished by public discussion. Subjects like racism, the place of foreigners in society, their economic role or access to the national community, and their rights have generated an awareness of belonging among the descendants of immigrants. This awareness has been reinforced by local and national policies and by targeted government practices. Studies of the United States after the 1960s show new widespread attention to ethnic concerns within public spaces and politics. This was clearly due to the influence of the civil rights movement on society at large and on legislation.[1] The search for equal rights introduced those identities into a mainly political struggle.

Therefore, although cultures are invented through their institutionalization within the framework of associations, they become politicized in their relations with the state. A simple consciousness of cultural differences is transformed into political action when it is based on demands for the state's recognition of those differences. The politicization of identities proceeds from the interaction between groups and state, from the struggle for recognition and representation within national institutions.

In France the liberalization of the law of association for foreigners in 1981 is the point of departure for the politicization of identities. In Germany, too, since the 1980s, activists among the descendants of Turkish immigrants have appeared on the public stage to demand recognition of a collective identity. From the point of view of the states, resources at the disposal of immigrants or foreigners go primarily for equal treatment and equal rights as a fundamental principle of democracy. From the point of view of the association activists, identities are now the element structuring a community in order to compete for state resources. Hence, the creation of associations is based on an obvious duality of objectives: developing a collective awareness of belonging and, at the same time, integrating into the structures of the state.

The ensuing policies are a priori far from affirmative action or any positive measure to compensate for inequality, as applied in the United States, where classifying ethnic groups by "chosen" ancestors elucidates a targeted policy. In France policies defending the idea and principles of universalism object to all identity differentiation. At least that is the official rhetoric, although it is contradicted by applied policies. The competition created by the state, which enables identities to be organized and expressed, results in a situation similar to the one in America, that is, the emergence onto the political stage of ethnic or religious communities seeking public recognition. In the United States the term *ethnicity* has now entered the scientific vocabulary and even the spoken language, and it no longer needs to be defined. But in a 1975 collection of essays with that title, Nathan Glazer and Daniel Moynihan, the editors, introduced it as a new term. They added, however, that it was not the word itself that was novel but the phenomenon of ethnicity it denoted. That phenomenon is defined as the expression of cultural, religious, and racial identities in the political realm, as they rally to demand recognition in the public sphere.

In France the term *ethnicité* is disturbing. It goes against the ideology of the republic "one and indivisible" because it refers to communities, other than the national community, over and against the state. It is therefore rejected. In Germany, since the word *ethnic* is associated with the nation, where individuals are bound through common ancestors, ethnic groups formed by foreigners do not raise any hackles. But in both countries, the hesitations of governments, on the Left and the Right, show cracks in the state, where so-called ethnic communities can be incorporated.

In France policies vacillate between a desire for continuity in political traditions, reinforced by a republican rhetoric, and a certain pragmatism toward pernicious results that fuel the political motivations of groups structured around identities. These policies consequently combine the symbolic with an electoral strategy. This chapter analyzes the mechanisms of the politicization of identities produced by constant interactions between individuals or groups and the French state. It attempts to show how, through policies concerning integration and the resources made available to the political actors who are the descendants of immigrants or to others, the state generates an ethnic market despite a rhetoric that rejects its presence. But at the same time a rhetoric about the French exception, redefined in terms of laïcité, leads the same actors to work out new forms of solidarity that would allow the constitution of a Muslim community and to develop a parallel discourse to locate themselves in relation to the state.

THE EMERGENCE OF NEW DIVISIONS

Republican Rhetoric

Tocqueville reported that in the United States "there are not only commercial and industrial associations . . . but others of a thousand different types—religious, moral." He linked the many associations in American social and political life with democracy, as limitations on the power of the state. In France, however, associations, which are encouraged by the state, are created with the aim of designating spokesmen for them, intermediaries between a group formed around common interests and the public authorities. This is the corporatist logic of the ancien régime, which in the republic recognizes labor unions, professional organizations, and other interest groups based on the collective interest. In its principle, this logic does not refer to identities—local, regional, religious, or ethnic.

Associations of foreigners fit into this scheme a priori, at least in its objectives, even if their content contradicts the principle of French corporatism, since French corporatism does not consider any cultural identity. As far as immigration is concerned, the implicit strategy of the state is to seek the emergence of an elite among the immigrants or their descendants, which can assume the role of spokesman for the concerned population, representing a collectivity with the public authorities. The declared objective of public authorities is to make public opinion accept "differences" and counter racism. Geneviève Domenach-Chich, chair of the Léo-Lagrange Foundation, affirmed in 1991 that "the French state entrusts the subcontracting of immigrants to the associations." The so-called immigrant associations were then considered the new stage of an integration policy, placed in the hands of association leaders.

Since the liberalization of the law of associations in 1981, foreigners active in labor unions, parties (particularly the French Communist Party), or other political groups have organized around special cultural features, invented and reaffirmed in their relation to politics. The discourse accompanying their action is supported generously by the Fund of Social Action, the largest source of funds for institutions concerned with identity. In the standard application for subsidies, the FAS has established a typology of their activities noting their "social" and "cultural" nature, defined as "community initiatives." These are the criteria established by the financial norms of the major public organization for integrating immigrants and their families. But faced with the "community drift" of the 1990s, a source of tension or even conflict between national institutions and certain associations, particularly Islamic ones, the FAS has amended its "requirements." The application no longer cites community initiatives. In a declaration in *Le Monde* on December

1, 1990, its director stated that a "recognition of communities is ruled out." At the same time, official reports, particularly those of the High Council on Integration, drew the attention of the association leaders and of public opinion to "French-style integration" or the "French model of integration." Association activists also altered their speech, rejecting any idea of ethnic or cultural community and its representation in the public domain; instead, they insisted on the role of representation assigned to individuals, the only intermediaries between a structured collectivity and the state. Both parts use the same rhetoric for their intentions.

Within the framework of so-called immigrant associations, these individuals are designated by virtue of being rooted in the milieu of a clearly defined group and in their networks of personal relations with specialized organizations. In the long run, they become indispensable spokesmen for the public authorities and social assistance, their only information network for social services. They explain the "specifically cultural behaviors" of North Africans (by country, regional or linguistic affiliation, or sex), Africans (of whatever ethnicity), Turks, and Kurds to the organizations that finance the associations. They demand treatment channeled and appropriate to their case to avoid the homogenization of differences by the state. In exchange, they adopt the views of the public authorities toward the group in question. They inform that group of desirable public behavior while spreading the message of the various governments about social integration as defined by the dominant model, particularly concerning the place of religion in French public life. During special days organized by the activists, their proposals are accepted or criticized but are mainly transmitted to the members or followers or simply to the occasional audience of the association.

Discourse becomes universalist in the struggle against racism. Faced with the National Front, which has campaigned against foreigners, assigning responsibility for "French ills" to immigration and immigrants and presenting them as a threat to society and French identity, the immigrant movement by and large is defined as antiracist. Racism becomes the most important element of mobilization in the associations and appears as the official theme of the descendants of immigrants in the struggle against the National Front. The parties of the center and the Left have gotten a second wind among immigrant youth and their electoral potential, and they promise to subsidize the associations.[2] The Socialist Party primarily, and its various trends, along with the centrists, channel their concept of immigrants and their expectations of the young people through the associations. The activists thus penetrate the political, and especially the electoral, mechanisms, responding to the electioneering of the parties, which is justified by the advance of the National Front.

The Emergence of an Ethnic Market

By institutionalizing collective identities through associations, the state gives "instructions" for differences in a republic. The aim, then, is to assimilate differences into a republican ideological framework and institutional structure. This is how rhetoric meets policy. The scope of mobilization within the associations and the rate of participation depend in large part on the totality of political life.

But the rhetoric and organization that make these differences instrumental produces new divisions. They are defined in cultural terms. They emerge in large part from political measures that add an identity element to traditional practices restructuring the society so that social demands are transformed into cultural or identity demands. This difference is based on a claim for the recognition of an "origin." Whereas in the 1960s and 1970s immigrants expressed their interests in terms of class, the younger generation expresses its concerns in terms of culture or religion, in an "identity of origin," reinterpreted within he framework of new collective actions. This identification does not exclude social affiliation but reinforces it. The abundant literature on ethnic groups in the United States emphasizes the link between religion, nationality, race, and class; and ethnicity is defined by a combination of all these elements. Similarly, positive measures of compensation to promote certain groups defined as minorities (as in affirmative action) are legitimated by an affiliation that is more social than national or racial, at least in discourse. Unlike the United States, however, in France a classification by origin or declared ancestors is excluded from the concept of national society and from census practices; yet initiatives aimed at immigrants, more precisely at North Africans, create a category that is informal but that does affect self-definition. This is one of the contradictions of the initiatives of the welfare state, whose concern for equal treatment produces an identity classification that becomes a new source of inequality.

In France most association activists, who themselves are descendants of immigrants, dispute the existence of a cultural division. Some criticize "the associations that live on those cultural resources" and challenge the role of the welfare state in the creation of that new division. Others complain of the dependence it creates, denouncing various organizations or ministries that present "their criteria" to them: a mixture of cultural and social standards that makes the association leaders or activists "the kept minions of society." Still others more specifically condemn the Social Action Fund for creating a separation copied from the identity criteria within society. "The FAS is the ghetto," said one association activist, adding: "As for us, they won't let a specific organization finance immigrant activities. That creates the notion of foreigners on one side and French on the other, in all areas. The FAS intervenes in culture, in jobs; now they make us employees of the TUC (paid community service); it's a terrific tool. . . . And initiatives that move toward integration, its mainstay, mean partition and marginalization."

Ultimately, social policies specifically for foreigners create a new market that can be defined as ethnic. This market, produced and maintained by the welfare state, does create new opportunities, but only for some immigrants. In the United States controversies over affirmative action deal precisely with that pernicious inequality, which, from the start, has worked to the advantage of the black middle class.

In France, with the proliferation of associations, a social category of cultural intermediaries has emerged.[3] Between thirty and forty years old when the association is created, whether of immigrant descent or not, they are self-declared coordinators, social assistants, and psychologists. Several so-called sociocultural associations prefer to appeal to Beur coordinators who are already trained as social assistants, who acquire that training on the job, or who are defined as such by their activity. They see the mutual aid, consultation, and legal information provided by their associations as social assistance in the categories of FAS financial norms.

The social trajectory of these new agents is delineated by and in the association movement. The role of association leader gives them economic advancement and a political career, thanks both to the existing networks and to those reinforced by their origin. In chapter 7 we will see that in the French municipal elections of March 1989, most of the young Beurs on the slates of the various parties were leaders or active staff members of associations.

Thus, whether economic, social, or political, these activists' integration is individual but is now based on a collective representation. They achieve a new social status because of their national or ethnic origin, which becomes communal in their action and in their role of representative. But that evidently does not hinder their individual rise, which is independent of the association movement. Yet individuals of various national origins have chosen "invisibility" and the "indifference" of the public authorities for their own advancement. Curiously, however, a growing number are asked to be advisers or consultants not only in the associations but also by influential political figures because of the "objectivity" or "rationality" of their knowledge and their social or economic success. The best-known example in France is Kofi Yamgnane, a first-generation immigrant of Togolese origin, a professional engineer and mayor of Saint-Coulitz in Brittany who is married to a Frenchwoman and was appointed secretary of state for Social Affairs and Integration in May 1991. This choice was not naive; the intent was to use him to symbolize successful individual integration. The example of French-style integration he embodies has a collective impact, both validating the role of republican institutions toward public opinion and immigrants and maintaining the hope of integration in the younger generations.

The existence of an ethnic market, like any market, makes the agents compete for identity or culture on one hand and the financial resources to promote it on the other. But using culture also leads to other divisions within the group. A divergence emerges between spokesmen and the rest of the immigrants for whom they are supposed to be speaking. The spokesmen were appointed or showed up as volunteers to ease tensions at the local level, and their relations with the public authorities have generated new internal conflicts within their own structures. The reference to the "we" who created an association to clarify a difference with regard to French society now implies something else. A new dichotomy is created between "us" and "them," "us" referring to the immigrants or their young descendants and "them" to the leaders of the associations, the "pros" (professionals of identity), as the immigrants call them.

This is a classic group phenomenon. In the United States studies on the mobilization of black or ethnic groups illustrate the professionalization of their leaders, who are sometimes even outside the movement and the group but are called upon as activists to mobilize human and financial resources. In other countries, in Africa, for example, these intermediaries are plainly called cultural entrepreneurs, and they play an important role in shaping states, where ethnicity is the major source of mobilization, by giving an ideological form to identities and by stirring nationalism.[4] What is new in France, however, is that such "ethnic entrepreneurs" are promoted by the state with a contrary rhetoric.

The intensity of a collective consciousness and the sense of belonging to a cultural or ethnic group depend obviously on the ability of those intermediaries to harmonize the codes of the host society and the cultural symbols they use to restructure the group. They are judged by their skill in mobilizing financial resources on one hand and human resources on the other, for both are indispensable to the survival of their association. The image of success they reflect is based, therefore, on their new function among the immigrants and on their talent for creating an identification with the individuals they appeal to and who accept them a priori as spokesmen. Hence, it is incumbent on them to represent and negotiate identities with the state apparatus and to maintain an identification with the populations to which they appeal.

Thus, the politicization of identity is closely linked with the emergence of that new "class" of intermediaries. It is actually a cause-and-effect relation. Manufactured to serve as spokesmen with the public authorities, these intermediaries trigger a realization of "basic" ethnic affiliation.

Forming a Community

Such an analysis of collective identity formation ascribes all responsibility to the state. More generally, the state, political parties, local or national policies, and governmental practices all contribute to that process of politicization of identities and to making it a demand for public recognition. In *The American Kaleidoscope*, Lawrence Fuchs has shown that local governments' promotion of black art and culture created a consciousness of their uniqueness and was a source of pride and mobilization. Similarly, subsidies to Puerto Ricans to create jobs in their neighborhoods intensified their sense of belonging to an ethnic group. Financing bilingual instruction in New York might produce a Hispanic awareness and even lead to the formation of a group of Latinos. These examples led Fuchs to emphasize that the nature of state intervention, on the federal or state level or with government programs, not only defines identities but can even change their content and boundaries.[5]

In France, since the 1990s, local government initiatives directed at North Africans and guided mainly by the "fear of Islam" have resulted only in "groping around" and countering the declared principles of the republic, that is, with the presence of communities in the public sphere.

"Thwarting Islam"

In France the mutual exploitation of identity or culture by activists and public authorities has enhanced associations on the local level. Each one invents a culture and traditions.[6] Specialized organizations, like the FAS, fuel the divisions created by temperamental and attitudinal incompatibilities between the leaders and ideological divergences concerning the country of origin. Activists' getting away from the original objective of the association or developing a new approach to immigrants is enough to dissolve one association while gaining the support of the specialized organizations to create another one.

Local authorities declare their intention of breaking ethnic solidarities and splitting apart a community welded by a single association. Their aim is to reinforce solidarities among immediate neighbors in order to separate ethnicity from the defense of common interests, and primarily to create a neighborhood community to harmonize with the discourse on republican principles. The main objective is to "reestablish the social bond" beyond differences.

Such intentions found a basis in the activities of local organizations. In the late 1980s, municipal councillors, school principals, coordinators of social centers, leaders of neighborhood social development programs, in short all local agents, increased and varied their mode of intervention. The leader of the FAS of the Moselle argued that local authorities justified subsidies by their desire to "thwart the Islamic associations." Municipalities then subsidized associations combining their activities with various operations in place at the level of neighborhood social development programs (DSQ), fairs, and so on. They made rooms available to the associations for conferences, discussions, exhibits designed to present a so-called culture of origin of the residents of a given place. Conversely, coordinators of cultural centers also organized meetings with immigrant parents or the children of immigrants. Local cultural centers even organized Muslim celebrations to attract observant families, whatever their national origin. For example, the cultural center of Borny, a suburb of Metz, which has a heavy concentration of Turkish and North African immigrants, organized collective prayers during Ramadan in 1991 "to weaken the influence of the imams in the neighborhood," according to its coordinator.

"Forming a Muslim Community"

The many subsidies to create new associations result in a fragmentation approaching "tribalism" in cities with strong concentrations of Muslim immigrant families. Fragments of exposed identities compete for both financial and human resources. Families feel forced to choose between certain associations and risk being judged by all of them. Even if they are hardly represented by the initiatives of any of the associations, families nevertheless take a stand on them and their members and define their own personal network within them or at the junction of several of them. Thus, this dynamic also contributes strongly to creating a community with politicized identities.[7]

In fact, competition shapes a community more than does solidarity among the individuals who compose it. The multiplicity of identity institutions strengthens the community system by offering its members a gamut of ethnic, social, and even political diversities, where more individuals can find their niche. The presence of associations of different and sometimes opposing tendencies leads individuals, whether they are followers or not, to participate in them, to locate themselves in relation to them. Conflicts between associations indicate that mode of individual participation and, consequently, identification with a community whose boundaries are defined by a play of rivalries, solidarities, and appeals to voters. A solidarity based on the struggle against racism, as developed by SOS-Racism in the early 1980s, for example, soon gave way to "interethnic" or interreligious conflicts between Jews and Muslims who were active in the association when the Muslims accused the movement of Zionism. These conflicts reinforced the religious identity of association members or sympathizers even though the association was based on universal values, with the struggle against racism constituting the main identification of its members.

Religious associations are not excluded from that field of confrontation. On the contrary, they are positioned as an alternative to cultural associations and contribute to closing off the environment. Created with the support of the country of origin, money from the Gulf states, and gifts from families and businesses, hence independent of public money, these institutions have developed in neighborhoods with high concentrations of Muslims. In most cases, they work with cultural institutions whenever their "social service" is in question, and their leaders also compete for access to human and sometimes even material resources from the local authorities. They appeal to the young, speaking to them of respect and dignity, morality and faith, peace and tolerance; they develop a discourse on roots and identity, as if to console them for their deception within the antiracist movements from which they have felt excluded. The imam of the Islamic Cultural Association of Épinay stated: "The young people understood that they were cheated by the current governments and all the 'spokesmen' associations describing themselves as France-Plus, SOS-Racism. As for me, I never considered myself a Beur. I am a Muslim Frenchman of Algerian origin. As a Muslim Frenchman, I feel completely integrated into French society, and all the young people who came to the association are all the young people who returned to religion. And the young 'Beurs' you've had problems with are those who don't know if they're Arab or French. They are completely out of sync, completely disoriented. This is the essential point that we have noted." Thus the term *Beur*, derived from the word *Arab* in the French pig Latin invented in the 1980s by the young descendants of North African immigrants in reference to their social and cultural experience, was rejected as soon as it was picked up by the media and the politicians, who, according to some of them, tried to give it a more social than cultural meaning.

Yet these young Beurs declared that they had found a framework of action within the association, admitted that they had been aware of a difference, and had mobilized to proclaim an identity. Today they feel excluded from assimilation and the institutions leading to it: school, work, the antiracist movement. Disappointment about the associations derives mainly from the "professionalization" of their leaders and a career "built on their back," as they say, and adds to their disappointment at the failure of the upward mobility they had hoped to achieve through education or the opening of the labor market. Moreover, since 1989, the leaders of cultural associations have demanded "the right to indifference," their slogan in the municipal elections of 1989. As if to mark a real difference, some young people today also assert that they no longer recognize themselves in the Beur identity, that "media identity that considers only successful immigrants, a success story," they say. Others express a feeling of rejection and recognize that they were even "used by their own people, for their own interest and advancement," to justify their connection with religion. Thus, whereas so-called sociocultural associations barely have forty or fifty permanent members— even if they receive twice that number when holding discussions or shows—Islamic associations number four hundred to five hundred permanent members and draw a much bigger crowd on holidays.

A division of social labor has now been established between the cultural and religious neighborhood associations, which shape a community just as much as the competition between them does. Whereas secular associations make do with social action, religious institutions take responsibility for identity, welcoming families, bringing the generations closer, and ensuring communication between them. In short, social assistance, as the public authorities define it, is reserved for secular associations, and cultural activities refer to Islamic religious associations. Sports, discussions of Islam as a religion, philosophy, doctrine, discussions of "current events concerning Muslims, like the case of Salman Rushdie or the head scarf," and educational support appear as much in their activities as instruction in the Koran or Arabic language courses. Sociocultural associations declare that they "salve the wounds of a catastrophic immigration policy," in the words of Nana Beur, the association chairwoman; religious associations, however, try "to awaken the young people to their identity, to help them discover it and say it," asserted the secretary-general of the Friends of Islam Association, whose headquarters is in Saint-Denis, a northern suburb of Paris.

Ultimately, cultural associations limit their work to administrative, "technical" work to ease the daily lives of young people. As for religious institutions, they develop an "ethnic" pride, a sense of community whose elements are drawn from Islam, its practice, its traditions, its values, and its mobilizing force. Their leaders also emphasize the capacity of their organization to adapt to the environment. This argument is based on the use of French in encounters, discussions, and even informal meetings: in short, French is the language of the collective. This is designed to achieve transparency with regard to the larger society, which is openly suspicious, and quite simply because French is the language of the young generation.

The universalist and republican discourse of the young descendants of immigrants who are active in the neighborhood association movements now deals with exclusion. They share this concern with other immigrant groups, Muslim or not, or quite simply with other young people who are defined by the same social criteria. "What a hassle" (*la galère*) is part of their vocabulary. The imams have also developed a republican discourse, alerting their audience to the situation of a de facto religious minority that requires a separation between the private and the public. "Our organization tries to explain to Muslims that they must not demand Islam as if they were in an Islamic country," said Ahmed Jaballah, chairman of the Union of Islamic Organizations of France, a federation created in 1983 based on the law of 1901, an umbrella group of about fifty Islamic associations scattered throughout France. "We appealed to Muslim sages to explain to them that the Muslim in a non-Muslim society has a completely private status. Islam presents itself as a complete lifestyle in a Muslim society; but in a non-Muslim society, religion must be applied at the individual and community level and that's all. French society cannot be asked to observe and adopt the obligations of Islam." Through his discourse he emphasized his "assimilation" of republican values and of French secularism (laïcité).

Influential persons in this framework are also defined as spokesmen. In most cases, they are specialized workers with a low level of religious education and are thirty-five to forty-five years old. They define their audience specifically: Muslims in general, but of the same nationality, even the same ethnicity. They appoint themselves as spokesmen to "inform the larger society about Islam," its calendar, its holidays. They set themselves up as moderators of local passions and tensions. Some even take on the mission of "showing teachers and educators how to discipline the young," as an answer to the violence that spreads in the public space, more specifically in schools. They create respect in the collective not only through their knowledge of religion, but mainly through their sense of authority and discipline, their power of negotiations with local authorities, to obtain permission to establish slaughterhouses or to build a mosque, for example.

Between the Mosque and the School

The mosque as a symbol and as a place that can shape a community is at the core of local conflicts. In Marseille, Grenoble, and Metz, several plots were bought, and the Muslim congregations are awaiting permission for the construction of a mosque. Regional, national, and even foreign media report on abortive attempts to build mosques, illustrated by "bulldozer" scenes. The mosque as an edifice with a minaret, desired by Muslims, disturbs citizens and politicians. The media call it a mosque-cathedral, an obviously intentional reference. According to *Robert's Dictionary*, a cathedral is the episcopal church of a diocese, but in current usage it represents any big and beautiful church. Consequently, a cathedral is imposing and occupies an important place in the urban landscape. Might that be the case for Islam? A cathedral is a historical monument marking "places of memory" as well as creating memories, whereas Islam is recent in France, and memories connected with it are located outside French history and territory. Is this, then, a way of concretizing how the history and landscape of the city have changed because of the permanent and structural presence of Islam?

In any case, the construction of a mosque-cathedral is primarily an important election campaign issue for mayors. In Marseille, in the legislative elections of November 1989, the National Front built its campaign on the slogan "No to the mosque," opposing the plan for the mosque-cathedral announced a month earlier by Senator and Mayor Robert Vigouroux. In Lyons, however, the newly elected mayor, Michel Noir, had to fight the National Front after he promised to build one in 1989, a battle that ended in the autumn of 1994 with the public opening of the Grand Mosque.[8] The question returns to the agenda in Strasbourg with the plan to build two big mosques, including a "mosque cathedral that would be reflected in the water and would be the counterpart of the famous gray sandstone cathedral on the other side of the river. . . . A whole symbol for the European capital."[9] Thus, one year after the municipal elections, a European dimension, a new opening for both France and the Muslims, is added to the local dimension.

Building mosques demonstrates the influence and negotiating success of the imams. Mosques reflect power relations between the public authorities and the local community forces. Local Islamic associations must overcome national and ethnic splits, and the imams must transcend rivalries and conflicts of power. In some cities, unity focused on a transnational and transcultural Islam is imposed as a solution, symbolized by the mosque. "We don't always get along with each other, we Turks, Moroccans, Tunisians, or Algerians, but we are all Muslims above all," declared the Algerian imam of Farebersvillers, in Lorraine, home to 2,500 Muslims from North Africa and Turkey. He added: "For the mosque, we have joined the styles of two Islamic cultures, one North African and the other Ottoman."

The polemics concerning mosques are limited to the municipality; just as important, if not more so, is the national issue of the head scarf in the schools. Excessive media attention poured oil on the fire and publicized existing tensions between national institutions and Islamic institutions, introducing a balance of power between the law of the republic and the larger society on one hand and the law of the Koran and the community on the other.

Politicians rallied around the issue of the head scarf, which strengthened the role of the imams or Islamic association leaders as representative spokesmen of a "dissident" community structured around Islam. Whether they were sent by the country of origin as part of the bilateral agreements with an official status recognized by both partners or they represented religious political parties like the Front Islamique du Salut (FIS) in Algeria or the Party of Prosperity (or Virtue) in Turkey, they were now established as the spokesman for their "community." But by choosing imams of all ideologies as spokesmen to calm tensions and persuade families to obey the laws of the republic, the state also increased the negotiating power of the religious associations by rejecting other associations or by forcing them to locate themselves outside the ground of Islam. Creating a new subject or object with as much cultural and ideological impact on the larger French society as on the groups in question made the choice easier for the families by placing religious identity at the core of their political interests.

THE RECALL OF THE UNIVERSAL

French Laïcité

In reaction to issues raised by the head scarf, French society redefined *laïcité*, which has become the very definition of French secularism. This principle of the republic has undergone several interpretations since November 1989, without reaching its final version, except that it is definitely the "official religion" of France. The subject of debates in the National Assembly, defended in formal or informal meetings held by (antiracist) association activists, intellectuals, and shapers of public opinion, the principle of laïcité and respect for it have jolted French society and its politicians. The scope of the polemic is similar to that of the church against the secular school established by Jules Ferry. In fact, it fills the role of foil played by Catholicism in the definition of *laïcité* in the early twentieth century and of its function and ideology in the school.[10] Today, Islam is at the core of the redefinition of *laïcité* and serves as its mirror.

The "case" shattered the politicians, the Socialist Party in power, by dividing its various currents and the teachers of the Ministry of Education. While some attributed a pluralist character to laïcité based on tolerance, others rejected the idea of a multireligious school as corresponding

to the secular school. But altogether, the public authorities, torn between a particularist pragmatism and universalist principles, were eager
to defend the republic by asserting laïcité as its fundamental value,
emphasizing its universal nature, and including it at the core of French
national identity.

One discussion gave rise to another. The Islamic head scarf was tied
to immigration and integration. A discourse of social peace made secularism its keeper and insisted on reinforcing the role of the school in
shaping citizens, consistent with national principles.

Islam in the Feminine

One important feature of the discussion of the head scarf has been the
defense of the rights of women, which have been difficult to achieve in
democratic societies. The case of the head scarf illustrates a community
pressure that has a greater impact on women, whose appearance in
public compromises the "honor" of the man, and consequently of the
family, in Mediterranean societies and in the transplanted community in
France.

Thus, a new rhetoric develops. Laïcité and the rights of women, both
linked with universal values and democracy in Western societies, have
generated new public initiatives in the 1990s, beginning with a change
of vocabulary and followed by an effort to channel the activities of
sociocultural associations. The issue is no longer spokesmen but mediators; the issue is no longer community action or social assistance but
mediation. Association requests for subsidies to mobilize public resources for the integration of immigrants and their families must be
reformulated in these new terms.

Although the concept of mediation has been present since the 1980s,
it has gained ground among the agents of immigration and clarifies the
conflict. "To say mediation is to say a potential situation of conflict,"
announced the report of the FAS working group on mediation, prepared
jointly by the delegations of social action and territorial action.[11] Public
authorities attempt to ease tensions by granting priority to mediation,
which, like conflicts elsewhere, has a territorial basis. Unlike association
leaders, mediators are individuals who have no political representation,
although their function, which emerged spontaneously, was quickly
used by local authorities and public institutions.

Yet in the 1980s, the FAS application for subsidies still ascribed
importance to spokesmen as liaisons between the structured collective,
such as the associations, and the state. Does the term *collective* now
refer to a religious community, a Muslim one in this case? In fact, families and the public perceive the status of spokesman, spontaneously

attributed to the imams, in terms of a structured religious community. Do the mediators now intervene mainly with individuals from their communities?

Since then, the "older brothers" have gained ground in the field of immigration, especially in the suburbs. They are responsible for taking the young people by the hand and leading them onto the right path to immigration. The terminology derives from traditional societies where social relations depend on the kinship and extended family dear to anthropologists. Its use and introduction into the language of public authorities, associations, and media are intentional, illustrating the essential element of trust lacking in relations between the state and the communities.

But more than mediators, the issue is of female mediators, "older sisters." Did the symbol of the head scarf feminize Islam and grant greater legitimacy to their presence in the field and to any social initiative they might undertake? Moreover, several studies on immigration have tried to show that women are agents of modernization among the immigrants, and other empirical studies have even demonstrated that girls performed better in school than boys and "integrated" better into French society. These women, themselves descendants of immigrants, were born in France or came there at an early age and thus were educated and socialized in France; now they constitute a new social category created and named by the public authorities, the "intermediary women": "women who have a college or secondary education and are eager to help develop the potential their male compatriots were deprived of, first by illiteracy and then by ignorance of the codes and practices both of the administration and of the neighborhood in the areas where they live."[12]

Reports on the subject claim that the expression "intermediary women" was spawned by the spontaneous activity of African women, "who drew on both their traditions and their abilities to develop under new conditions of life."[13] These women influence families who have close and distant bonds, because they are reasonable and embody an example of adaptation without a total loss of traditions. Their role is even seen as traditional. In the case of African immigration, they have spoken out against sexual mutilations, condemned polygamy, and rationalized their stand. In 1982 their activities in the field were encouraged by Yvette Roudy, minister of the condition of women.

Today their function has been accepted and extended to other groups, representing other problems of adaptation. Once again the issue of the head scarf has served as a catalyst. In September 1994, as a result of reactions to the circular of François Bayrou, minister of education, declaring "the prohibition of ostentatious signs" in public schools,

Simone Veil, minister of health, social affairs, and the city, who was invited to Radio Telé-Luxembourg (RTL), stated that she had suggested to Bayrou "male or female mediators who might perhaps help in the field. . . . There are young women, basically Muslims, who have come to terms with themselves, but who could also explain very well, I think, why wearing the veil, in the current situation, might prevent those girls from succeeding, from doing what they want to."[14]

In fact, these intermediary women, who are between thirty and forty-five years old, embody a successful image of immigration. They state that they have to be "emancipated" by education in the republic, like the "earlier waves" of immigrants in France who now serve as a reassuring example of the effectiveness of the nation's principal institution. They come as "teachers of society" to repair the "evil" the girls in question as well as French society might suffer because of the head scarf. They are supposed to act individually with the girls, who are often of the same national, religious, or ethnic origin. They praise laïcité and individual freedom and criticize the oppressive nature of the religious communities. They pose as an example of compatibility between Islam and the West, between tradition and modernity, emphasizing their attachment to their roots and to their religious, national, or ethnic culture and also to the universal values embodied by Western democratic societies. Is it a strategy of the public authorities to convince families that the issue is not assimilation into French society but assimilation into modernity and universality?

Thus, the politicization of identities is a product of relations with the state and its institutions, which provide form and content and locate them on a field of competition for power. Politicization or ethnicization? The relationship is in fact very close. Even if the term *ethnicity* is disturbing for ideological reasons, it was a reality experienced in the 1980s and 1990s. The appearance of Islam in public corresponds to a form of ethnicity, as defined in the United States, and efforts to shape a religious community and institutions demanding public recognition correspond to the definition of *ethnic community* in France. The development of the discussion in the United States, influenced by multicultural quarrels, shows a further shift away from an ethnic division and toward a racial division that reduces society to a field of confrontation between a "black community" and a "white community." In France every reference to identity or to a community now refers to religion, and in the case of immigration, to Islam.

When identities are politicized, they assume new ways to express old grievances. In the United States the history of slavery, rooted in memory, mentality, and institutions, is analyzed as the origin of social inequalities today. In France Islam, linked to the colonial history of the past and to immigration today, constitutes the line of ethnic demarcation. Its presence recalls not only the Christian identity of the West but more particularly the tensions between religion, which was rejected when the republican state was constructed, and the identity of the French nation. Today laïcité reappears in the public debate as an unresolved question in France.

But the real problem is inherent in the fact that the ideology guiding the wise principles of the French state becomes a source of contradictions with unexpected results. Although encouraging the creation of immigrant associations was originally only a means of "controlling" society and perhaps a way to tame and even homogenize differences with the political socialization they guaranteed, the political mechanisms spawned by the settlement of immigrants in the 1960s ultimately lead to the formation of communities.

At the same time, the acquisition of political know-how within the associations in the communities pits the communities against the state. In this confrontation, the role of the state is reduced to its instrumental utility, since the search for identification is done by services provided by the welfare state and sums paid to the community or identity institutions. Moreover, the ideological and governmental institutional void in the religious area is liable to leave the field open to all the pressure that might be exerted by a Muslim religious community.

CHAPTER SIX

The Politicization of Identities in Germany

*Die im Grundgesetz angelegte Spannung zwischen
weltbürgerlichen und nationalstaatlich-völkischen
Verfassungsnormen ist bis heute nicht aufgelöst worden.*
The tension between cosmopolitan and ethnonationalist
norms that were initially incorporated into the fundamental
law has not been resolved to this day.

—Dieter Oberndörfer

THE 1980s MARKED A TURNING POINT in the treatment of immigrants in Germany, too. Public authorities seemed to realize that "the guests are here to stay." And the Turks[1] abandoned the discourse of return and replaced it with talk of permanent settlement with political rights. In the same vein, some associations have issued pamphlets inviting families from Turkey to "see the errors of the past [in Germany] more clearly" (that is, living in Germany as if they were in Turkey because of the myth of return) and to stop thinking about going back, since that idea confined them to a reclusive identity.

Yet, as in France, specialized institutions encourage the Ausländer to organize around their differences. In France *difference* was defined in cultural and religious terms, and the associations found a legal ground to express it publicly. In Germany *difference* is described not only as cultural but also as structural. Individuals with a different nationality or religion live as a separate group. In addition, Turkish or Kurdish activists demand the "right of permanent presence" and not the "right of difference," since difference is perceived on both sides (Germans and Turkish nationals) as permanent. Citizenship thus becomes a means of guaranteeing residence and the political rights associated with it and not of ensuring a cultural integration. There is no clear intention to combine citizenship and cultural integration or even identity.

Consequently, the concept of the presence of foreigners or immigrants is quite different; at least it is formulated in different terms in the two countries. In France social policies aim at integrating workers and their families, whereas in Germany the policy is that of foreigners (Ausländerpolitik). Similarly, the French state intervenes in the associations, and the German administration encourages foreigners to create their own associations (*Selbsthilfe*).

At the same time, while the United States constitutes an antimodel for France, where the American nation is perceived as split into ethnic communities, for Germany the American model represents a democratic model, where different cultures can organize and express themselves (as German immigrants experienced in the United States). Public and academic discussions as well as political measures concerning the organizational styles of foreigners in Germany thus relate to analyses inspired by American references to ethnic groups or minorities. In this perspective, unlike France, German public authorities show their desire to see the Turks organize into an ethnic community united around common interests, beyond their ideological, religious, ethnic, and linguistic divisions, that is, all conflicts specific to Turkey, transplanted and expressed in Germany.

The Committee on Foreigners (*Ausländerbeauftragte*), the equivalent of the French FAS, was created in 1981, initially in Berlin and later on the federal level, precisely to encourage associations to "be open to the world," one of the criteria for financing their activities. Independent of all government ministries, this committee counters the isolation or marginalization of foreigners in the social, cultural, economic, or political arena to help them coalesce in communities and to focus all their activities on Germany. As in France, the explicit goal is to encourage the emergence of an elite and/or a spokesperson, speaking on behalf of an ethnic community structured around a shared identity and interests, committed to addressing demands to Germany, thus indicating a permanent residence in the country. All the measures introduced conform to this objective and correspond to a permanent acceptance of foreigners in the Federal Republic as an inevitable reality. Thus German policies toward immigration or the settlement of foreigners vacillate between *Ethnos* and *Demos*,[2] that is, between an idea of the nation defined in terms of ethnic criteria (Ethnos) and the requirements of a democratic state (Demos), the other aspect of German identity.

However, as in France, competition for resources available to foreigners to construct a community makes cooperation between groups and associations difficult. This rivalry affects a population that shares the same nationality and also jeopardizes the idea of a unified Turkish-Muslim ethnic community which the public authorities desire. Moreover, policies developed in this area are ambiguous about the ethnic community's sharing its loyalty with an allegiance to the German national community.

As with the French case cited in the previous chapter, in this chapter I will analyze the mechanisms of politicizing the identities of Turkish nationals in their interaction with the German state, the ambiguities of discourse, and the inferred and pernicious effects of social policies in the construction of an ethnic community. As in the French case, in this chapter I will try to show the role of public powers and social policies concerning immigration and integration, as well as the self-perception of German society in the definition and nature of the reconstituted community.

RELIGIOUS PLURALISM AND ISLAM

Between the Head Scarf and the Crucifix

The Committee on Foreigners defines *community* as in the constitution, namely, "a group of persons who feel connected to one or several deities and whom they possibly worship." This religious conception of community dates from the early nineteenth century, when the religious freedom granted to both Catholics and Lutherans assumed a corporative nature, "granting equal rights only to communities formed as corporations."[3]

This is what distinguishes German secularism from French laïcité. Although both are based on the separation of church and state, a principle declared by article 137 of the Weimar Constitution and maintained by the Federal Republic, they differ in their relation to the public sphere. Whereas laïcité in France excludes religion from public life, German secularism has not stopped Catholic and Protestant churches from forming legal corporations recognized by public law. Hence, the social and moral function of churches is recognized legally, and they are assisted by the state, which levies a tax on every citizen who belongs to a community of believers. As semipublic institutions officially recognized by the state, churches still play an important role in the stability of German society.

French laïcité is the result of long conflicts between church and state and was not established in national and public institutions until the late nineteenth century; traces of German secularization, however, date from the treaties of Westphalia of 1648, which not only put an end to the Thirty Years' War but also declared the supremacy of territorial allegiance based on the principle of *cujus regio, ejus religio* (the religion of the prince is the religion of the people) and the decline of the political role of religion. Even today, French laïcité systematically produces an antireligious discourse, whereas German secularism leads to the institutionally sanctioned denominational duality of the public sphere. The result is a melding of the ecclesiastical, social, and political structures, which maintain their denominational nature even now. The historian Étienne François has emphasized the permanence of identities in denominational mentalities and behavior, "thus giving the denominational fact an anthropological, social, and cultural dimension that goes far beyond the specifically religious sphere."[4]

In two distinct ways, religion thus remains the prickliest question in both countries, as indicated by the passionate discussions on the place of religion—either Christian or Muslim—in schools. In Germany, more precisely in politically conservative Catholic Bavaria, the case of the crucifix in August 1995 was similar to the case of the head scarf in France. The outcry was provoked by a ban on the crucifix in classrooms imposed by the constitutional court of Karlsruhe in response to a complaint filed by followers of an anthroposophic group inspired by Steiner, on the principle that "no religion can be favored with respect to others" and that, consequently, the symbol of Christianity could not be displayed in the classroom if parents complained about it.

The decision of the Constitutional Court was as vague as the 1992 ruling of the French Council of State or the 1994 circular letter of François Bayrou, minister of education. The Bavarians saw it as a second *Kulturkampf*. "The War against the Catholics" was the headline in *Die Zeit* of August 25, 1995. Reactions were unanimous on one point: the cross or the crucifix is part of national culture, especially in Bavaria, as emphasized by an article in a special issue of *Der Spiegel* devoted to the subject. "The cross is as much a part of culture in Bavaria as the clock of the town bell tower," even if the court considered that religious symbol "a constraint and not a choice."[5]

The debate is basically akin to the one in France in the last century on "the removal of God" from the primary school: a "school without catechism and without holy history or Gospel," "a school without a crucifix or any other religious symbol," which was forbidden by Jules Ferry and his supporters in the name of denominational neutrality, the motto of laïcité. The opponents, who saw Christianity "at the base of our civilization," defined the procedure as an imposed laïcité and considered it based on an "intolerant and despotic" jurisprudence.[6] Significantly, that argument recurred just as emotionally in the recent public debate on the independent or private school or on the case of the head scarf.

The same terms have reappeared in Germany and in France during arguments about the crucifix, religion, and neutrality of the state. But in Germany religion is part of the curriculum, and the names of two political parties, the CDU (Christliche demokratische Union) and the CSU (Christliche soziale Union), include the adjective *Christian*, explicitly expressing their close relation with the church (particularly in the case of the Bavarian CSU). As chairman of the CDU, Chancellor Helmut Kohl has even stated that "the cross as a symbol of the Christian faith does not constitute a threat but a help, an orientation established by Christian values for the majority of people," adding that the CDU "will continue to work for the Christian values of German society";[7] and this was how he later defined the opening of a pluralistic society.

A Place for Islam

Yet when the issue of the Islamic head scarf provoked an existential crisis in France, German politicians found the French response exaggerated. The German press mainly reported French anxieties about the threat to the republican tradition, just as the French press confined itself to reporting only the facts about the issue of the crucifix in Bavaria. Nevertheless, an article in *Der Spiegel* raised shrewder questions about the argument over "respect for common traditional norms in the public schools" in France. "What common norms, Islam is the second religion in France!"[8] exclaimed the journalist, who was surely alluding to the fact that Islam is the third religion in Germany, and the everyday sight of girls in head scarves in school and elsewhere seems natural there.

There are two ways to interpret the amazement of German public opinion at the scope of the debates over the head scarf in France. First, the concepts of separation of church and state and the internalization of religious pluralism are different in the two countries, as indicated by the decision of the Constitutional Court of Karlsruhe. As a journalist of the *Frankfurter Allgemeine Zeitung* emphasized: "What would happen [here] if Christian parents complained that Muslim girls wear the head scarf?" The second interpretation is that the German refusal to accept foreigners as part of the general society, and even more so of the nation, results in an indifference about anybody's clothing habits. Should that indifference be seen as a recognition of the idea that foreigners form a separate population? If Germany is not a country of immigration, the religious customs of the guests do not matter as long as they do not disturb public order, since there is no question of the cultural integration of the foreigners. Interestingly, a few years later, during the great discussions on the reform of nationality, the head scarf worn by young Muslim girls from Afghanistan created the same uneasiness in Germany. This raised the question of the bond between belonging to the nation—either German or French—and the publicly declared affiliation to Islam.

Yet, since the 1980s, the German Committee on Foreigners (*Ausländerberauftragte*) has been studying ways to include Islam in its religious pluralism. It considers organizing Turkish Islam around political trends or brotherhoods connected with Turkey, which is incompatible with the currently abundant discourse of permanent settlement, the idea being, as in France, to define an Islam independent of external influences. In the case of the Turks, the issue was to remove the influence of the ideological rifts between a religious political ideal promoted by the Islamic party, which was amply represented and firmly established in Germany, and the present Turkish state in the religious area through its associative organization, the Diyanet.

The committee's idea of a Muslim community is obviously based on the official place of religion in Germany and the role of the churches in taking care of foreigners, as during the 1960s, when the needs of workers from the entire Mediterranean basin were handled by denominational charities. As mentioned in chapter 3, the Catholic Caritas was mainly concerned with Catholic immigrants, whereas the Protestant Diakonisches Werk took care of Orthodox Greeks or Serbs; and an organization affiliated with the SPD, the Arbeiterwohlfahrt, was created to welcome the Muslims. But after three decades of Islam in Germany, this model now seems even more inadequate. As a result, Turks looked to Turkey to help find their bearings. This includes unofficially promoting a political-cultural blend of Islam transmitted by imams imported from Turkey.

The "indoctrination" of children by imams from Turkey who support their worldview with practices that the Committee on Foreigners labeled antidemocratic is another indication of the urgency of new measures in this area. The question is how to grant Islam, "the third religion of the country," the same rights as Protestantism and Catholicism, especially in the area of religious instruction in public schools. Not only must it be adapted to current laws and practices specific to each Land, but responsibility for the public instruction of Islam must be controlled.

Since the 1990s, attempts in three *Länder* have represented three attempts to integrate Islam in the public schools. In Berlin, since religious instruction by and large is associated with the churches, instruction of the Koran had first been placed under the supervision of the Turkish state through the intermediary of the Diyanet, its official organ. Dependent on the prime minister of Turkey, the Diyanet, the state secretaryship in charge of religious affairs, is represented in Europe by an organization called Religious Affairs for Turkish Immigrant Workers (DITIB), which recruits and distributes imams to the public schools of large European cities. Along with Turkish secular teachers, their presence is acknowledged in the bilateral agreements that initially dealt with Turkish language classes and since 1984 with religion classes, both of them outside the curriculum.

The second attempt is that of Hamburg. In that Social Democratic (SPD) *Land*, language teachers, although of Turkish nationality, enjoy the status of civil servant and have established instruction in Islam within the *Religionspedagogik* program that applies to all religions. The third, adopted in northern Westphalia, makes teachers of theology, scientists, and Christian pedagogues responsible for implementing a curriculum of Islam.

Neither the Turkish population nor the German authorities are satisfied with these methods. In Berlin opponents of the Turkish government reject the Diyanet and its agency, the DITIB. And so, a planned Koran school in Berlin, associated with the Islamic federation there, hence in principle independent of the Turkish government and open to all Muslims of the city, was proposed in the late 1980s. It obtained permission to take over religious instruction in 1997, even though discussions raised by that thwarted initiative revealed the personal connections between the principal of the school and the chairman of the Islamic federation of Berlin, who was a member of the religious party in Turkey; and that is obviously one of the reasons for its failure.[9]

In Hamburg Turkish religious associations oppose Islamic instruction by secular teachers who do not know their particular kind of Islam; and in northern Westphalia, public authorities expressed their fear of the development of an orthodox rather than a secular Islam.

But again, German federalism makes these experiences local, and teaching the Muslim religion in the public schools still raises the more general question of its recognition alongside the Christian denominations. In this vein, on March 1, 1979, the central committee of Islamic cultural centers presented a demand for recognition as part of the legal framework of the corporations of public right (*Körperschaft des öffentlichen Rechts*) enjoyed by the other religions in Germany. But it failed because the authorities expressed distrust of organizations attached either to the Turkish government or to political parties in Turkey, perceived by and large as undemocratic.[10]

THE CONSTRUCTION OF AN ETHNIC COMMUNITY

The Impossible Religious Community

These developments affect Islam's ability to organize a community defined substantively by the German constitution as a gathering of persons linked by common concepts and a consensus. Even if it is part of the same national group, a divided and politicized Islam contradicts the idea of "a gathering" but not necessarily that of a community. As in the case of the associations whose proliferation, instead of dividing a collectivity, gathers it around common references, ideological, political, and religious divisions make Muslim Turks members of a community that is segmented, where relations between individuals are contentious even though they share national and religious references. In the spring of 1980, in Berlin, young Turkish girls wearing the head scarf to school infuriated some of their immigrant compatriots who adhered to the secular principles of a Turkish republic founded on the values of Kemal Atatürk, who in 1926 had banned such symbols in Turkish schools. So, it was not Berlin politicians who opposed the Muslims of Berlin but rather Turkish nationals, some of whom defended Kemalist principles as staunchly as the republicans in France defended theirs, and others associated religion with a Turkish or Kurdish identity, generally under the influence of the religious parties.

Such incidents reflect ideological divisions and multiple identifications within a community defined not only by membership in a religious denomination but also by membership in the same nation. The demarcation line is obviously blurred. The identity fragmentation specific to immigration reveals several religious (Sunnis, Alevis), national, and ethnic (Turkish, Kurdish) affiliations of Turkish nationals in Germany, each corresponding to particular organizations. Yet this does not undermine the community structure. As in France, internal conflicts within the group are signs of its encapsulation rather than its disintegration. Membership is asserted even more strongly in Germany, where the common reference to Turkey and the status of foreigner unites immigrants from Turkey by their nationality, characterized from the start as a community, even though it is divided by ideologies; ethnic, religious, or linguistic identities; and different interests.

The major trends spawning religious groups are also transposed from Turkish political life. In fact, the community of the believers and the pious is just as divided there among rival organizations either supporting or opposing the Turkish government. Some immigrants have chosen the more open and democratic Germany and Europe in general as fields of action. Several other associations have emerged between the two main organizations—National Vision, representing the religious party, and Diyanet, or DITIB, mentioned earlier, representing the official view of the Turkish government. In between are popular associations called Turkish cultural centers, which also form a network and were created by the *Süleymanci*, the disciples of Süleyman Turhanan, leader of a brotherhood in Turkey since the beginning of Turkish immigration to Europe. Their establishment in the host countries in the 1970s might have looked like a reaction against Kemalism, which banned brotherhoods and sects in republican Turkey, but followers of that trend were supported by Turkish consulates and were influential, especially among the immigrants. They were the first to weave a whole network of cultural centers in Germany and Europe (hence the adjective *cultural*) to ensure the teaching of the Koran to children. Using an apolitical language of religion, they drew families who did not want to be burdened by a political label that could have made it hard to go back home.

Since the 1980s, after the army's intervention in Turkey, an increasingly politicized Islam has gained ground simultaneously in the homeland and among the immigrants. The imams, some of them religious attachés in Ankara, even changed their approach when they came to Germany, especially most of the leaders of the Süleymanci. Even more amazing is the career of Cemalettin Kaplan, "the caliph," leader of the association called Anatolian Islamic Federated State. Kaplan, who died in June 1995 in Cologne, had been attaché of religious affairs in Ankara and vice-president of the Diyanet: he then became the Muslim clergyman assigned to uphold the law (*müftü*) in Adana until 1981; moreover, in 1977, he was a candidate of the Party of National Salvation, the forerunner of the current Party of Prosperity. When he retired, Necmettin Erbakan, chairman of that party, sent him to Germany to work with National Vision. But in fact, Kaplan shaped his view of Islam in the wake of his trip to Iran in 1983, and later, returning to Germany, he created his own association to preach an Islamic Turkish state in the image of Iran but adapted to Turkish-Ottoman history, where he would be appointed caliph.

Turkish families, however, are not remote from politics in Turkey. In fact, they choose sides according to the regional, ethnic, and political identity of their association, as well as their personal ties with an imam or authority. This partly explains the proliferation of Islamic associations competing for followers and activists, and hence for the financial resources linked with their membership, creating rival prayer halls in the same neighborhood and justifying their usefulness more generally with the services they provide or the availability of their buildings.

Even the Islamic federation created in Berlin in 1982 did not prevent divisions. Despite efforts at neutrality, the chairman of that umbrella organization of various Muslim religious associations of all nationalities could not obscure his Turkish nationality or his membership in the Party of Prosperity or Virtue. The federation, therefore, looked like a national organization representing a religious party that was just as Turkish. Thus, some Turkish nationals joined the federation, and others opted for its rival, the one representing official Turkey (DITIB), or for National Vision, or for Kaplan's movement, or even for the nationalist trend of the Gray Wolves.[11]

In Search of a National Community

Divided and politicized Islam prevents German public authorities from advancing very far in forming a religious community. The question becomes: under those conditions, who in fact would be the spokesman of the community? And of what community? If neutrality is a criterion, how can a partner emerge who is the expression of neither the Turkish state in general nor of any one of the successive governments or opposition parties? Must unity be sought according to the criterion of nationality? Must *community* be defined by a history and interests based on a national affiliation, or on religion, or on political ideology? Barbara John, leader of the Committee on Foreigners in Berlin, stated that "the state is willing to help the Turks form a group uniting individuals with different interests, beyond the religious, ethnic, and ideological divisions . . . that prevent the community from forming." "There are 7,000 Greeks in Berlin, and they are organized into 13 groups, the 33,000 (ex) Yugoslavians are structured into 6 groups, and the almost 125,000 Turks are divided into more than 100 groups." "They do not constitute a community," she added.[12] In 1987 Ertekin Özcan listed more than three thousand Turkish associations of all kinds, political, athletic, cultural, and social.[13] The same ideological, religious, linguistic, and ethnic differences explain their diversity and proliferation.

However, neither the diversity of Turkish immigrants in Germany nor their segmented organization presents an obstacle to their sense of belonging to the same community, which is, paradoxically, reinforced by internal divisions. Turkish nationals certainly organize, act, or simply take a position for or against the official representation of their country. They accept or reject any given ideology, accept or refuse the current governments or their policies. But their point of reference remains fixed in Turkey as a common element. In sum, their criteria of ethnicity refer to a Turkishness or Kurdishness from Turkey, to an ethnic community in both cases based on Turkish nationality but willing to be independent of official Turkey.

German party politics has played an important role in separating associations on the basis of nationality and in the integration policies that maintain them. When immigration began, each trend transposed from Turkish politics and re-created in Germany found support in German parties. As if the bilateral agreements between the two countries were also based on their political allegiances, groups on the Left and Right allied with a German partner of the same bent. Thus each of the big parties, such as the SPD and the CDU, had its own Turkish organization and leaders. The Progressive Volkseinheit der Türkei in Berlin West e.V. (the popular progressive group of Turkey, or HDB, the Popular and Revolutionary Turkish Union), created in 1973 as a branch of the SPD, was active especially in West Berlin. In 1985 the CDU sponsored a vast association, the Freiheitliche Türkisch-Deutscher Freundschaftsverein e.V. (Liberal Turkish-German Association, or Hür Türk, translated literally as "the Free Turk"), with headquarters in Bonn. This association refuses all members of extremist parties on the Right or Left in Turkey and Germany, is led by a German CDU representative and a retired official of Turkish General Information, and claims to "conform to the constitutions of the Turkish republic and the German republic." The stated objective of both sides is to unite moderate splinter groups and to ensure their democratic functioning.

The creation of these two structures can be seen as part of a strategy to control the political activities of Turks in Germany. In any case, both perceived themselves as intermediaries between the German and Turkish states, as well as among the parties of both countries. Donations by their respective members have enabled them to finance parties in Turkey, among other things. The same holds for National Vision, which has been feeding the coffers of the Party of Prosperity, but with no equivalent in the German political gamut. The party is just not considered an official spokesman by either the Turkish state or the German state.[14]

Thus, the concept of spokesman has referred and still refers initially to a state-to-state relationship. Algerian associations in France also appropriated the role of intermediary between French and Algerian state authorities concerning immigration. In both cases, these organizations were involved, from the very start, with politics in the home countries, and then developed social and cultural campaigns to help their nationals maintain ties with their "origins." In both cases, the notion of spokesman highlights the idea of a return of the state of origin. Although it has been implicit in France, this approach was explicitly included in the bilateral agreements between Turkey and Germany. But unlike France, where the associations affected only the first generation and have no influence on young people today, the organizations set up as spokesmen in Germany are still trying to increase the awareness of all Turkish immigrants, of all generations. Perhaps this is because Germany did not see itself as a country of immigration, the presence of foreigners has been seen as temporary, and the young generation of Turkish descent still holds Turkish citizenship; hence the Federal Republic accepts only the Turkish state or at least the associations representing it in Germany as spokesmen.

But the policies of integrating foreigners (Ausländerpolitik), put in place in the 1980s, tip that balance somewhat. The Committee on Foreigners rejects the term *Gastarbeiter* in an attempt to emphasize their permanent presence. The Greens have introduced the term "foreign fellow citizens" (*ausländische Mitbürger*). Under these conditions, spokesmen for the whole Turkish community should be chosen. In Berlin, at any rate, the committee proposes to help them reshape their networks beyond political interests channeled toward Turkey and to unite in defense of economic, social, and political interests in the Federal Republic; in short, to develop their "social capital," by granting social workers the role of spokesmen and no longer the function of advisers to the public authorities seeking information about the mores and customs of foreigners of Turkish nationality, their settlement, and their plans to return to their country.

ETHNIC OR MINORITY COMMUNITY

Political measures concerning foreigners now originate in the logic of an ethnic community and are accompanied by an attempt to channel available resources that have traditionally subsidized official organizations that absorbed foreigners (like the Caritas, the Red Cross, the Evangelical Church, and the Arbeiterwohlfahrt) to the foreigners themselves as a way to promote their own organization (Selbsthilfe). The idea is that foreigners should create their own organizations to combat delinquency, poverty, and crime, a procedure reminiscent of American liberalism, which sees voluntary associations emerging from ethnic communities as mutual aid or welfare institutions serving their members and handling the social problems that affect them most. But this logic of a structured and integrated ethnic community taking care of itself implies a parallel struggle for the recognition of equal rights.

Therefore, the issues of such a restructuring are important both for the Turks and for Germany. The Turks must now present an image of a community that is no longer segmented, divided, and contentious, but on the contrary, of a collective united by common interests, better equipped to fight the prevailing discrimination and racism. The association activists take up the discourse of the public authorities and follow their orders to organize or shape that ethnic community. They muster their forces to create umbrella associations in each *Land* intending to form a community (*Gemeinde*) and to consolidate all Turkish nationals. In the view of public authorities, this becomes the only way to achieve legitimacy and make "their presence felt" as a group united by a single objective: permanent settlement and equal rights. When all is said and done, the ethnic community is defined by its program of political action, and this is the framework the associations and their members use to express their identification.

For Germany, helping the foreign population link the networks between the various groups to break their isolation and destroy their internal divisions is part of a program of social "peace." But more than social peace in the strict sense, it is mainly concerned with preserving democracy by warding off policies and practices that keep the foreign population apart. Discussions of citizenship and nationality have also taken this direction since 1985.

Since the racist acts of 1992, the question of citizenship has become even more important. The arson that killed five persons, including two children, in Mölln in November 1992 and a Turkish family in Solingen in April 1993 alerted public opinion to the situation and the political rights of foreigners who had been living on German soil for three generations. Moreover, granting citizenship to foreigners is viewed as a moral obligation based on equality of rights, insofar as the Aussiedler, populations demanding a recognition of their German origins, see the right of naturalization attributed in fact, without being socialized in Germany, and in most cases without even speaking the language. Thus, there is a rift between foreigners by culture (social and political) and foreigners by blood. Moreover, racist attacks have increased since the reunification of the two Germanys and have widened the gap between Turks or foreigners in general and Germans, each group withdrawing and marking the borders of its identity and even its territory.

Neighborhoods inhabited by Turks have almost become fortresses where not only can "skins not penetrate" but where others also feel like "tourists." In Berlin the walls of Kreuzberg are decorated with the portraits of young victims of racist acts, as if to mark the territorial limits of the neighborhood and the borders of a collective identity. Similarly, every formal or informal gathering held by the associations, sports events, or other events begin with a minute of silence in their memory. Special editions of bilingual magazines published by Turks in Germany deal with racism, listing the chronology of violent acts and the names of victims. Some extremist associations, such as the Anti-Fa, also call for vengeance; more moderate ones distribute pamphlets calling on the Turks to break their silence and act; and still others hold discussions to condemn the passivity of the politicians and the ineffectiveness of the police toward the perpetrators of that violence, holding the German state responsible for the waves of xenophobia. The common interests that cement the ethnic community now relate to the struggle against racism, which has become the major element shaping the collective identity.

The Construction of a National Minority

The expression *türkische Minderheit*, "Turkish minority," has become part of the language of intellectuals and activists affiliated with the SPD. More broadly, what the public authorities call an ethnic community elicits a response when transformed into the idea of an ethnic minority among the association leaders or activists among the Turkish immigrants in Germany. For them, this term indicates the structural presence of a culturally different population, amounting to almost two million individuals in all social categories: the unemployed, skilled or unskilled laborers, students, executives, merchants, and manufacturers, who express their sense of belonging to various regional, linguistic, or ethnic cultures. All of them constitute "Turkey in Germany," wrote Faruk Sen, chairman of Turkish Studies in Essen, who thinks that the expression "'a Turk from Germany' will be imposed on public opinion." "Our artists, our businessmen, our culture, our religion, our television, our press, are only one aspect of Turkey in Germany. We have also established an internal communication network with seven daily newspapers, one weekly, and one monthly journal published regularly in Germany," he adds as if to assert the presence of a structured minority trying to become more solid.[15] Such arguments make him use and propose the term *türkische Minderheit* in political discussions as a member of the SPD.[16]

Thus, the *idea* of a Turkish minority finds a basis in nationality, a common denominator among the population who migrated from Turkey to Germany. Of course, the reason for this must be sought in the definition of Turkey itself as a nation-state and its internalization as such. But there is also a question of whether German national identity defined by descent is what leads non-Germans to consider themselves the same, to define themselves first in terms of the same ethnic criteria and then to form a minority. Or is it the political environment and legal status that maintain the difference of nationality as a constituent element in the construction of a minority? Or, in Uli Bielefeld's words, does "the logic of state control of ethnicity"[17] lead other ethnic communities to becoming institutionalized as ethnic minorities, on a basis of nationality or ethnicity, or both?

The discourse of activists from Turkey about minorities initially was based on the American example, which was developed within the framework of sociological studies on race relations in the United States, where the use of the term *minority* changed its meaning and target in different periods. In the 1930s the term referred to ethnic minorities of European origin, but it took on a political dimension in the 1960s, beginning with struggles for equal rights and laws modeled on blacks and their "fundamental difference."[18] The politics of affirmative action and more specifically its translation in the census as "ethnic ancestry" gave an official status to minorities designated by policies, categorized by quotas, and protected by the law. Favoritism based on compensation for previous inequities has made American Indians, blacks, Hispanics, and Asians "minorities eligible for Affirmative Action," in the words of the U.S. federal government.

The discourse of Turkish activists highlights this inspiration when it claims a recognition of equal social rights, and especially political rights for "minorities." But there are two considerable differences. One concerns the past of the so-called minorities in the United States and of foreigners in Germany, the specific histories of their immigration and their different relations with the state. The other difference, equally if not more important, concerns the legal status of so-called minorities. Groups defined as minorities are not all citizens of the United States, but citizenship is accessible to minorities and/or their children, whereas Turkish guests are foreigners and remain foreign in Germany for at least three generations, a difference that defines minority on different bases in the two countries: an ethnic minority, defined by national or racial origin or gender in the United States, and a mainly national criterion in Germany.

The discourse of activists on minorities is also influenced by Europe and European institutions, particularly the European Council and the program for minority rights. Yet this program, which is based on the Charter of Regional Languages, refers to the historical and territorial minorities of the populations in Europe and not to the descendants of immigrants. Yet activists have reformulated their demands, emphasizing the cultural aspects of a minority, particularly when they demand recognition for the Turkish language and its instruction in public schools. The combination creates total confusion about the definition of *minority* but nevertheless leads to a common demand, whatever the criteria: the demand for a recognition of the national, ethnic, linguistic, and even religious differences.

Thus, an ethnic minority does not constitute a given in itself but is constructed around common interests expressed in identity terms, ranging from the desire to preserve a culture to the need to survive against racist aggression. But its context is defined primarily by relations with the authorities. As Henri Giordon has emphasized, "There are no minorities per se, they are defined only structurally. They are groups put in a minority situation through relations of power and rights which subjects them to other groups within an overall society whose interests are taken care of by a state."[19]

Turkish nationals in Germany take the Jews as a concrete example of a minority, in terms of their history and organization. This reference concerns two contradictory but complementary elements. First, the Jewish minority initially is considered a bad example of assimilation, since, in the Turkish nationals' view, cultural and political invisibility did not prevent their extermination in the past and the hostility of the present.

A slogan written on the Berlin city hall in 1981 established a parallel between the Jews and the Turks: "What the Jews left behind is what is to come for the Turks." This slogan was considered a warning to the Turks of what might be in store for them.

The second element concerns the Jews' organization and their communitarian structure. In fact, the Jewish minority is considered an example of unity and of the organization of a pressure group with national and international influence. Surely this is what the association leaders and the Turkish state are aiming for: to organize increasingly around transnational networks on the European level and even beyond and to draw international attention to the fate of the Turks in Germany.

The Turks see these elements as a twofold lesson for these reasons: first to make sure they do not suffer the same history as the Jews of Germany, and second to unite to fight more effectively against racism, inequality, and political marginalization. Different leaders and activists use these criteria to shape an ethnic minority out of all the social and cultural diversity of the Turkish nationals in Germany, including groups of businessmen as well as youth clubs, sports teams, folklore groups, mosques, associations of regional culture, and even political groups. All these groups are seeking a common platform to express themselves, going beyond their social or cultural features, which are initially fragmented, in order to (re)constitute themselves in that new perspective later on.

The minority is defined by its nationality within an umbrella organization (*Dachorganisation*), trying to respond to the wishes of the public authorities and the political parties, with the motto "Let's get rid of internal divisions and unite," as expressed by Hakki Keskin, an SPD representative in the Hamburg parliament, a professor, and a leader of a federation of Turkish associations in the same *Land*. Thus, organizations called unions (*Vereine*) appear, each combining about twenty associations and appointing themselves mouthpieces of the Turkish community of such and such a *Land*. This development expresses the extension of the corporate system, characteristic of a civil society of noncitizens based on residence and concern for equal rights corresponding to a form of citizenship I will analyze later. In addition, it expresses the immigrants' desire for integration. They claim to be organized as a minority that fits into the social structure of Germany as a quasi-public institution and in the general scheme in which such institutions play an important role in political decisions.[20]

Racism, violence, and exclusion are many factors that influence the definition and structuring of a minority. In 1984 the murder of two young Turks by skinheads impelled Keskin to create the Union of Turkish Migrants of Hamburg (Bündnis türkischer Einwanderer). To give an internal legitimacy to the organization, he stated: "We have eliminated all extremist organizations of both the Left and the Right and assembled those organizations based in Hamburg, including a religious association formed by young students affiliated with the Party of Prosperity. We have thus assembled about twenty of the most democratic associations."

But the model derives from the *türkische Gemeinde zu Berlin* (the Turkish community of Berlin, TGB), an organization created in 1983 in the image of the *jüdische Gemeinde zu Berlin* (Jewish community of Berlin). Its founder was an engineer who directed the professional training of young Turkish immigrants in Germany. Its current chairman is also a Turkish educator. He was appointed by Ankara to serve from 1976 to 1982, but then settled in Berlin. He presents the TGB as the favorite mouthpiece of the various German trade union and charitable institutions and the official representatives of the Turkish government. He thus illustrates the shift in the concept of official spokesman, since issues concerning the presence of the Turks on German soil are settled no longer between governments but through official representatives cropping up in civil society, even if they display their affinities with the home countries.

The türkische Gemeinde zu Berlin cites its bonds with the SPD as well as with the CDU and the FDP to show that "the interests of 140,000 Turks entrenched in Berlin go beyond partisan orientations." By mentioning its potential influence in Berlin elections, the TGB mobilizes to exploit it by giving priority to the struggle for the recognition of equal rights for Turks. It also acts as an office of communication between Turkish nationals in Berlin, in the rest of Germany, and even in Europe. It sends messages to foreign institutions affected by issues of immigration and the situation of minorities to inform them, for example, of racist acts overlooked by the local or national press, of its discussions and meetings, of diplomatic relations between Turkey and Israel, and of its relations with the jüdische Gemeinde zu Berlin to show by the same token its openness to other communities or minorities. This rapprochement may have something to do with Turkey's foreign policy and its relationship with Israel; but such a relationship between the two so-called minorities is clearly intended to prove both to German public opinion and to the group's own followers its efforts to shape a minority in order to make them aware and to convince them of the reality of the TGB's struggle against racism.

Note, too, that this Berlin model has created competition. Since 1992, the türkische Gemeinde zu Berlin has been competing with the Union of Immigrants from Turkey of Berlin-Bradenburg (BETB). This organization was created by three activists who had come as students in the late

1970s and were active in the SPD as well as in the association movement. It stands as an example of the internal dynamics of the immigration and settlement of the Turkish population as well as its relations with the German government. The leaders of this new association claim to be interested "solely in Germany," whereas "the TGB is an organ of the consulates, which are trying to form a lobby." The BETB intends to form a pressure group to define an immigration policy and ways to adapt national institutions to the reality of a multicultural society, to formulate an antidiscriminatory law to be included in the constitution. They are pleased to see that "the CDU is open to immigration and that its discourse admits the presence of foreigners," although they clearly display their affinity with the SPD, the FDP, and the Greens (*Bündnis 90*), "who attach more importance and reserve more space in their campaign for subjects relating to immigration or the presence of foreigners."

Thus, the use of a so-called identity of origin in France defined by nationality and expressed through its connections with the authorities in both the home country and the host country is a source of competition between various organizations in Germany. In both countries, they all respond by and large to the expectations of the public authorities, with their leaders repeating the same rhetoric and achieving the same control. Different processes in the two countries produce relatively identical results. In France the implicit strategy of "splitting the communities" results in a fragmentation and politicization of identities, which, because of competition between organizations, leads to a sort of tribalism on the local level. In Germany the strategy of forming a community, which the public authorities have adopted, does not prevent divisions either, despite consolidations on the state level. Barbara John, chair of the Committee on Foreigners in Berlin, did note "some 'progress' in the organization of the Turks." "They are assembling in the left center and right center. The right center is dependent on the consulate, the left center on the German welfare state," she declared. Progress here is indicated by an aspiration to shape representative organizations of a "community where consensus prevails" as defined by the constitution, rather than having several conflicting formal or informal groups.

Yet, as in France, allocating resources to these rival structures whose projects are partly subsidized by the same organizations leads to divisions that highlight individual strategies rather than concern for the collective representation of a minority. The question is knowing whether to use existing political divisions to create a community dependent on German public authorities, who would thus appoint their own spokesmen in order to grant legitimacy to their structure.

This approach contradicts the principle of self-organization of the foreigners protected by the committees for foreigners and eliminates the idea developed by the activists that a national minority can exist in the Federal Republic. A preliminary report submitted on March 12, 1993, by the Committee of Berlin to the associations for the approval of new measures concerning foreigners was initially titled *Bericht über die Lage ethnischer Minderheiten* (Report on the condition of ethnic minorities). But on March 3, 1994, it was published under the title of *Bericht zur Integration und Ausländerpolitik* (Report on the integration and policy for foreigners), a change reflecting disagreement between the various ministries, parties, and the committee. In this connection, the committee spokesman in Bonn revealed that he preferred the term *Turkish nationals (die türkische Staatsangehörige)* to *Turkish minority (türkische Minderheit)*,[21] because, he explained, the word *minority* has a cultural meaning synonymous with *lifestyle*, and not a political meaning indicating specific rights.

These terminological hesitations are not neutral. On the one hand, they refer to the very conception of German democracy, and on the other, to the allegiance of foreigners to that state. In fact, the very concept of minority refers to the idea of political inequality. In the United States, where it was based on racial discrimination and measures designed to compensate for it, use of the term has already given rise to ideological arguments. Americanism as an ideal, found on an equality among its citizens, rejected the notion of a minority based on nationality because of its moral implications for democracy. In Germany the existence of a national minority recognized as such would risk making the status of foreigner permanent and structural as well as confirming Germany's view of itself as a nation formed by descent.

Further, the concept of minority refers to multiple allegiances; as many allegiances as identity references. From this point of view, the minority formed by Turkish nationals would be defined by its divided allegiance between the German state and the Turkish state, corresponding to the dual citizenship that all associations demand regardless of their political orientation. But the most interesting aspect of the efforts of the activists shaping a national Turkish minority is the gap they emphasize between various strategies of the German public authorities, of the associations they lead, and of the Turkish government. Whereas the German government seeks the possibility of finding representative spokesmen in the community and the ethnic group, Turkish nationals rely on such a structure to demand recognition of their presence in the form of specific rights, and even of their existence as a national minority defined by their connection with the German state and society. The Turkish state, by contrast, aims at forming a Turkish lobby in Germany to defend the image of Turkey in Europe and its supranational institutions. These distinct strategies are also found in the methods of organization: ethnic community, national minority, or Turkish lobby all refer to a structure centered on nationality. But the relations of Turkish immigrant leaders with German civil society are generating a new identification and bringing another focus to their activity. The leaders of cultural or religious associations, of federations of associations, the intellectuals and businessmen who partly support the organizations of identity and give them important donations, particularly to build mosques, are increasingly taking on the role of "ambassadors of Turkish immigrants in Germany."

A Minority in the Minority

Not all Turkish nationals identify with the idea of a national minority. Kurds, for example, who see themselves as an ethnic and linguistic minority in Turkey, claim recognition as a minority within a minority in Germany. The same is true for *alevîs* (Turkish Shiites), who consider themselves a religious minority in Turkey and therefore in Germany. This fragmentation of identities that arise in immigration leads them to demand the same treatment as the Turks, whom they consider another ethnic-linguistic-religious community. They create their own cultural associations and demand access to radio and television, language courses, and religious instruction. In short, through their activists, the Kurds and the alevîs seek separate recognition as a community, each with its own culture and history, distinct from that of the Turkish community as a whole. This differentiation exists in Turkey, as a cultural and ethnic transmission, and shows the intense social and political interactions between the two countries through immigration. But in the German context, this display of distinct identities puts the Kurds in the position of a minority in the minority, although they are not recognized as a minority in Turkey.[22]

Official German institutions, subject to the logic of nationality and religion, obviously did not distinguish the Turks from the Kurds either ethnically or denominationally. Immigration based on the bilateral agreement of the two states could in fact depend only on the official definition of its population, as referred to the principles of the nation-state of the country of origin as well. But today identity reappropriations have led to the demand for institutional rearrangements even with separated political strategies. For some immigrant groups, Germany and Europe in general constitute a democratic political sphere allowing them to get rid of political taboos imposed by the formation of religious and linguistic homogeneous nation-states and political groups seeking representation abroad.

This results in demands that go so far as to clash with diplomatic relations between Turkey and Germany. Conversely, some regard the German reluctance to recognize a Kurdish community as falling within the scheme of the Federal Republic's foreign policy.[23] Yet an attempt to create the "Kurdish community of Berlin" (*kurdische Gemeinde zu Berlin*) in the summer of 1994 was intended as a way to unite about twenty associations of four nationalities (Turkish, Iraqi, Iranian, and Syrian) to demand recognition of a Kurdish minority in Germany like its counterpart, the Turkish minorities, and within the same Western conception of human rights and of democracy. The Kurdish demand, political in Turkey and cultural in Germany, is part of a movement that is generally nationalist and seeks support from the Berlin public authorities to grant the kurdische Gemeinde zu Berlin the same legal status as other associations of foreigners. As for financing their projects, according to the founder and chairman of the kurdische Gemeinde, it was to be based on a distribution of resources granted to the Turkish associations, calculated according to the number of Kurdish members in these associations.

But the kurdische Gemeinde zu Berlin was short-lived. Recognition by the Committee on Foreigners of Berlin would have signaled a distance from the official position of Turkey on the subject. But it also might have allowed the Kurds to create a different political sphere of identification from the one offered by the radical wing of the Kurdish movement, the PKK, to keep them away from any reference to Turkey, and, as with other associations, to channel their demands toward the country of residence and not toward self-determination and territories to be conquered.

It remains to define who is Kurdish. "One who defines himself as a Kurd, whose parents are Kurds, is part of our 'community,'" said the founder of the kurdische Gemeinde, who declared himself a "Kurd from Turkey." This definition superimposes individual membership and ethnic belonging based on declared ancestors, since there is no sign in official censuses or on documents of a national identity indicating a Kurdish category, at least for Turkey, and therefore for the immigrants from Turkey. Even the language, the core demand for recognition in Turkey, is not a criterion of "belonging" because of the assimilation of the Kurds living in central or western Anatolia.

But the politicization of a minority identity within a minority poses a problem of identification, due mainly to the German perception of the Turks. "Racist attacks don't target Kurds and Turks separately," the Turkish association leaders like to explain by way of emphasizing a common struggle and common interests that should unite them. But more than a problem of identification, politicizing the Kurdish identity in Germany, like the structure of the Turkish minority, raises the question of allegiance: allegiance to a Kurdish identity, allegiance to German society, or allegiance to the German state, since the Turkish state is in the adversary camp.

The choice and the institutionalization of a Kurdish identity are inevitably located once again in the extension of Turkish politics and are a source of new ethnic and political divisions among the Turks in Berlin, elsewhere in Germany, or in Europe. Moreover, a minority's efforts to unite and its desire for representation result in splinter groups that find legitimacy in international opinion. From this perspective, the leaders of the federations, eager to build a structure and obtain the status of national minority in Germany, and consequently sensitive to the rights of minorities even in Turkey, have developed a discourse on the importance of the unity of the Turkish nation. They accuse the German public authorities of using "divisions to break national solidarity and to weaken its strength as a minority." Representatives of federations make statements in the Turkish and German press about the Turkish nation-state, the citizenship status of the Kurds or the alevîs, and the need for a national cohesion that may be stronger in Germany than it is in Turkey.

In both France and Germany, the politicization of identities thus illustrates a power relation between an emerging community and the state. The interaction between the political logic of each country and the groups concerned defines the constituent elements of such a structure. In France the scope of the discussion on laïcité or the place of religion in the public space sets Islam at the core of construction plans for a community of Muslim groups, mainly descendants of North African immigrants. In Germany, however, the struggle against racism and the search for spokesmen among the Turks leads these spokesmen to define themselves on an ethnic-national basis (including religion) and as a result to demand the status of a minority with equal rights. So in Germany, "nationalization" of the Turks arises, whereas in France, "Islamicization" of the Muslims appears. But although the Turkish minority in Germany draws its identity references from the Turkish state and its representatives, the Muslims in France locate themselves in both relation and opposition to the French state. The difference of national references is a difference in content but not necessarily in form.

In both countries, the strategies of the states waver between principles based on the representation of political traditions and pragmatic measures to reestablish a social cohesion, and they are accompanied by a flood of pernicious results. Establishing a community in Germany with regard to the welfare state moves in the direction of corporatism, as in professional interest groups, trade unions, and churches. Such an approach encourages a "structural" integration while contributing to the development of a separate collective identity. In France arrangements initiated by the welfare state have the same effect on the immigrant population's organizations, but with the major difference that the state declares an explicit strategy of cultural and political integration. Nevertheless, in Germany, as well as in France and the United States, recognizing such structures raises the same question of allegiance toward the political community. The line of demarcation—religious in France, national in Germany, and "racial" in the United States—refers in the same way to the question of identification with the national community by reducing relations with the respective states to their utilitarian function.

CHAPTER SEVEN

The Negotiation of Identities

> There is the hope, not always vivid in the minds of
> negotiators, that the process of negotiation will give rise to a
> shared commitment to tolerance, equality and mutual aid.
> —Michael Walzer

THE TWO PRECEDING CHAPTERS dealt with the politicization of identities. I showed that identities operate in relation with the respective states and are the basis for structuring ethnoreligious communities in France and Germany. This led me to maintain that the states, with their policies, public discourse, and the contradictions between rhetoric and political action, which vacillate between ideology and pragmatism, contribute to shaping such community structures. Moreover, the states even give these communities their content, that is, they define their elements of identity. Their recognition or simply the search for their legitimacy leads to negotiation on both sides.

This chapter shows the process of negotiations between states and communities thus created. In fact, public discussions lead to negotiations with states for recognition. From the point of view of the activists, demanding recognition of a collective identity is the logical consequence of the politicization of identities. Based on the principle of equality, the issue for individuals or groups is struggling against every form of exclusion, political, social, or cultural, which ends in a demand for recognition. Confronting the emergence of communities trying to organize and win legitimacy, states either redefine or reinforce the fundamental principles that had prevailed at their inception as a way of setting limits on that recognition while placing identity demands within an institutional framework and establish the limits of their recognition and legitimacy.

The question is how France, which retrospectively calls itself a country of immigration, and Germany, which has until recently missed no opportunity to point out that it is not a country of immigration, are beginning to negotiate with the descendants of immigrants. Several phenomena answer these questions.

Building these communities encounters contradictions that appear in the discourse relating to the shaping of nation-states, as well as contradictions between discourse and policies. Eager to appoint spokesmen, the French and German governments have chosen to regard these associations as representative of communities. But far from representing the descendants of immigrants as a whole, with their cultural, national, ethnic, and religious divisions, to say nothing of the diversity of their social ambitions and political demands, these associations are perceived by French and German society in general as the community as a whole. This is the distortion that applies when their leaders are consulted by politicians and the media; they participate in national debates about them, affect public opinion, and influence governmental decisions by informing national awareness.

Thus, immigrants are no longer identified solely by their economic function. Whether they remain "foreigners" in Germany or are defined as being of foreign origin in France, a political function is assigned to them. These questions appeared in polls during the 1980s: "Would you oppose the election in France of a president of the republic of Muslim origin; the election of a person of Muslim origin as mayor of the commune where you live?" Or: "Do you think the Muslims of France should have representatives at the national level to speak on their behalf?"[1] These questions directly pose the problem of recognizing a cultural or religious identity in the public domain, and they implicitly pose the problem of membership in a specific community—even though 75 percent of the French questioned opposed the election of a president of the French Republic of Muslim origin and 63 percent were against a mayor of that origin.

In Germany, too, even though most Turks do not have civic rights, political parties still use polls to "measure" their voting preferences. Such polls imply political recognition even if they are not accompanied by real representation.

This recognition opens the way to identity negotiations. It concerns negotiating new ways and means of including immigrant groups in the political community; therefore it raises the question of citizenship. It also leads to a redefinition of a balance between the community structures that are taking shape and national institutions.

As for the identity elements structuring a community, France, confronting the visibility of Islam in the public space, has been led to redefine the relation between the state and religion, in this case, to reconsider the link between citizenship and identity. In both cases, these negotiations have been established in the name of equality of rights and treatment, especially since the militants who were first active in implementing identity structures and who confronted the state were socialized in associations that were encouraged and recognized by the respective states. They acquired the "identity of a citizen," a type of "social capital"—according to Robert D. Putnam—in their political commitment, which was manifested in participation in national and local life in the respective countries.[2]

These modes of participation demonstrate a multiplicity of allegiances to the group, the community, and the state, which are not necessarily in conflict, and lead to a redefinition of the concept of citizenship and of its bond to nationality and identity; bonds that are to be negotiated. The multiplicity of allegiances necessarily undermines the classic bond between the cultural community as a source of identification and political membership as a right of civic participation with equal rights.

Negotiations of identity between states and immigrants raise the question of the state as a legitimate framework of citizenship and of recognition. Negotiating identity leads its redefinition through an "institutional assimilation" of differences in the public space in order to generate a social recomposition and to reestablish mutual trust between states and immigrants.

The Question of Citizenship

The concepts of citizenship and nationality—two interdependent and "interchangeable"[3] concepts in the framework of the nation-state—are defined as the individual's belonging to a political community. This belonging takes shape through social, political, and cultural rights and the duties that embody the very idea of citizenship. The legal act that makes this principle concrete implies including "foreigners" within the national community whose moral and political values they are supposed to share. They are also supposed to adopt, even appropriate, historical references as proof of a complete adherence and loyalty to the founding principles of the nation, which, according to Weber, is the only community born of the modernity. At least, those are the expectations.

The social practices of citizenship, however, led to its extension into other areas, such as health, education, and access to social advantages in general. Soon after World War II, the British sociologist T. H. Marshall reconsidered citizenship in terms of social class; and since the 1980s, it has been included as a major subject of the social sciences at the junction of law and political theory and has been the focus of the European discussion of immigrant workers and their rights.

As a general social right, citizenship is ultimately located in the continuity of political rights. But for foreign workers and their families, as Y. Soysal noted, upon arrival in France and Germany, workers were settled into a "social citizenship," with access to the same social advantages as nationals.[4] Particularly in terms of human rights, nationals and foreigners are protected by the constitution in the same way. This is what Habermas calls a "passive citizenship" and finds its legitimacy in the development of the welfare state. The transition from this social citizenship to the so-called active legal citizenship[5] is done by naturalization, which considers length of stay, contribution of labor and service, as well as a "natural" identification.

Nevertheless, citizenship, as social practice, is manifested by direct or indirect participation in public life by both individuals and groups, both immigrants and the larger population. In this sense, it is expressed by a sense of commitment to the political community.[6] The main difference between France and Germany inheres in the laws regulating citizenship and affecting both the means of participation and the strategies of the agents. But in both countries the process of politicizing identities has led immigrants, whether legal citizens or foreigners, to act in the public sphere, that common area of communication, socialization, and exercise of power, and thus to demonstrate at least their de facto commitment and belonging to a political community.

Citizenship and Political Commitment

In France, soon after the municipal elections of March 1989, the newspapers reported that more than five hundred young people "of North African origin" (especially Kabyles) had been elected, including fifty-four deputy mayors.[7] The newly created France-Plus association was named the ambassador of civic rights and congratulated on the results.[8]

Municipal elections obviously represent an important issue for groups confined to urban areas because of their social or cultural origins. The elections of March 1989 allowed the Beurs to implement the political function of the associations by appropriating their "territory of identity" (see chapter 3) and acting as an organized force. In view of the progress of Le Pen, their discourse was set at the national level and even had international repercussions because of the Rushdie affair. The activists feared that Muslims rallying around the Rushdie affair in Great Britain would influence French public opinion, which was ready to link Islam with immigration. Any agitation around the Rushdie affair would pave the way for the National Front to turn it into a bugaboo and achieve a result close to that of the 1983 elections. "Something has to be done," said the young activists in the associations, thus justifying the existence of their organizations, which they defined as "political weapons."

At that moment, several associations were created, and their leaders appeared on the slates of various parties of the Center Right or Left. France-Plus and SOS-Racism, the biggest media machines of immigration, on one hand, and the local associations, on the other, competed for places on those slates that were really "open" (or not). The rivalry spawned by the parties' electioneering made them use the leaders of the big national associations in cities with a heavy concentration of the descendants of 1960s immigrants. The small local associations also sought to be included. In Saint-Denis, for example, the Generation Beur association competed with SOS-Racism for a good place on the socialist slate.

Moreover, some associations with a strong local base presented independent slates composed of "French of French stock and French of Italian, Algerian, and other origin, a real mixture," according to one of the representatives. Despite the criticism of those who define these slates as a "ghetto," young people used them to illustrate a local reality and to draw the attention of the authorities to the fact that the demands of Parisian associations such as SOS-Racism and France-Plus did not fit their experience or suit their needs. The public powers and the media began to consider these big associations as the voice of the young descendants of immigrants, whereas the small groups aimed at creating a primarily local identification among the young and at getting them to participate in the politics of their "housing project" (the term used most often).

This mobilization marks above all a political commitment to the national community. It is produced by the transition from a *civil participation*, demonstrated mainly within the associations, to a *civic participation* that results in the act of voting. It is in fact a transition from a citizenship previously defined by a commitment limited to community institutions to a citizenship that integrates the immigrants directly into the political community.

As far as foreigners—those with no legal citizenship—are concerned, the absence of civic participation leads them to seek indirect ways to integrate into the political community and thus to prove their commitment in France as well as in Germany. This is exercised especially on the local level, for example, where some associations have rallied for foreigners' right to vote in municipal elections.

But in fact that commitment becomes a concrete reality with the establishment of the advisory boards for foreigners in Germany (*Ausländerbeiräte*) or the extramunicipal committees of immigrants and the associate advisers in France. These organizations allow "nonnationals," as they are officially termed in the Federal Republic, to get involved for the common good, in this case, that of the city. In Germany the advisory boards, created in the mid-1970s and now set up in most urban centers, have guided foreigners to organize on behalf of common interests, particularly schools, day-care centers, green spaces, and businesses. The establishment of independent slates of candidates in these cases generates strong competition and sometimes creates interethnic tensions, both within and between the associations; but, by and large, the mobilization of Turkish candidates indicates a desire to participate in a democratic game to start a process of representation.

Nevertheless, the purely symbolic jurisdictions of these boards prevent their elected members from exercising influence on community decisions. In fact, all they do is submit problems faced by foreign merchants or students to the local authorities or present reports that cite the malfunction of the offices. Yet there is a tremendous interest in their election. In Bamberg, for example, in the autumn of 1994, the participation rate of foreigners in nominating the advisory board was 48.5 percent in general and 78 percent among the Turks, whose candidates won four seats.[9]

A similar procedure was instituted in France with the extramunicipal committees and associate advisers, mentioned earlier. One associate adviser, despite his purely advisory and symbolic role as in Germany, said: "We vote, we give our point of view"; another added: "You have the feeling and the pride of appearing in the proceedings."[10] As in Germany, these advisers in fact vote as nationals; they participate in discussions on foreigners in the city, appoint spokesmen who are supposed to represent them, and, naturally, demand equal rights for everyone.

Thus, participation in general institutions in which civic virtue is supposed to be acquired leads to a de facto commitment in national political life. It ushers in the exercise of citizenship itself and the implementation of a new identity of a citizen built by the commitment of individuals and engendering a sense of pride caused by integration into established (communal or national) institutions. In short, shaping that new identity is a process of "political acculturation," that is, the internalization of the national values and rules of the political game of the host country. "The identity of citizen" is based in the struggle for universal values: a struggle against racism, against exclusion, and for equality. These elements, which cement the reconstituted cultural community, also constitute the values that integrate them into the national community.

Citizenship, Nationality, and Identity

Shaping the identity of a citizen, expressed in both communal and national institutions, conflicts with classical analyses of citizenship. These lump together political commitment and national feeling, since citizenship is systematically attached to the nation-state, where its political and identity aspects merge. But whether citizenship is political, juridical, social, or economic, and whether its identity content is cultural or legal, this combination is summed up in a feeling of loyalty toward the group, the community, civil society, and the state. The strategies of the agents emerge in the interpenetration of these entities: in France an increasingly collective strategy appears in the vote; and in Germany there is, of course, a collective but compensatory strategy, in which the citizen's identity does not make him or her a "spectator who votes," in the words of J.-J. Rousseau, but an agent trying to influence governmental decisions through its action on public opinion.

In France the 1989 municipal elections were a catalyst for the young descendants of immigrants who realized that they belonged to a specific category, like the Beurs. Their mobilization clarified a collective strategy of integration as young people of North African origin. "Our vote counts, we must vote effectively," said the association leaders. This strategy, which located the "I" in the "we" in a confrontation with power, drew its resources from the struggle against racism and the National Front, which had targeted them and seemed to force them to appear as a group. The "we" was merely a way to distinguish themselves from the general French electorate. During the presidential elections of 1988, "a new type of correlation between the Le Pen vote, inclusion in the slates, and the Beur vote was taking shape."[11] Similarly, in the municipal elections of June 1995, when the subject of immigration was reintroduced after the National Front won 15 percent of the vote in the first round of presidential elections held the preceding month, some association leaders on the party slates developed the same arguments. In the departments of Nord and Pas-de-Calais, independent slates were formed as in 1989, but other candidates of North African origin appeared on other slates, adding that "they no longer wanted to be considered token Beurs" (as they thought they had been regarded by the Socialist Party in 1988). They therefore tried to get rid of the label Beur so as not to represent a target population. This must be seen as a new strategy of invisibility in the municipal elections of 1989. In June 1995 the journalist Philippe Bernard noted in *Le Monde* that "there are going to be more elected officials in the municipal elections who are descendants of immigrants . . . [but] without a label."

Yet, both in 1989 and in 1995, the discourse of the elected officials of North African origin concerned the republic, universal values, and their duty to represent all the inhabitants of the community, and they claimed that their election was not the result of a "community vote." Yet their political commitment, originating in the struggle against the National Front and racism, asserted a collective identity and an "ethnicity" facing the same social problems perceived and experienced by everyone because of a common origin. This development was confirmed by the competition not only between associations but also between political parties and even between internal tendencies within the parties.

This fast-growing collective strategy does not contradict the individual strategies examined in previous chapters. It complements them, challenging the representation of the French model of integration and not the politically defined status of citizen. Yet in the 1989 municipal elections, the discourse of the activists introduced the idea of a "new citizenship," defined as "a citizenship no longer reserved solely for nationals, but open to all Frenchmen and foreigners who demand the exercise of it on the basis of residence." In Saint-Étienne the Magic Grain association presented an autonomous slate in this vein: "For an active urban citizenship" or "A citizenship against the mess." These subjects surfaced again in 1995. But then the content of the concept of citizenship changed in public discourse. Whereas in 1989 it was equivalent to a right and a political identification, in 1995 it was defined as the exact opposite of exclusion. This explains its social aspect without disregarding its political, legal, and even identity aspect.

Statistics, paradoxically, still show an increase in the acquisition of French citizenship. Declarations of nationality and naturalizations increased by 3.5 percent in 1985 and 1.8 percent in 1989, and they have continued to grow by 2.2 percent a year.[12] This phenomenon is partly explained by demography: the young descendants of immigrants born in France or who came as children have come of age. But another factor has also intervened. In 1987 the public debates of the Committee of Experts on the Code of Citizenship made these young people aware of their automatic access to French citizenship. In 1988 presidential elections accelerated the naturalization of some young people and motivated those who already had French citizenship to register to vote, mainly because of the campaign of France-Plus, which toured the suburbs supporting these steps. This was stated by the representative of the National Association for the Immigrant Generation (ANGI): "When the association was created [in late 1981], everyone had Algerian citizenship. Then, little by little, people changed their citizenship, requested naturalization, perhaps because a moment had come when the choice was imposed. Now most people have French citizenship, not yet all, but we'll get there." That development clearly has something to do with the debates between the leaders of various political factions organized by independent local radio stations, which coupled them with information programs to teach civics to the "new French."

The rate of naturalizing foreigners or of acquiring nationality has not stopped growing since the 1990s. An exceptional increase was noted in 1994 because of the acceleration of the procedure and the handling of files in stock. The show of will that the 1993 law demanded among young people born in France of foreign parents did not stop the momentum of the transition to French nationality. Since then, the number of people who have acquired French nationality, no matter what the procedure, has been about one hundred thousand per year.[13]

In Germany at the same time, in view of the conditions of acquiring citizenship, activists developed different strategies, which I call strategies of compensation. These have not excluded integration from their agenda; quite the contrary, they have led to seeking indirect ways of reaching it. The lack of voting influence was offset on the local level by a form of citizenship that derived especially from its social practice and was defined by forming groups of foreigners to confront the federal state or the *Land*. Moreover, increasing numbers of Turks are now active in German political parties, particularly the SPD and the FDP, and they have participated for some years with the Greens, even though their presence as active members is not accompanied by any power of representation.

As for the voting rights for foreigners on the local level, although the parliament of Hamburg granted them in 1987, the Constitutional Court threw out that measure in 1989, on the grounds that only German citizens had the right to vote on the local or federal level as in France, where "voters are all French nationals, of legal age, both sexes enjoying their civil and civic right as voters," as specified in article 3 of the constitution. But the difficulty of acquiring German citizenship for "foreigners by blood" keeps young people whose parents or grandparents came from Turkey in their nationality of origin and consequently out of voter participation.

Yet, in 1990, a new proposed law on foreigners (*Ausländergesetz*) introduced for the first time the criterion of socialization for the grandchildren of Gastarbeiter who are candidates for citizenship. According to this law, young foreigners can obtain citizenship as a right if they submit a request for it between the ages of sixteen and twenty-three, have resided in the Federal Republic of Germany continuously for eight years, have attended an educational institution for six years, with at least four of those years in a general school, and have not committed a felony. Moreover, the price of citizenship, which used to vary between DM 3,000 and DM 5,000, was lowered to DM 100 for these young people. The flexibility introduced into the procedures of acquiring German citizenship is visible in statistics indicating an upsurge in naturalizations from all nationalities, from 37,000 of in 1980 to 101,377 in 1990.[14] The rise is particularly spectacular in Berlin, where the number of naturalized citizens increased from 1,843 in 1982 to 7,056 in 1990 and 9,200 in 1992.[15] The number of naturalized foreigners, which var-

ied between 20,000 and 30,000 a year between 1973 and 1989, reached
101,377 in 1990. In 1993, with the effective application of the law,
more than 29,000 foreigners acquired German citizenship through regu-
larization and 44,900 through naturalization based on discretionary
decisions by the German authorities, and these figures continue to rise.[16]

Further, in 1994 the new coalition government announced a more
advanced measure concerning the third generation of children of Turkish origin, taking the form of what the association leaders call child
citizenship (*Kindesstaatsangehörigkeit*). The objective of this proposed
law is first to grant German citizenship at birth to a child born of foreign parents if one parent was born in the Federal Republic. This introduces, in brief, a dual citizenship, but it comes with a restriction: the
married couple must furnish proof of residence in Germany for at least
ten years before the baby's birth. Moreover, at the age of eighteen, the
child can retreat and choose between German citizenship and the parents' nationality. Finally, note that although the statement of intent is
favored, as in the French measures of 1993, the ban on dual citizenship
imposes the choice of a single citizenship in Germany. A passionate
debate took place in 1998 after the new SPD-Green coalition government proposed to the *Bundestag* a new citizenship law accepting dual
citizenship in order to facilitate the integration of immigrants. The con-
servatives opposed particularly to dual citizenship mobilized a petition
campaign against it. After the CDU wan the *Land* election in Hesse in
February 1999, the government retreated and agreed instead for jus soli
as the basis of citizenship for children born in Germany to foreign parents. The law that has been in effect since January 1, 2000, has effectively introduced the jus soli, that is, every child born on German
territory of foreign parents who themselves were born on German soil
or who had arrived at the age of eight is German at birth. Nevertheless,
between the ages of sixteen and twenty-three, that person will have to
choose between German nationality and the nationality of his or her
parents, that is, between "remaining German" and "becoming a foreigner." Naturally, it is too soon to measure the results of this law, but
for the moment the difference in the procedures of granting citizenship
to foreigners or children of foreigners in the two countries has an indis-
putable effect on modes of civic participation.

In France, although the strategies of the agents become increasingly
collective and the concept of citizenship comes with the awareness of a
specific identity, participation in community politics remains individual.
In Germany, by contrast, despite strong participation in associations
and in the elections of advisers in some cities, the status of nationalities
by and large actually leads to a greater political isolation of "non-Germans." Active participation in civil society through mobilization within

associations does not lead to inclusion in the civic community. Further, the advisory boards, the only channels of representation of non-nationals in the cities, tend, on the contrary, to maintain the separation. The result is a hodgepodge of foreigners divided into nationalities, thus producing new segmentations that keep each national group in its own sphere. The proof of that situation is that the Turkish candidates for councils are beginning to form separate slates following partisan trends in Turkey, with no thought of representing all foreigners in the city; rather they are concerned with settling their own scores within a community that is certainly divided but nevertheless real. In an editorial in the community newspaper of Ulm, for example, a Turkish imam accused the candidates on the slates for "union" and "equal rights," as presented by his secular compatriots, of not responding to religious currents. Citizenship, like identity and commitment, is thus limited to the group with no access to the general political community or any connection to the neighboring community and other foreign groups.

So, if a "social citizenship" that includes the foreigner in the existing corporatist structures results in direct participation in civil society, this participation is only indirect with regard to the political community. Only "legal," that is, political, citizenship grants the right of full participation in the political community. Nevertheless, in both countries social reality tends to disrupt the overlapping of the national community and the political community, the bond between identity and right, and between culture and politics. In France and Germany, in fact, lists of affiliations and political commitment show that the practice of citizenship breaks away from a conception bound exclusively with national identity.

In France the concept of citizenship somehow replaces that of "civilization," a memento of greatness no longer shared by everyone or in the same way. In the discourse, the concept of citizenship is bound with the phenomenon of exclusion, and access to citizenship appears mainly as a measure of social compensation for social exclusion through politics and law. So for immigration between the two world wars, Émile Témine, in *Histoire des migrations à Marseille*, reports the testimony of an Italian immigrant in Marseille who declared that he had not "known any special problem either in settling in or in his professional life, [and] has thought of requesting French citizenship only after half a century of residence in Marseille."

Today this citizenship is increasingly limited to a right of civic participation and theoretically no longer excludes the expression of collective identities, even if that challenges republican ideology. The principle of new ethnic identifications, even defined in religious terms in a secular state, has become, in short, an issue of citizenship to be negotiated.

In Germany, however, the refusal to integrate national or religious groups other than the "Germans" into the political community can only further accentuate the particularism of the nation as conceived in that country. Identification with the ethnic community then finds its place only in civil society where citizenship is practiced. *The right to participate in the exercise of power* through legal citizenship remains to be won there. The dual citizenship the Turks demand is based in a logic that refers nationality to an identity and citizenship to a right that would allow negotiating a moral ethnonational personality. Such a personality is built on a double reference to German civil society through residence, along with the rights and duties connected to it; and to Turkish nationality—for those who share that—at the level of identity, which leads to the construction of a national minority. This ethnic identification expressed by the status of minority has become the issue of citizenship to be negotiated.

A Question of Recognition

The question of citizenship is even more important because it coincides with that of recognition. In both France and Germany, demands clash with the founding principles of the states. But asking for recognition as a minority aims at allowing groups that declare a specific identity to emerge from their political marginality and thus expresses a struggle for emancipation. But unlike the emancipation of the Enlightenment, which separated religion from public life and the individual from the community to guarantee an essential *identification* with the national community, the demand for recognition in this case is spawned by a *wish for participation* with equal rights recognized for a religious or national community within the structures of the state. Consequently, recognition refers to the recognition of a religious institution, particularly a Muslim one, in the same capacity as other religions, and it raises the question of institutional equality in France. In Germany recognition refers to a foreign community, in terms of the nationality of origin.

A French Islam

On January 11, 1995, "M. Pasqua recognized a Council representing the Muslims" and declared at the inauguration of the Mosque of Lyon in early 1995 that "the issue of Islam must be treated as a French issue."

In fact, the recognition of Islam is as serious as it is for other religions, but it has arisen almost a century later. In November 1989 the case of the head scarf crystallized the issue in a power balance between

French national identity on one hand and that of the last waves of immigrants on the other, the former remolded around laïcité and the latter around Islam. Politicians realized that one more religion had moved into society and its institutions, particularly the public school. Islamic association activists experienced it as an assertion of the immigrant population. What they had to negotiate with the public authorities was the permanent and structural presence of Islam and its cultural expression. In that situation, some political leaders and intellectuals felt it incumbent on them to remind the French of the fundamental principles of the republic as the hard core of the national character, and to remind the immigrants of the rules of behavior imposed on them in a state whose laïcité had become a sort of "official religion," the founding value of the nation-state and the pillar of social cohesion.

The assertion of Islam, like the emergence of an ethnicity already crystallized through certain modes of political participation, contradicts the doctrine of a nation characterized by its cultural unity and the common identity of its citizens. This principle of unity claims to obscure all cultural, regional, linguistic, and other differences in the public domain. This was confirmed by the Constitutional Committee's rejection of the term "people" as applied to the Corsicans, emphasizing that the expression "the people," applied to the French people, must be considered a unifying category and was not open to any division by virtue of the law."[17] The idea of assimilating a "foreign body" defined by its nationality obeys that logic of the integral inclusion of naturalized foreigners or their children who are French either at birth or at the age of sixteen.

Yet, according to Danièle Lochak, "the state's ignoring of differences is confined to religion."[18] The author states, in fact, that although France rejects the notion of "minority," the term appears in legal texts only in reference to a "religious minority." This is proved by the fact that there is no problem of recognition and representation for the almost four hundred thousand Portuguese, who form all kinds of associations and whose bonds of village solidarity are undeniably characteristic of a community organization. But the Portuguese are invisible to public opinion because they adhere to the same religion as the French, even if they attend separate churches. Similarly, reference to the community of Italians, Poles, and Armenians in the past were meant only from the angle of an ephemeral, local structure facilitating the transition between past and future and did not mean a permanent structure leading to its recognition.

But this view of community disappears when religions are perceived as being different. The separation of church and state confers institutional legal status on the Catholic clergy, the Protestants of the National Federation of the Protestant Churches of France, and the Jews governed by the Consistory created under Napoleon. This recognition is seen as an expression of respect for freedom of religion and the neutrality of the secular state. Even though the politicians mobilized around the head scarf issue in the name of laïcité, that mobilization elevated Islam to the core of the collective identity of the descendants of the North African immigrants. The place of Islam in France revived the old duality between religion and state in the public discussion.

In fact, the demand for the recognition of Islam has led association activists to reorganize. At the local level, they have attempted to go beyond the national, ethnic, and ideological divisions to define common elements uniting all Muslims, by building a mosque, for example. At the national level, the Union of Islamic Organizations of France was created in 1983, followed two years later by the National Federation of Muslims of France. "We realize that representatives are necessary," said the founder of the federation, challenging the representative status of the Mosque of Paris, the only Muslim institution officially recognized by the state, and its rector as sole spokesman, appointed initially by the French government and by the Algerian government after 1963. "It is better if representatives emerge from the community," he added. Shaping a "community" now becomes "an option"[19] in order to define an identity of action or reaction and to assert it publicly through representative institutions recognized by the state.

After heated discussions about the place of religion in French society generated by the case of the head scarf, in 1990 Minister of the Interior Pierre Joxe created the Council of Thought on Islam in France, or CORIF. Is representation assumed to be the prerequisite for "thinking" about means of adapting the requirements of Islam to the norms of society, or vice versa? "Unable to represent Islam, I have withheld a suggestion of Jacques Berque, who told me that it was possible, on the other hand, to symbolize Islam," Joxe explained in an interview in Débat.[20] As if the state wanted to structure its opponents' mobilization beyond their national and even religious diversity, it tried to assemble the Muslims of France "symbolically," through CORIF. "The idea is that the Council might become the embryo of a representative structure of Islam for the public powers, on the model of the Episcopal Conference or the Protestant Federation of France."[21]

In 1994, shortly after the publication of a circular by François Bayrou, minister of national education, banning all ostentatious religious symbols in educational establishments, Charles Pasqua officially recognized the representative Council of Muslims of France (CRMF), created the previous year, and appointed its chairman, Dr. Boubakeur, the rector of the Mosque of Paris, as official spokesman. A physician by profession, author of a charter on the Muslim religion in France, Rector

Boubakeur granted an interview to *Le Monde* on May 31, 1995, in which he asserted his independence with regard to Algeria, his homeland: "Muslims intend to work for the emergence of Islam in France . . . not following any foreign authority." And Minister Pasqua declared: "I have always wanted Islam to go from the status of a tolerated religion in France to that of a religion accepted by everyone as part of the French spiritual landscape." Thus, Islam has been integrated into a scheme that Lochak considers "a pragmatic handling of differences," consisting of "gradually introducing the minimal dose of institutionalization needed for a concrete resolution of the practical problems created by the existence of 'minority groups,' who want to end up with 'official recognition,' which would then produce the institutionalization of differences."[22]

This process clearly aims at orchestrating a shift from an Islam in France to an Islam of France, from a simple presence of Muslims and the practices visible in public space to an Islam that is expressed and developed within national institutions, assuming its freedom from "foreign" influences, especially those of the homeland. This can be done only by an "institutional assimilation," a form of institutional recognition in the framework of legitimacy of the state as well as in its historical continuity of a concern for equality, yet without affecting the cultural and/or religious identity of the represented collectivity. One leader of the National Federation of Muslims of France commented in this respect that, with CORIF, "Joxe's goal was clear: he no longer wanted Algeria to monopolize Islam in France. He made Sheikh Haddam [rector of the Mosque of Paris at that time] equal to other associations. One among others."

"Islam of France" transforms relations between the concept of the authorities and that of the general public. In Muslim countries this relationship places believers, whether citizens or not, vis-à-vis national authorities closely connected with religion, except in Turkey. When believers immigrate, they no longer confront anyone except an imam, who has become the leader of a primarily local community, and their institutional representation on the national level granted them their political role.

The discussion is far from over. "Nationalizing" Islam, making it a "French Islam," "institutionally assimilated," might introduce a liberating process while responding to the demands of the principles of equality but also to the expectations of the concerned populations. This was how the shift from the "Jews of France" to "French Judaism" took place, even if only in its terminology. In both cases representation obviously brings a legal protection more broadly guaranteed by all the representative organizations initiated by the state, which, in this case, intervenes both as arbiter and as dispenser of official recognition. This experience makes existing representative organizations, particularly Jewish institutions, which are older and were created and developed with respect to laïcité, the reference of associations of non-Islamic immigrants. France-Plus, for example, proposes the creation of a Muslim consistory, one of its activists arguing that "secular Islam is completely compatible with life in France." The chairman of the Federation of Muslims of France, however, rejects this plan precisely because of the argument advanced by France-Plus: "They want us to copy the model of the Consistory made up of people who are Jews but not religious." Note that the same quarrel divided observant Jews from secular Jews when the Consistory was centralized, and its leaders insisted on secularizing it by removing all religious content.[23]

And note also that Muslims now refer to the legal status of Jewish institutions, and some Jews increasingly draw on the claims for Muslim recognition to express a sense of belonging to a "Jewish community," signaling the rejection of the concept of French Judaism in favor of "Jews of France." Inspired by Muslim aspirations and the permanent redefinitions of laïcité they suggest, even the Church of France has revived the discussion of its relations with the state. This approach has resurrected the problem of independent education through the revision of the Falloux law, which had to do with the status of private schools vis-à-vis the state. The demand for a recognition of Islam has thus created a "snowball effect," in which they are carried away by the flood of public demands and declarations. But it has also spawned a general revision of the place of religion in the public sphere, challenging the concept of republican secularism, its universality, and its practices, as well as the connection between church and state in France.

The institution of representative structures of special groups or communities is justified by the role of conflict mediator ascribed to every modern democratic state, since the plethora of public interests, identities, and allegiances is an inevitable source of tension and even of violent conflicts in some cases. Whereas the majority opinion views the recognition of Islam as generating conflict, Muslims experience it as compensation for rejection. And, as if to assert a historical continuity, the state takes refuge behind an inclusionist strategy that leads it to encourage representative institutions to make their chairman its main spokesman and consider their members full partners in the political community. Recently, and with the same point of view, Minister of the Interior Jean-Pierre Chevènement also tried to create a representative institution and has encountered the same difficulties described in the preceding chapter.

The stake of such recognition is high, depending, among other things, on the size of the "Muslim electorate," no matter how sociologically varied and politically differentiated it is. How else to interpret the ostensibly surprising absence of any mention during the presidential campaign of 1995 of the "distance" of Islam as a cultural or a political system, both described as communal? Quite simply, it is because cultural and political acculturations have made inroads that the representation of a group of French citizens of the Muslim denomination has made itself felt, even if it is not expressed in those terms. The issue is so important that it has revived public discussion of the conditions of granting citizenship, which, since the Committee of Experts of 1987, has constantly returned, particularly when there is a change of government. The Left wants to return to the "automatic" right of being born on French soil, the conservative Right remains silent on the "choice" of nationality at the age of sixteen, which it introduced, and the extreme Right advocates the right of blood. On television, Jean-Marie Le Pen particularly lamented the fact that citizenship is "granted too easily" and pleaded for a citizenship that is "inherited and earned." Emphasizing what he defines as the indissoluble bond between nationality, citizenship, and identity, the chairman of the National Front intends to eject "the new citizens" from the collective identity of the French nation, which he would like to see transmitted by inheritance, as in Germany. Even more surprising was Valéry Giscard d'Estaing's use of the term *invasion* to describe immigration. He recommended including citizenship in the right of blood as in Germany. In his report that led to the new law of 1997, Patrick Weil sought a consensus among the differing interpretations of citizenship.[24] We can thus see how the rules of citizenship are in fact "negotiated."

A Turkish Minority in Germany

In Germany the demand for recognition is more complex. It bears on the status of an ethnic minority, based on both a Turkish national identity and a Muslim religious identity, two elements perceived as foreign in the German collective identity. The national minority is defined by its foreign legal status and the religious minority by the marginalization of Islam with regard to other religions enjoying an official status. Nevertheless, the Turks' demand for recognition has intensified under the impact of spectacular racist attacks since 1990, placing it at the core of the discussion as a right of protection against the "hatred of foreigners" (*Ausländerhass*) or "hostility toward foreigners" (*Ausländerfeindlichkeit*). The difficulty is that the demand for this right depends on the sort of citizenship that favors the legal aspect by neglecting the identity aspect. Hence, the extra step toward an acceptance of dual citizenship, which would directly affect the fundamental German law by merging citizenship and nationality, has become an element of conflict that has been negotiated.

The Turks' demand for dual citizenship introduces clear distinctions between nationality, citizenship, and identity. Even if nationality and citizenship are interdependent, as in France, this distinction does exist in political terminology. Citizenship (*Staatsbürgerschaft*) and nationality (*Staatsangehörigkeit*) refer to the state, but the former as an instrument, the latter as belonging. The reference to dual citizenship is based on that duality: the "minority" in question demonstrates a desire for integration into the political community with the demand for citizenship, and it expresses its "attachment" to its nationality of origin.

But these ambiguities are reinforced mainly by expressions that indicate uncertainty about how to call foreigners who have struck roots in the national territory: either the term "non-Germans" for the moderate Right or "foreign fellow citizens" (*ausländische Mitbürger*) for the Greens. These two expressions emphasize the bond or the lack of a bond that some people would like to create or reinforce between citizens and nationals. And the content of the discussions concerns conditions of access to citizenship, which also depend on a reexamination of the concept of the state and its relation to the definition of the nation. By demanding recognition as a minority, the Turks are defining citizenship as a legal tool to allow political representation, and nationality as an ethnic identity like the one the Germans shape for themselves. The status of minority basically keeps the respective identities separate, and the discussions of dual citizenship end up defining a double reference of identity and rights.

But recognizing the Turks as an ethnic minority forces the Germans to admit the permanence of their presence and the ethnic-national and religious differences this involves. German politicians have started to reject the official discourse that "Germany is not a country of immigration" and have agreed that Germany, like other European countries, has become de facto a country of immigration where about six million foreigners live permanently. Only if this reality is accepted can the "non-German" groups hope to achieve political representation, since they have lived in the Federal Republic for generations.

Yet, as in France, the subject of foreigners, immigration, and citizenship was strangely absent from the German election campaign in the autumn of 1994. Nevertheless, soon after the elections, the protocol of the new coalition government developed a formula for the third generation of children of Turks, "childhood citizenship" (*Kindesstaatsangehörigkeit*) mentioned in chapter 6, and reintroduced dual citizenship into the public discussion. Note that this formula stipulates that at the age of eighteen young Turks would have to choose between German nationality and the nationality of their parents. In fact, this new formula again recognizes dual citizenship until the legal age as an "experiment," a test of the practice of citizenship and of dual citizenship.

"Citizenship by eye-dropper!" exclaimed the Turkish newspapers, and the spokesmen of various Turkish organizations reacted vehemently. In fact, like the demand for dual citizenship, that formula once again revealed the mutual distrust between the German state and the Turks. Germany not only regrets the nonidentification of the Turks with the German nation in the case of the acquisition of citizenship, but also expresses its distrust about the exercise of their duty as citizens, since that can take place only at the age of eighteen, the legal age. Moreover, in a rather revealing way, naturalizations that are discretionary demand that the candidates declare loyalty.

For thirty-five years German governments called Turkish residents "guests," and have suggested, sometimes more, sometimes less subtly, that their true cultural and political home is in Turkey. Is it therefore so surprising that these Turks themselves sustain a sense of belonging to their country of origin? This leads the Turks to justify their demand for dual citizenship by arguing that only being granted German citizenship can put an end to the racist acts committed against them. Thus, after that sort of violence was perpetrated in Mölln and Solingen, their press expressed that feeling with these headlines: "The Nazis Torch and Germany Sleeps" and "Another German Crime." Similarly, the Turkish press reported the verdict handed down against the criminals of Solingen in terms that raised doubts about German justice and defined the Turkish state as "the protector of the rights of its nationals," as if to remind German public opinion that "their state represents [both legal and identity] safety." Moreover, this feeling is reinforced by the arrival in Federal Germany of Aussiedler and asylum seekers. Aussiedler from Eastern Europe and Russia are naturalized de jure because of their German ancestors.

The Turks' power of negotiation in Germany draws most of its strength from their economic integration. If citizenship, by definition, is a status that allows influencing political decisions, Turkish nationals are trying to demonstrate their potential on an economic basis. A 1991 report published in Brussels estimates the direct or indirect economic contribution of the Turks at about DM 57 billion, a sum that exceeds the expenses of the welfare state for foreigners, which amounts to only DM 16 billion.[25] In fact, the 1.8 million Turks in Germany included 35,000 entrepreneurs in 1992, from restaurateurs to manufacturers, who employed a total of 150,000 Turks and 75,000 Germans, whose annual receipts amounted to DM 25 billion and who paid DM 1 billion in taxes in 1991.[26]

Some of these economic agents not only play an important role in relations between Germany and Turkey but also control the fate of German investment projects in the Turkephone republics of the former Soviet Union. "We have opened offices for Turkish and German products in Azerbaijan and Kazakhstan," said a Turkish manufacturer of Berlin. Several have also invested in the former East Germany.

But even more interesting, "Turks consume more than Germans," according to an article in *Der Spiegel*, subtitled: "The Turks Are the Future of Germany."[27] "Many of them drive Mercedeses, own tape recorders, hi-fi systems, computers, even better investments." As a result, an increasing number of German businesses are advertising on television networks or in the local Turkish press. Moreover, during the winter of 1992–93, the anti-Turkish violence of Mölln and Solingen seems to have stirred businesses more than it did politicians. Many companies published messages of solidarity with the foreigners. Lufthansa, for example, stated: "We are foreigners every day." BMW noted that "Without foreigners, we are poor." And Siemens asserted: "We cannot tolerate intolerance." It went on: "We take a stand because we are foreigners in 150 countries. We will always be concerned where our foreign fellow citizens are concerned."

The economic contribution of immigrant groups is not easily perceptible by French statistics. Once French citizenship is acquired, these groups are classified as "French by acquisition" and become numerically invisible. That shows the different styles, even different concepts, of integration in the two countries. But in Germany, can security based on an economic presence compensate for political insecurity? Turkish business people wonder about the risks to the German economy if they should withdraw their investments. One Turkish manufacturer of Berlin stated: "I have invested in the new Länder of the former DDR, but I haven't yet gotten a *Pfennig* of interest, and we are insulted and beaten up there. Why continue?"

Although the French state finally recognized a representative Council of Muslims to appease social tensions, will the fear of economic instability generated by racial conflicts persuade German politicians to recognize the "Turkish minority" and grant it political rights? In other words, can the Turks' economic integration pave the way for political representation and give them the bargaining power to negotiate their collective interests? A partial answer to that question can be found in the nineteenth century, when economic circles were able to integrate Germany into international economic competition during the depression of 1873–96. Thus the economic sector achieved importance and exercised political influence. Following the same logic, various occupational groups, like the organization of Turkish physicians since 1990, and subsequently associations of business people of various Länder, are now preparing to act as pressure groups to negotiate collective interests ranging from protecting social and cultural rights to measures against xenophobia. Remembering the role economics played in redefining German identity after the war, they also rely on their financial success to become a political force. They carefully avoid presenting themselves as victims; instead they draw attention to their contribution to German society and thus elicit respect among German authorities.

"The hard core of German identity is the economy," stated Barbara John, leader of the *Ausländerbeauftragte* of Berlin during an interview in May 1993. Does this mean that the "economic miracle" and prosperity have somehow given new content to German identity beyond the old ethnic references? Or does this approach return to premodern understanding of the citizen as *Bürger*? In Germany this notion of Bürger relates more to civil society than to allegiance to the political community; civil society there is defined, in fact, as "civic society" (*die bürgerlische Gesellschaft*) and is not only distinct from the state and its institutions but opposed to them. In this sense, every individual who participates in public life dominated by economic competition can be considered a citizen. "That suggests that citizen is synonymous with civic, two sides of the same coin," wrote Ralf Dahrendorf.[28] The term *ausländische Mitbürger* (foreign fellow citizens), introduced by the Greens, should be interpreted within this logic, since the formulation amounts to admitting Turkish nationals into German society through economic citizenship in the absence of political citizenship. Is their "gentrification" then a step toward naturalization, as the German term *Einbürgerung* implies, even if it is used with reference to the state (*Staatsbürger*) and not to the city, as for the citizen?

This very specific concept of citizenship makes economics serve politics, unlike in France, where politics prevails over economics, at least in discourse. But that means that the Turks in Germany, who are citizens without being citizens, have more political influence than the North Africans in France, who are legally citizens, especially the younger generations. In Germany the children and grandchildren of Turkish immigrants express their identification with the general society with regard to the success of their parents or grandparents, or of those Turks seen in each case as the source of "ethnic pride." The discussion of immigration in France has been embedded in the debate on social exclusion and the suburban phenomenon, which leads to a sense of self-denigration and anger. In Germany, however, an image of economic success has become a motivation to legitimate the claim to a status of minority and permits a conspicuous attachment to the home country and an introduction of the discussion of dual citizenship. Entrepreneurs, in particular, pose as intermediaries between both Turkish and German politicians and manufacturers. They mediate in economic negotiations between Turkey and Germany, sponsor Turkish-born painters who trained in Germany, and invested in the promotion of cultural life in Turkey. They also support the associations according to their political affinities and their position in relation to Turkey. In sum, their efforts by and large are directed toward forming lobbies recognized in both countries, based on community institutions not only determined by Turkish political life but located inside or in opposition to the German system, reacting to every declaration of the government regarding Turkey.

The outcome of this duality is decisive for both countries. For Turkey, the outcome is the object of a recovery of considerable economic and political consequences, particularly with European institutions. So the concept of dual nationality has been integrated into the Turkish constitution, recently even ascribing Turkish identity to a young person born in Turkey who no longer possesses nationality or to a young person born in Germany whose parents were born in Turkey. For Germany Turks represent an important voting bloc, and political parties compete to define the place of non-Germans in the political community. A 1994 study on how the Turks would have voted in the elections if they had been German citizens revealed that 49 percent would have voted for the SPD (down from 67 percent in 1986),[29] 11 percent for the Greens, 10 percent for the FDP, and 6 percent for the CDU.[30] Although the number of German voters of Turkish origin was no more than thirty-five thousand, political parties published propaganda in the community newspapers as if they wanted to realize an electoral investment. The FDP wagered that the Turkish vote would go beyond 5 percent. The SPD supports their big associations to keep their activists from joining other parties. This is why German political parties express their opinion on the political situation in Turkey or on the relations they intend to develop between the two countries.

Ultimately, these behaviors demonstrate mainly that the image of the Turks has changed. They are no longer perceived simply as foreign workers but are considered citizens belonging to civil society and participating in democratic social, economic, and political interactions. They are even accepted as political agents. Aside from association activists or those who are influential within German political parties, there are four elected delegates of Turkish origin: one in the parliament of the *Land* of Berlin (Green), another in the parliament of Hamburg (SPD), and two (one SPD and one Green) in the federal parliament in Bonn—now in

Berlin. Cem Özdemir, a Green delegate in the Bundestag, was born in Germany. His election in 1994 was announced in the Turkish press with the headline "We Have Conquered Bonn." The German press by and large preferred to attribute a southern German (*Schwabe*) regional identity to him: "He is a *Schwabe* Turk who has nothing to do with German identity, but with *Schwabe* identity." And Özdemir explained himself thus: "I have fun raising my regional compatriots' consciousness by speaking to them in their dialect; it's a way of disarming their racism" (interview of March 1995).

Basically, Özdemir defines himself primarily as a "new native" (*neuer Inländer*), as he calls the young people of his and future generations, emphasizing the contrast with the previous generation, who were considered Ausländer (foreigners) or sometimes *Einwanderer* (immigrants). "The *neue Inländer* are an important part of our republic. They have known the freedom of a civil and urban society; they are sure of themselves and go their own way; they don't give in to the pressure of their parents or to external influences," he declared as if to prove their identity as citizens. In fact, more of these young Turks have been educated in German schools (*Bildungsinländer*, or "trained inside"), are steeped in the local culture, have passed the *Abitur* (the German matriculation exam) in West Germany, and have even graduated from German universities. "But all that without a passport," noted the delegate from Bonn. Hence acquiring German nationality, which is synonymous with citizenship, is imposed not only as a right but also as a duty. This association of duty and citizenship demonstrates an identification with German society, as asserted by the young parliamentarian: "I tell the young people that the problems of Germany are our problems, that we have something to say and we must contribute to the search for their solutions." These are the bases for a current campaign to persuade all generations of Turkish nationals to apply for German nationality.

Yet the reality is more complex. Pragmatism and emotion are blended with regard to both Turkey and Germany, as indicated by a community newspaper published in Ulm. On the front page of the March 1995 issue are two passports, one Turkish and one German, with a block headline: "You Have Nothing to Lose, You Have a Lot to Win." Inside, four pages explain to the Turks the advantages of acquiring German citizenship without damaging their "interests" in Turkey. "The right to elect and to be elected, the freedom to choose a profession, no expulsion, free movement in the European Union, access to all rights and duties of Germans," it argues. And, in addition, "you don't lose your rights to your property, your money, your inheritance, your insurance premiums in Turkey."

So, in this sense, the issue is no longer Turkish identity but rights in a

Turkey now on the same level as Germany. Yet demands remain linked, since they affect equal rights and the recognition of a collective identity constructed in Germany on the basis of an identification with Turkey. Association activists, members of advisory boards, and delegates take responsibility only for civic instruction about the administrative steps to acquire German citizenship. For the rest, Turkish identity is always present in cultural activities and in the language or religion courses provided by the associations. Recognition for the Turkish language is demanded within the framework of a bilingual education, inspired by programs for Hispanics in the United States, or within public religious institutions. Moreover, that identity generates the demand for citizenship and representation when its goal is to raise a barrier against racism. It then results in the demand for an antidiscrimination law, for professional equality, or equality in housing. The demand of a right is clearly linked with identity.

Identity negotiations between states and communities are thus visibly included in a historical continuity of the role of the state in France and of civil society in Germany, as well as relations between the two countries and their respective immigrant groups. Yet despite the differences of political traditions that encourage participation in a so-called republican political community in France, in civil society in Germany identity negotiations challenge the definition and practice of citizenship: a citizenship against social exclusion in France and the United States, and a citizenship for political inclusion in Germany. The two approaches go beyond a concept of citizenship limited strictly to the nation-state and hence separate citizenship from nationality, reducing the former to political rights and giving the latter a dimension of pure identity, which is developed in negotiations for its recognition. The abundance of identifications and cultural, ethnic, or religious allegiances deriving from them lead to a shift of the boundaries between what was defined as private and what was defined as public, and was based on the bond between church and state in France and nationality and state in Germany. By and large, the discussion ultimately leads to the relationship between culture and politics and new definitions of belonging.

CHAPTER EIGHT

The European Union:
New Space for Negotiating Identities

> Europe has unity only in its multiplicity. It is the interactions
> between people, cultures, states that have woven a unity that
> is itself plural and contradictory.
>
> —Edgar Morin

ALL IDENTITIES ARE NOW to be negotiated within the framework of the
European Union. Whether they are national, regional, linguistic, religious, majority, or minority, identities are redefined by the complex
interaction and identification among states, nations, and regions, as well
as groups in the European space. Nation-states cling to historical
achievements and reinforce their special features by including them in
models they want to defend: a model of sovereignty, a model of a
nation-state, a model of integration, a model of citizenship, a model of
nationality. Paradoxically, these models are especially in demand, since
policies of immigration, integration, and citizenship appear to converge.
Efforts to establish a European political agenda seem to trigger the promotion of national uniqueness at the same time.

The activists among immigrants seem to rely increasingly on the idea
of a political Europe to intensify their quest for recognition. Some
leaders of associations involved in building transnational networks of
solidarity in terms of a nationality (of origin or current) and a common
religion mobilize beyond and across borders. These networks, like those
of professional groups, form the threads of a spiderweb covering the
European space, that "space without internal borders where"—according to the Single Europe Act of 1986—"the free circulation of wealth
and capital is guaranteed." For descendants of immigrants, a transnational organization has become a way to bypass national policies and
negotiate a recognition beyond the limits set by national models in the
states where they reside.

The negotiation of identities and rights on the European scale reveals
an abundance of memberships and allegiances divided between the
country of origin, the country of residence, and Europe, and it leads to
a new concept of citizenship, questioning its link to nationality. The

same is true with the Maastricht Treaty, signed in February 1992. The treaty stipulates that persons holding citizenship in one of the countries of the European Union have the right to vote in local elections. This immediately introduces a separation between citizenship (the exercise of a right according to residence), nationality (membership), and territory (where citizenship rights are applied) even if the treaty projects its national conception at the European level: a person is a citizen of the Union if he or she has nationality in one of the member countries of the Union (article 8). The practical application of this Union citizenship illustrates the diversity of situations and the multiplicity of allegiances for the citizens of the Union as well as for the descendants of the 1960s immigrants, some of whom of non-European origin are sometimes citizens of their country of residence and other times are legally foreigners.

The political reconstruction of Europe creates paradoxes within the nation-states that compose the European Union. Its supranational institutions and the transnational organizations it generates lead to a redefinition of the political structure of nation-states, accelerating their process of negotiation both inside and outside their territories. For immigrant populations, these increasingly appear as a crucial structure for negotiating the claimed and represented identity and interest ultimately with the state. The state constitutes the only concrete protective framework for rights. Shaping transnational networks becomes a way to influence states from the outside while keeping the "idea of a nation" for mobilization. All these relations between Europe, the nation-states, and the foreign immigrants with a European identity lead to a redefinition of the concepts of universality, particularity, nationality, and citizenship—concepts that shape a European identity and its effect of multiple negotiations, which show even more in transnationality.

UNIVERSALITY AND PARTICULARITY

The universality of the nation-state is based on the Declaration of the Rights of Man and Citizen, at least in France. The Universal Declaration of the Rights of Man, proclaimed by the United Nations in 1948, is addressed to all individuals. Its scope is "more global and universal and conveys an apparent consensus of international society, a good collective conscience *urbi et orbi*."[1] So the citizen is the individual. Using this approach, the universality inherited from the French Revolution must be reinterpreted in its general application to other European countries through European institutions, particularly the European Council. The same applies to the concept of human rights or citizenship at a more specific level. A poll published in June 1993 by *Eurobaromètre*, a bulletin of the European Commission, showed that 81 percent of Europeans think that decisions about the "rights of man" should be made in common (between country and Union), and 79 percent think the same about the "rights of the citizen."[2]

Thus, united Europe introduces a "normative supranationalism" that extends beyond the framework of the nation-states and is even imposed on them.[3] Even if the issue of human rights remains the exclusive jurisdiction of the states, they are forced to accept the new legal norms formulated by European institutions, since the European Convention on the Rights of Man entitles the European citizen (in this case, one who has nationality in one of the states that has accepted the right of individual appeal) to apply directly to the European Council, and it entitles a foreigner (who does not have nationality in one of the states of the Union) to appeal to the European Court of the Rights of Man. In case of deportation, for example, the foreigner can oppose the national decisions on behalf of the right of respect for family life (¶1 of article 8), after exhausting the paths of internal appeal. Thus, the principle of the convention is based on the idea that "the individual, previously isolated and ignored in relations between states, becomes a citizen in the community of European nations."[4] There are a great many individual petitions to the European Court of the Rights of Man. As for public opinion, 50 percent of the interviewed members of the Union think the decisions of the court should be obeyed, and 22 percent think they should not.[5]

Rights of Solidarity, Rights of Minorities

Attorneys are also considering a classification of rights: civil and political rights first, followed by economic, social, and cultural rights, and finally "rights of solidarity."[6] Rights of solidarity refer to freedom of collective action in a community and are based on the idea that "only in a community is the full development of the individual personality possible."[7] Introducing these rights of solidarity thus emphasizes the ambivalence between individual rights and collective rights, a new concern of states and groups that appears not only in public opinion but also in political discourse.

The rights of solidarity for immigrants might refer to the rights of minorities. Hence their challenge to nation-states. In the European context the concept of minority has been developed since the fall of the Berlin Wall in reference to the social, cultural, and political reality of the countries of Central and Eastern Europe. Since 1989, the problem of democracy in these countries has been posed in terms of recognizing minorities and has generated the application of minority rights in the European institutions of other countries of Western Europe. Yet this concept is so ideologically charged that it is hardly portable. For example, on November 10, 1994, the European Council developed a framework agreement guaranteeing the individual freedoms of minorities without infringing on the unity and cohesion of the state. France did not sign the agreement because its minister for European affairs judged the text "incompatible with the constitution."[8] By the same principle, France also rejected the recognition of regional (minority) languages recommended by the *Charte des langues régionales*.

Yet the term *minority* is ambiguous. Does it designate cultural, linguistic, territorial, and officially recognized minorities, like the Catalans and the Basques in Spain, Bretons and Corse in France, or does it refer to minorities composed of immigrants but also officially recognized as minorities, as in the Netherlands? The definition proposed by the Convention of Human Rights is broad: "The term 'minority' indicates a group that is numerically inferior to the rest of the population and whose members are moved by the desire to preserve their culture, their traditions, their religion, or their language."[9] In France, whether it is regional or religious identities, or collective identities expressed by individuals or groups of immigrant descent, the term is rejected. In Germany it refers only to German minorities living outside the territory. Nevertheless, when Turkish nationals claim minority rights in Germany, placing the maintenance of their language and its introduction into public education at the core of a community structure, they no longer refer explicitly to the United States, particularly affirmative action, but tacitly to this agreement.

Yet, at the same time, in discussing immigration, politicians in each country insist on the unique aspects of tradition as far as citizenship and nationality are concerned. In fact, although European public opinion is increasingly considering immigration as a subject within the jurisdiction of the Union at the intergovernmental level, like the right of asylum, its tangible aspects inevitably challenge the models specific to each state.[10] In *Le Monde* of March 10, 1994, for example, Jean-Pierre Chevènement (chairman of the Citizens' Movement) and Anicet Le Pors proposed redefining the Maastricht Treaty, "relying on the founding values of the French nation: the culture of public service, secularity, the French model of integration, based on the principle of equality against the logic of minorities and a wide role for the right of citizenship by birth on French soil." As for Germany, the unexportable model of citizenship justifies the lack of discourse in this area. Can the French model be considered the one most easily universalized?

Between Market and Union

Yet France and Germany glorified "the myth of 1992," of a vast unified space, a place where products and resources circulated, which involved a duty to build a political union. Thus, for Raymond Barre "to make the European Union one of the great powers of the future, maintaining its rank without any illusory pretense to dominate it, is a new form of historical struggle of our country to control its own destiny."[11] François Mitterrand, who presented his New Year wishes in 1995, also repeated that "the future of France is through Europe." Since then, any political or economic project cannot overlook or neglect the European aspect; its anticipated implications are in fact incorporated into the discourse. From now on, national sovereignty and pride are measured through Europe and its important share in its achievement. In Germany as well, participation in the European construction is often felt as an element of self-respect, perhaps even a way of belonging to a political nation (Europe) and not only a cultural nation (Germany). In both cases, the common plans were seen as proof of a "desire to live together" and to have a "common destiny," despite the diversity of "heritages." As Edgar Morin emphasized, "Europe is not emerging from a past that contradicts it; it is barely emerging from the present because it is the future that commands it."[12]

Yet in 1992, during the ratification of the Maastricht Treaty, both public opinion and politicians were reserved. France ratified the treaty with only 51 percent of the vote in the referendum in September of that year. In Germany ratification of the treaty was not submitted to a referendum—as in Belgium, the Netherlands, and Luxembourg—but was not a foregone conclusion. It was accompanied particularly by questions about the constitutionality of the treaty and its compatibility with article 38 of the Basic Law guaranteeing the "[German] people" the subjective right to participate in the election of delegates to the Bundestag, and it turned that into an inviolable democratic principle that cannot be overruled by the accepted and acceptable transfer of tasks and jurisdictions. As a result, the judges of the federal constitutional court of Karlsruhe insisted on the "constitutional sovereignty of the BRD [Bundesrepublik Deutschland]" and the need to protect its "democratic vitality."

Paradoxically, along with being a source of pride in each country, the construction of Europe is thus accompanied by nationalist discourses based on a rejection of the operations of the Union. As Jean Leca emphasized: "Men, even modern ones, don't live only on the welfare state, the market, and contractual bonds."[13] In fact, they seek a community of belonging where their collective identity and emotions can be expressed, and in the European space, this community is still the nation. For most individuals, national identity continues to take precedence over European identity. They declare that they are first French (63 percent) or Germans (55 percent), and then Europeans. Similarly, only 47 percent of the French think it is "a good thing" to belong to the European Union, and 40 percent feel that France has not gained any advantage from it.[14]

The Issue of Sovereignty

But what is the identity of a state if it is not connected with its sovereignty, which is weakened by external European coercion? In the French presidential campaign of 1995, Jacques Chirac felt it necessary to emphasize his vision of a European Union "that respects the sovereignty of the states."[15] More generally, resistance to European unification stresses the predominance of national distinctions and the need to redefine them in a supranational political space that increases interactions between countries. Does that explain the paradox in the contrast between the openness embodied by the idea of the European Union and the nationalist withdrawals expressed in discourse that tries to reformulate the founding principles of the nation-states and illustrate their particularity? This paradox is created by the ambivalent relations between the various states of the European Union and is fueled by feelings of both trust and distrust. Trust is expressed in a common project and in the inevitable harmonizing of the various processes to "manufacture" Europeans. And distrust is shown toward neighbors whenever there is an issue of protecting borders, hence, whenever there is an issue of immigration.

The case is more complicated, since the challenge to immigration policies, political asylum, and access to citizenship in each of the countries conveys and blends a distrust of two categories of foreigners: those from outside and those from inside. The speeches of Interior Minister Charles Pasqua in the debates on his new measures concerning the law of nationality, identity checks, and immigration, are revealing in this respect: "To keep control of its identity, France intends to define its own situation, the quality and origin of those who are or will be associated with the national community in the spirit of the values of its republic, in the framework of its constitution, and in the respect of the international law it has freely accepted."[16]

In Germany, article 16 of the Basic Law concerning asylum seekers was also a hot subject in the early 1990s. Debates on revoking that article included speeches similar to those of the French interior minister: "It is the right of self-determination of nations, a right that prevails over the right of residence. That right of self-determination derives from the sovereignty of the state; it is independence from all foreign authority, the power to decide the political, economic, social, and cultural development of one's own country."[17]

Ultimately, each of the two countries has developed an argument dictated by its own conception of an "evil" resulting from the presence of foreigners: France fears the nonidentification of the French of foreign origin with the national community; Germany suspects asylum seekers of abusing the right of residence. Moreover, there is also a xenophobia that finds justification in the economic depression affecting all European countries. In sum, that "evil" from elsewhere leads to the assertion of a "right of self-determination" that restates the rights of minorities or oppressed peoples within Europe, a development that increases existing tensions between immigrants, the majority, and the states. The loss of trust in the universality of the nation-states among immigrants or their descendants makes them resort to another concept of universality, of a space where foreigners who reside in Europe, or even citizens seen as foreigners, are included in a plurality of cultures just like those cultures that refer to traditional national identities. This, at least, is their new representation of Europe.

Transnationality and Nationality

In the early 1990s, more than 13 million "foreigners" (non-Europeans) were living legally in the twelve countries of the European Community. Sixty percent of the foreigners in France and 70 percent of those in Germany and in the Netherlands are citizens of countries outside the European Community. Of this group, France has absorbed most of the North Africans (820,000 Algerians, 516,000 Moroccans, and 200,000 Tunisians), and Germany has taken the largest number of Turks (almost 2 million). In the Netherlands, the Turks (160,000) and the Moroccans (123,000) constitute most of the non-European immigrants, and Great Britain is characterized by a preponderance of groups from India (689,000), the West Indies (547,000), and Pakistan (406,000).[18]

These groups are increasingly organized into transnational networks and find a fulcrum in the new political space of the European Union. In fact, even if immigration and integration policies still refer to national jurisdictions, the descendants of immigrants take refuge in the solidarities expressed by a common nationality, ethnicity, and religion, which cut across boundaries. This was especially apparent at the signing of the Maastricht Treaty, when some activists among the immigrants demonstrated their desire to go beyond European national frameworks and spoke of a thirteenth population or a thirteenth state or even a thirteenth nation to emphasize their membership in a "transnational community."

Some of the networks that fuel this border-crossing vision are the result of local initiatives, others are established by institutions of the European Union, particularly the European parliament, and still others are promoted by the home countries. But all of them help the activists develop political strategies and mobilization beyond states. "We have to get used to addressing supranational organizations, to achieving an organization in Strasbourg or Brussels that will be European and will cut through," said one association leader in Marseille.

Transnational Strategies and National Realities

Yet, as we have seen, the initiatives that immigrants undertake mainly indicate their desire to integrate in the country of settlement. Even if efforts carried out for that purpose have contributed in some respects to shaping "separate communities," immigrants regard such communities as indispensable structures for negotiating with the public authorities for the recognition of collective identities constructed in national frameworks. The objective is clear: a political representation to defend the rights of residence, housing, and employment connected with consideration of that identity. This goal can be defined and obtained within the national framework. However, initiatives on the transnational level are located a priori beyond interactions and negotiations with states. In addition, the associations also rely on the process of constructing a united Europe, especially on its expected development in a political space open to other negotiations. As one association leader in Marseille stated in an interview: "It was harder to negotiate the plan with the Departments or the District than with the European Community, which accepted it at the outset, while we couldn't get a meeting with the lowest official of the District."

Thus, every demand at the national level now implies a simultaneous pressure at the European level. Similarly, every claim at the European level may affect the national decisions of each member state. As one of the leaders of the Union of African Workers in France said: "We immigrants from 'third world' countries have to organize and defend ourselves, raise high demands, because most of our recommendations that are accepted by the European Community and often favor us are not always looked on with favor by the member countries. . . . Let us act so that what is positive on the European scale can reverberate in the individual countries."

In short, consolidating transnational solidarities may influence states outside the Union. But the expectations this conceals among immigrant networks emphasize the paradox of transnationality. In fact, if the objective of a border-crossing structure is to reinforce the states' representation at the European level, its practical goal is mainly to end up with national recognition. Needless to say, even leaders who are most active at the European level depict the states as the only opponents they have to contend with in the final analysis.

This predominance of the states is also felt in the associations' difficulty in coordinating their activities and demands. How can they define a common denominator that can unite the various initiatives? Initially, the act of shaping networks was legitimated by social, economic, political, and legal motives corresponding to the main concerns of European public opinion—both immigrant and nonimmigrant—unemployment (67 percent) and racism.[19] Thus, associations whose activities are most supported by the welfare states of the member countries are those that mainly attempt to organize into transnational networks. As for their leaders, they develop a discourse on equal rights and the universality of human rights, seeing the transnational effort as a way to fight racism and xenophobia globally.

The Immigrant Forum

The budgetary policy of European Union institutions makes their task easier. Since 1986, the European Parliament, in particular, has made funds available to so-called immigrant associations to coordinate their activities. This initiative generated a new transnational structure, the Immigrant Forum, which aims to become a "place of expression for noncommunity groups living in Europe, in which they can share their demands but also circulate information from European authorities."[20] According to the monitor of the Immigrant Forum for the Committee of the European Communities, the goal is to obtain for nationals of Third World countries "the same opportunities and rights as the natives, and thus to compensate for the absence of democracy." The explicit objective is to mount a legal opposition to the rise of racism in various European countries.

In principle, the Immigrant Forum unites the associations of immigrants formed primarily by nationality of origin and not legal affiliation, as, for example, associations of young descendants of North African immigrants in France, who are mostly French citizens, or of blacks in Great Britain, who hold British citizenship. The issue, however, is not nationality but ethnicity. Moreover, the organization's ability is measured by the multiplicity of nationalities represented, the number of branches, the extent of the networks, the plurality of sectors they cover (economic, social, cultural), and, of course, how representative they are in the countries where they are located.

These criteria recall not only the ambiguity of a European identity to be defined, which will be analyzed later. Nor do they correspond completely to the real motives of the activists. The stated objective of European authorities forces them, in reality, to conceal their identity concerns in their strategies of recognition of "non-European Europeans." British activists, for example, reject the term *immigrant*, considering it inappropriate to their situation. They want to see a law on the equality of the races appear in Europe as in Great Britain; an organization named SCORE (UK), for Standing Conference on Racial Equality, emerged in 1990, expressing publicly the fear of a Europe that would define its own identity by exclusions, in terms not only of the legal status of foreigners but also of race and racism.

In reality, the main criterion of the network structure comes down to identity. Presumed identities of origin, or an identity of circumstance, to use Jean Leca's term again,[21] constructed in relation with the states and institutionalized through associations, do in fact form links in the boundary-crossing chain. This is confirmed by the local activities of some associations, which now include cultural exchange programs such as concerts and discussions throughout Europe to delineate a sphere of identity and to define their social and legal position in the Union.

Do they all agree on the meaning of *transnationality*? For the Algerians in France, for example, *transnational* refers mainly to relations between France and Algeria.[22] The Turks, however, "are overrepresented in the Immigrant Forum," said Giuseppe Callovi, the specialist in European immigration policy within the European Community. The difference is obviously explained by the influence of the past, which hangs over initiatives, curbs the activities of the Algerians because of their relation with France, and shows Turkey's historical indifference toward the countries of immigration, hence their dispersion throughout Europe. But in most cases, all associations are created and developed in reaction to the French, German, British, or Dutch contexts, and by and large, they have trouble finding a common base with which to coordinate their activities at the European level.

The Informal Networks and Islam

And Islam? If identity provides the cement of the networks, Islam is the hard core. Representatives of Islamic associations work mainly in conjunction with the home countries or with the help of international organizations or both. The home countries try to rally their nationals to obtain the European authorities' recognition for their (extracommunity)

country. Thus, they reactivate their loyalties through religion and contribute to the creation of a transnational community. The international
organizations interested in Islam in Europe mobilize resources to allow
Islam to go beyond the national diversity of Muslims living in the various countries of the Union, to create a single religious identification
and a transnational solidarity based on that. Because of this policy,
these denominational networks have fitted into the European system
and rival the sociocultural associations on a local level.

Yet coordinating the Islamic networks in Europe may be even harder
than coordinating the associations defined as social, because, although
the Islamic associations are autonomous with respect to the welfare
state of the various European countries, they relate like the so-called
cultural associations to the public authorities of the countries of residence. "I try not to take a position that goes beyond the borders. We
are in France, and our goal is to defend Islam in France," said the leader
of the National Federation of Muslims in France. Similarly in Germany—as in the Netherlands—the Islamic associations are part of the
federations of associations grouped by nationality that are seeking representation as a minority in the country of settlement.

Another difficulty comes from the diversity of the nationalities, sects,
and ethnocultural groups among the Muslims in Europe. Some association groups are concerned about European representation and present
themselves as multinationals, collecting several nationalities of origin
while branching out in the various countries of the Union, like the
Jamaat-Tabligh organization, which is also called Faith and Practice in
France. This organization is of Indian origin and was first established in
Great Britain in the 1960s. Since then it has extended its networks into
France and Belgium, and recently into Germany and the Netherlands,
sending missionaries into local communities to promote the faith of the
Muslims and, obviously, to get them to support the organization.[23] This
movement "transcends not only material boundaries but also sects,
legal schools, and Sufi orders in their ideological conception," and its
activists express the desire "to be good citizens," avoiding all political
positions, since according to them "politics divides Islam."[24]

However, other Islamic associations openly express the political position of Islam in the international system. Nevertheless, most of them
remain confined to the nationality they represent, and especially to the
political parties they serve as spokesmen in Europe. This is the case, for
example, of the National Vision, the affiliate of the religious Party of
Prosperity in Turkey (Refah Partisi) and later Party of Virtue (Fazilet),
which created the Organization of the National Vision (AMGT) in
Europe, with its twenty-eight foreign offices, ten of them in Germany,
and its own "multinational vision." Opposing the consular network of

religious affairs of the Turkish state (Diyanet), the organization's activists are trying to create a transnational solidarity based on a political identity expressed through religion, which actually remains Turkish. Algerian networks of the Islamic Front of Salvation or those of its armed branch, the GIA, pursue the same objectives of political legitimation with their followers. If these networks are necessarily transformed into structures of absorption in the name of the religious or political identification they share with Muslims in other countries, their presence affects both Europe and the home countries, especially overall relations between Europe and the entire Muslim bloc.

In short, Islam in Europe is seeking unity in its diversity. But since the organizations claiming to represent it are generally outside the formal networks of the Immigrant Forum, they intensify their development of a system of solidarity based on religion. Yet, as with social and cultural networks, their strategy is to obtain recognition of identities that are primarily national and ethnic. Despite the influence of the home countries or the international organizations that endow them with political importance, their claims are adapted to the European context. They also raise a question of representation in European institutions, especially since the European Convention of Human Rights (ECHR) recognizes freedom of religion. Article 9 of the ECHR states that "every person has the right to freedom of thought, of conscience, and of religion. This right implies the freedom to have or to adopt a religion or conviction of one's choice, as well as the freedom to demonstrate one's religion or conviction, individually or collectively, in public or in private, through worship and instruction, the practice and performance of rituals."[25]

"POSTNATIONAL CITIZENSHIP" AND EUROPEAN IDENTITY

The networks of transnational solidarity have introduced a new practice of political participation both into united Europe and into the nation-states, allowing non-European resident national agents to assert their autonomy with regard to territorially defined state systems. By demanding equality of rights and treatment, they are trying to promote their status as European citizens in the new political sphere that is taking shape.

Several discussions of European citizenship, nationality, and identity have accompanied the gradual transformation of one big single market in a political sphere. Jean-Marc Ferry has proposed a postnational model to emphasize that the nationalist principle was swept away by the construction of a political Europe.[26] And Jürgen Habermas has developed the concept of constitutional patriotism to underline the separation between the sense of belonging implied by national citizenship and its legal practice beyond the frameworks of the nation-state.[27] Considering immigrants of non-European descent, Yasemin Soysal defines as postnational the adoption of international norms referring to the person or residence, and not to legal citizenship.[28]

This postnational concept of belonging generates normative discourses concerning the necessary definition of a new model of citizenship. But European projects do not always follow these discourses. Legally, the Maastricht Treaty maintains the bond between national citizenship and citizenship of the Union. In particular, article 8 of the treaty states that any person with nationality in one of its member states is a citizen of the Union. Thus defined, the citizen has the right to move about freely in the European space, the right to stay freely on the territory of the member states, and even the right to vote in municipal and European elections in a member state where he or she is not a national but simply a resident. The last point reduces citizenship to a political practice (partial voting rights), separates it from nationality (national identity), and introduces a de facto notion of extraterritoriality of citizenship.

The Maastricht Treaty also mentions that the "states must specify, for information, what persons must be considered as their nationals." This is what Germany has done by defining *German nationals* (*Staatsangehörige*). Note that in official German discussions this concern for precision has led to an increase in the use of the term *national* in reference to foreigners, particularly Turks. Further, Germany seems to have been increasingly inspired by European norms when dealing with immigrants. Is this a substitute (if only a linguistic one) for the ethnic reference to German citizenship and nationality that would grant East Germans the status of citizens of the Union, since they claim German ancestry, which gives them the right "to be German"? In this case, would the "Turkish nationals" living in Germany since the 1960s be returned to their nationality of origin, as another "ethnic" identity?

Institutional Practices and European Identity

Nevertheless, the practices that challenge the adaptability of national citizenship within European legal frameworks are far from designing a postnational citizenship. Europe has been built instead on supranational institutions whose conception and functioning are opposed to the postnational concept. Whereas postnationalism would lead to a recognition of cultural diversity and an acceptance of pluralism as a foundation of European membership, supranationalism maintains national models, as exemplified by the European parliament's creation of the Immigrant

Forum. In fact, like the welfare states of the member nations, the European parliament has devoted funds to launch competition between various local and national associations, either independent or organized into federations of associations, as long as they represent non-European immigrants according to their nationality (even a nationality of origin for those who have acquired citizenship in the country of residence).

However, the criteria for admitting associations to the Immigrant Forum reflect several contradictions about the concept of European citizenship and identity. The terminology itself illustrates the ambiguity of the definitions of *immigrant* and *foreigner*. The term *immigrant* refers mainly to representations of a real or imaginary social situation. So, the forum uses it to designate immigrants from outside the European community and hence distinct from the "European national," and the term *foreigner* simply indicates the national of a Third World country. But does this concern only immigrants who have no political rights either in their country of residence or in their non-European community nationality? Considering the differences of citizenship laws in the various countries of the European Community, can the descendants of immigrants acquire nationality in the host country? Or, considering colonial relations, even if another group does have citizenship in the host country from the beginning, do its members experience the same rejection as foreigners because of their religious, ethnic, or racial characteristics? This is the case, for example, with some North Africans in France, blacks in Great Britain, and Surinamans and Indonesians in the Netherlands. Or is the whole group simply excluded from a European identity both because of its present or past nationality and because of its color or religion, which for immigrants from outside the European Community often corresponds to nationality? Is this not the construction of a European identity based on the rejection of the Other, a foreigner within, or a "foreign minority" in contrast to regional minorities?

Where do we place the emigrants from European countries that exported manpower in the 1950s and 1960s? They came from Spain, Portugal, Italy, and Greece, countries currently represented in the European Parliament but whose nationals live in France and Germany, to mention only those two countries. These groups qualify as immigrants because of their social status, are perceived as foreigners in their host countries, and are as affected as non-Europeans by the social problems resulting from that status. Yet these European immigrants and their associations are not part of the forum.[29]

The very fact that the forum includes only associations representing immigrants from Third World countries amounts to excluding them from the incipient European identity. Yet, just as in the United States, a country of immigration since it was founded and where the various waves have contributed to defining the American nation, in Europe non-European immigrants feed the hope held out by the European Parliament to participate in the construction of Europe and to contribute to forging its identity. This hope stems from their perception of a European identity as "soft" in contrast to the "hard" national identities that are the product of common experiences rooted in memory and history, and hard to penetrate for immigrants. But, in practice, by forming the Immigrant Forum, the European parliament has created a gap between European immigrants and non-European immigrants. A future can at least be imagined when the permanent presence of these non-European immigrants would create an official status of European resident with specific political rights. But for the time being, official European initiatives have been producing only a minority.

Nationality or European Citizenship?

This minority is defined by a current or original non–European Community nationality, and its representation by the Immigrant Forum assumes an ethnoreligious aspect. In this sense, it reinforces the nationalist sentiments expressed by the member states confronting the European construction. But the immigrant activists' political commitment to equal rights on the national and European levels is accompanied by a new language about citizenship. "We are European citizens; we are part of the European landscape," said one association leader. They see the European landscape as only a spiderweb of networks of solidarity and interests spread over a territory that now covers fifteen countries. They maintain that their presence in that web confers a right to participate in shaping Europe, which is justified by their commitment to a new political space offering everyone the legal status of citizen of the Union, or at least, of a European resident in one of the member nations, often for nearly thirty years.

"European residents" active in shaping the transnational networks who identify with European society clearly refers particularly to the relations of the Turks with German society. The difference between Germany and united Europe is that the Turks came to Germany long after the state was built and are not part of the nation. But as European residents, they are on German territory at a moment when a political bloc is being established, and they contribute to shaping its identity. Their exclusion from political projects resembles the exclusion of American blacks in the eighteenth century, owing to the Revolution that prevented them from shaping the national identity. For the "non-nationals" of one of the member nations, citizenship thus implies a responsibility in shaping the new "community of fate."

However, association activists who claim to be European residents have trouble defining a suitable status. "Somewhere we are Europeans, citizens of Europe. If we are not European citizens, at any rate, we consider ourselves citizens of Europe," said one association leader. "As for obtaining nationality, we would have preferred it to be a European nationality in order to move freely," he added. While nationality in the framework of a nation-state brings identity and the right of citizenship, in that leader's discourse, the right of citizenship assumes a legal scope in the sense that access to Union citizenship would have to involve the right of free movement.

The confusion is significant. Imbued with a republican tradition, the confusion refers to citizenship on a cultural basis and to nationality as a source of rights. Alain Touraine also stated this: "I want to acquire a European nationality and keep French citizenship." Touraine's reasoning was based on the separation of state and society and connected nationality to the state and citizenship to society.[30] But by separating nationality from citizenship, which are inseparable in republican logic, he comes close to a liberal tradition that defines citizenship, according to Habermas, as "conceived on the model of belonging to an organization that guarantees a legal position and locates the individual outside the state."[31]

Thus, discourses about political Europe pile up, and they are similar or they clash. Their polysemy illustrates the upheaval of the model of the nation-state and the difficulty of breaking away from it, and it emphasizes its incompatibility with European reality. A model of a European state and of a European society necessarily covers a multitude of national, regional, ethnic, and religious affiliations. According to this logic, it is up to the individual, the citizen, to combine and classify loyalties. As the leader of the Association of Moroccans in France put it: "Today we must no longer consider ourselves 'Moroccans,' but as belonging to the European community, Frenchmen of Moroccan origin." He could have added "of the Muslim denomination" without threatening either French laïcité or secular Europe but simply to express an attachment to a religious culture, which, like "Moroccan origin," conveys an attachment to a tradition, a history, and, of course, a religion. Those of Algerian, Tunisian, Turkish, or any other origin might also be part of a "minority belonging to the European community": an ethnic-national, and not a regional, minority determined by the norms of the European Council or a Muslim religious minority in a Judeo-Christian and multidenominational Europe.

The principle of these multiple identifications deriving from the logic of the idea of a political Europe generates the passionate arguments that have accompanied its construction. They illustrate the weakness of the nation-states confronting the demands of identity expressed both within national boundaries and through the intra-European competition created by distinct political projects.

But at the same time, the irrationality of national sentiments reduced to ethnic belonging contrasts with the rationality of European institutions. Eager for harmony, these institutions define legal norms, particularly in the areas of human rights and minority rights, which now affect "foreigners inside" more than the nationals of a member nation of the Union. The supranational institutions that produce norms and the transnational organizations that produce identity put the nation-states at the core of the negotiations as a condition of their permanence as a framework for political legitimacy.

Conclusion

PARADOXES

Relations between states and immigrants are often expressed in terms of conflicts of identities and allegiances. These raise questions about the nature of the national community, about boundaries between the universal and the particular, and about the concept of democracy. In practice, managing identities elucidates managing the paradoxes generated by the discrepancy between principles and reality, between discourse and action, between rhetoric and policy. This makes the definition of a model difficult and rather irrelevant. Republicanism or liberalism as rules shaping models remains a set of abstract ideas leading to programs of political action that are often "irrational" even though they rely on a historical narrative that is rational. Practice, however, leads to policies of adjustment. Resorting to pragmatic measures becomes the only way to allow the definition of a new historical compromise. This is even more so in the European context, especially since building a political Europe raises the problem of transnationality and of communities that might enjoy certain advantages without having a guaranteed political status in the framework of the nation-states.

This leads to negotiations that guide the political actions of both the states and the groups. These negotiations are about developing new codes of coexistence by redefining some values or reinforcing others in order to calibrate the idea of a united nation-state with the de facto pluralism of modern societies and its institutional representation, to guarantee a historical continuity, and to recognize the unique features that crop up in the public space; in short, to reestablish the bond between the state and civil society, ending in a reconstruction of the social and political pact.

The option of negotiation appears a priori as a moderate solution. It seeks primarily to respond to a conflict that is itself moderate. In fact, both the identity demands of the descendants of immigrants in Western Europe and their modes of organization are altogether different from the nationalist revival movements that have produced territorialized ethnic conflicts in the Balkans, Lebanon, and Turkey. Demands for the recognition of the special religious features of the North Africans in France or of an ethnic-national identity of the Turks in Germany are integrated by and large into the framework of political expression, which are under pressure from national and international efforts and move simply toward a "right of difference" as a new basis for the democratic method. Indeed, the idea of emancipation, based on assimilation as a principle of equality, justice, and modernity that once characterized the shaping of nation-states and implied the universal participation of individuals in the many social and political interactions demanded by citizenship, no longer corresponds to current expectations. Now emancipation refers to the recognition of cultural, religious, and ethnic differences as the criteria of democratic societies,[1] and this demand leads Western states today to define compensatory measures for those "excluded from assimilation."

This produces a series of pernicious results and paradoxes which are ultimately tantamount to the paradoxes of democracy itself.[2] Although a "policy of difference" and the recognition it implies go beyond the division between the private and the public, they create other divisions concerning identities. In France, in the 1980s, the devices promoting a social integration of immigrants relied in large part on public aid to allow cultural diversity to be organized and identities to be asserted. In Germany, where the foreigner is perceived primarily as belonging to an ethnic-national group, plans for integration aim to include him or her in German corporatism as a vehicle of communities of interest. Thus, in both countries, policies to remove social inequalities stemming from cultural differences have shown identities to be the only legitimate bases of political action. From this perspective, prior shaping into communities—ethnic-cultural and religious ones this time—has become a tactic necessary to ending up with an ultimate legal recognition of declared special features and to negotiate these with the authorities. Hence, the states have been led to evoke the founding values of the nation they still protect and to negotiate them with the groups that express other identifications and allegiances. But in return these groups had to provide a firmer definition of identity elements, which they could use to form themselves into a community in their search for a recognition whose limits were included in the legitimacy of the host states. From this perspective, the North Africans defined solidarities around Islam confronting laïcité in France, and Turkish nationals have formed as an ethnic minority confronting the concept of German citizenship and nationality.

As a result, the French and German states determine not only the immigrants' social and cultural organizations but also an identity around which such an organization can be structured in order to be officially recognized. But at the same time, in France and Germany, the demands that correspond to this choice reflect a malfunction of the state, which challenges the representations of national traditions and, in some respects, produces a power balance between a community seen as dissident and the national political community. In France, discussions of laïcité and the church-state relationship, which is ambiguous but highly charged, have led Muslim groups to take a position on the religious field as a legitimate one. In Germany the "dream of unity" has led the Turks to react by demanding recognition as an ethnic minority as part of the Turkish nationality but that also implicitly includes the Muslim religion. They thus challenge the identity-citizenship bond, which is as central as laïcité in France. In the United States, the criterion of race was also permanently established after discussions of multiculturalism and policies of affirmative action, which attempted to develop equality of opportunity between the various communities, particularly between blacks and whites.

THE LIMITS OF RECOGNITION

Negotiating identities depends on defining the limits of the possible recognition of differences. The recognition of a national minority, as the Turks demand in Germany, would maintain separate identities, and the lack of a right to citizenship also emphasizes that separation and thus challenges the meaning of democracy and endangers its practice. However, the recognition of a Muslim "religious minority" in France, where some citizens would express their commitment to Islam, would not conflict with secularity either empirically or normatively if it is defined as state neutrality toward denominational issues. On the contrary, recognizing Islam officially would allow it to develop within the framework of representative institutions away from the influence of the home country. Not recognizing it, however, raises the problem of equality and representation among the various religions in France. In Germany recognition of Islam would also be integrated into the religious pluralism that is already constructed institutionally and in which a large majority of the Turkish population might be recognized. In both cases, it remains a question of a balance between civil society and the state, or of a bond between cultural diversity and citizenship, which does not threaten either civic principles or the final identity of the collective as a whole.

Nevertheless, the demand for recognition is a source of tension fueled by mutual distrust, which generates increasingly exclusive discourse. This is why, in France and Germany, public or quasi-public social or cultural institutions are perceived only in their strictly utilitarian role or results. Although they have guaranteed the political socialization of the immigrant actors they have rallied, they have not managed to persuade the activists to identify with the national political community. On the contrary, because the function of these institutions has been limited to "favors" of subsidies in the cultural field, they have reinforced the identity assertion within the community organizations created by their initiative. This phenomenon is accompanied by rhetoric referring to the "imagined traditions" of the public authorities who have removed the immigrant, the foreigner, from the historical narrative of the assimilationist host nations by creating an identity "reappropriation" of its own in that narrative. As a result, this process feeds the political campaigns of parties hostile to announced or demanded "differences" and contributes to transforming the subject of immigration and identities into a battlefield where other parties take positions. At the same time, the lip service of government measures for or against immigrant groups reinforces the identity divisions that then appear in the classic dualism of victim and hero. In short, compensatory policies that aim at reducing social inequalities paradoxically promote the expression of cultural differences and identification.

INCLUSIVE INDIFFERENCE

This is the dilemma that indicates the limits of the democratic method. If recognition of differences also leads to the glorification of "exclusivity," can an "inclusive indifference" be imagined? An indifference that, as far as identity is concerned, corresponds to a principled refusal to distinguish any origin at all, either religious, cultural, or linguistic, within the process of assimilation (article 2 of the French constitution). But when, precisely in those circumstances, the identity expression is based on social arguments such as unemployment and poverty, that notion of indifference then raises the problem of collective responsibility. The persistence of ethnicity in urban zones with a heavy concentration of immigrants appears to be the product of social immobility and raises the problem of social justice and the reallocation of resources. From this perspective, indifference perceived and experienced as political indifference toward social inequalities can no longer be described as inclusive.

The desire to reject differentiation a priori is certainly a legitimate response to a need to monitor distinctions that are promoted by social, political, or media discourse and that prevent the descendants of immigrants from identifying with the state and its institutions. For, as Charles Taylor has correctly emphasized, "It is hard to conceive of a democratic state that really lacks every identifying dimension."[3] And the political agents among the descendants of immigrants express a desire to be part of the political "we" and are careful to refer to their commitment to the "general interest." They try to demonstrate their appropriation of values defined as republican and universal in France or as democratic in Germany. In France they outline projects that combine a certain "laïcist particularism" and a "negotiated Islam." In Germany they attempt to reconcile the exercise of citizenship and dual nationality, a citizenship that refers to a legal concept of territorial rights as a means of access to political rights, separate from nationality, which refers to the country of origin, as a sociocultural reference, separate from the citizenship that is demanded.

Nevertheless, in that vein, belonging to a separate community, shaped mainly by government policies, does not undermine allegiance to the nation-state. On the contrary, in both Germany and France, it takes shape within the institutions recognized by the nation-state to such an extent that the phenomenon of recognition responds to a form of emancipation in principle. But unlike the emancipation of the Enlightenment, which separates religion from public life and the individual from the community in order to guarantee the individual's "essential identification" with the national community, the demand for recognition expressed by some immigrants is generated by a desire for participation based on equal rights recognized for religious or ethnic identities, but within the framework of the state with regard to its own legitimacy. Such a concept of recognition is thus part of a new path to political assimilation, interpreted both as an individual and a collective means of access to modernity.

Thus, state policies engender most of the paradoxes between discourse and action or between principles and reality in the treatment of identities. But, as T. H. Marshall has emphasized with relation to social citizenship, "social behaviour is not governed by logic, and . . . a human society can make a square meal out of a stew of paradox without getting indigestion."[4] In the area of identities, the issue is discovering means that can establish mutual trust between states and the descendants of immigrants which would satisfy the immigrant groups' need for identification and combine the verbal indifference of political principles with a practical differentiation recognized as legitimate within national institutions. In fact, the states constitute the only identity frame of reference with enough individual or collective legitimacy to allow dialogue and citizenship, the only political power that allows identities to be negotiated. Even if the construction of a political Europe shatters the classical outlines of the nation-state, it is still the states that will ultimately negotiate the limits of recognition of differences and, as a result, the identities that can be expressed.

Notes

INTRODUCTION

1. For a philosophical elaboration of the discrepancy between ideas and facts, see Dunn, *Contemporary Crisis*.

2. It would be impossible to cite all the works on this subject. See ibid.

3. This is the title of a collection of essays by J. Habermas in its French translation (Paris: Fayard, 2000).

4. See the works of Jean-Marc Ferry.

5. E. Renan, *Qu'est-ce qu'une nation? et autres essais politiques*, ed. J. Roman (Paris: Presse Pocket, 1992).

6. Brubaker, *Citizenship and Nationhood*.

7. Since this book has appeared in French, several comparative studies have made the same observation as well as an analysis of convergences both in policies and the rights of foreigners in various European countries. See Joppke, *Immigration and the Nation-State*; Favell, *Philosophies of Integration*; V. Guiraudon, "Citizenship Rights for Non-Citizens: France, Germany, and the Netherlands, 1974–1994," in *Challenge to the Nation-State*, ed. Joppke; Kopmans and Statham, "Challenging the Liberal Nation-State?"

8. See Weil and Hansen, *Nationalité et citoyenneté*. The articles in this book demonstrate a convergence in policies and laws about citizenship among European countries.

9. See Horowitz and Noiriel, *Immigrants in Two Democracies*.

10. From the perspective of political philosophy, James Tully views these negotiations as a means (without conflict) of arriving at a "constitutionalism of cultural diversity." James Tully, *Strange Multiplicity*.

11. See Skocpol, *States and Social Revolutions*. Evans, Rueschemeyer, and Skocpol, *Bringing the State Back In*. W. Sewell Jr., "Ideologies and Social Revolutions: Reflections on the French Case," *The Journal of Modern History* 57, no. 1 (1985).

12. It would be impossible to cite all the works on the crisis of the nation-state. As a rough guide, see Dunn, *Contemporary Crisis*; some works forthrightly announce the end of the nation-state, and others develop scenarios for "after the nation-state," as indicated by the title of the French translation of a collection of essays by J. Habermas, *L'après État-nation: La nouvelle constellation politique* (Paris: Fayard, 2000).

13. See C. Tilly, "Reflections on the History of the European State-Making," in *Formation of National States*, ed. Rokkan and Tilly.

14. For a typology of the state with different definitions of minorities, see Kymlicka, *Multicultural Citizenship*, especially chap. 2, "Politics of Multiculturalism." The author distinguishes multinational states (states composed of

linguistically and territorially defined national entities) from polyethnic states (the presence of several ethnic communities resulting from immigration), a useful typology for distinguishing two social realities, but not necessarily encompassing every minority situation or pertinent to the nature and degree of mobilization.

15. Soysal, *Limits of Citizenship*.

16. See J. Leca, "Individualisme et citoyenneté," in *Sur l'individualisme*, ed. Birnbaum and Leca.

17. Kymlicka, *Multicultural Citizenship*.

18. Leca, "Nationalité et citoyenneté."

19. The title of an article by R. Debray in *Le Nouvel Observateur*.

20. W. R. Brubaker, ed., *Immigration and the Politics of Citizenship in Europe and North America* (Lanham: University Press of America, 1989), and *Citizenship and Nationhood*.

21. This is the position of Schnapper in *La France de l'intégration*.

22. Schnapper, *La communauté des citoyens*.

23. Todd, *Le destin des immigrés*.

24. M. Wievorka, ed., *La société fragmentée: Le multiculturisme en débat* (Paris : La découverte, 1996).

25. This discussion, of course, extends beyond the context of immigration. It is based on gender studies as well as on regionalism. It refers to all the phenomena of groups that demand recognition in political life. The equality of women in politics or the status of Corsica as an autonomous region has led to the same review of the republic and the idea of the nation-state.

26. See Blondiaux, Marcou, and Rangeon, *La démocratie locale*; Neveu, *Espace public*. And for a comparative perspective of France and the United States, see the works of Loïc Wacquant and Sophie Body-Gendrot.

27. For a collection of several of Habermas's essays on nationality, citizenship, Europe, and the republic, see *L'intégration républicaine*.

28. See the most recent work of Bade and Oltmer, *Aussiedler*.

29. See Ireland, *Policy Challenges of Ethnic Diversity*; and Soysal, *Limits of Citizenship*.

30. This concurs with the idea of a republican and liberal citizen, developed by R. Dagger, which expresses the attachment both to the national community and to a collective identity other than national. See *Civic Virtues*.

31. An institutional assimilation is also a partial answer to the questions raised by W. Kymlicka and W. Norman about governmental policies to promote civic virtues and guarantee a sense of belonging. See W. Kymlicka and W. Norman, eds., *Citizenship in Diverse Societies* (New York: Oxford University Press, 2000).

32. See Lichbach and Zuckerman, *Comparative Politics*.

33. Kastoryano, "Paris-Berlin."

34. I have taken this formulation from Joel S. Migdal, "Studying the State," in *Comparative Politics*, ed. Lichbach and Zuckerman, pp. 208–37.

35. See Berezin, "Fissured Terrain."

CHAPTER 1
THE WAR OF WORDS

1. Aron, *Dimensions de la conscience historique*, chap. 1.

2. Quoted by Weil, *La France et ses étrangers*, p. 62.

3. V. Giscard d'Estaing, "Invasion ou immigration," *Figaro-Magazine* (September 1991).

4. Duroselle, *"L'Invasion."*

5. Y. Lequin, "L'invasion pacifique," in *La Mosaïque France*, pp. 335–52.

6. C. Guillaumin, *Mots*, no. 8 (1984): 43–51.

7. See the same phenomenon in terms of the word *racism*, analyzed by Taguieff, *La force des préjugés*, p. 125.

8. Kastoryano, "Paris-Berlin."

9. V. de Rudder, "La tolérance s'arrête au seuil," *Pluriel-Débat* (1980): 3–15.

10. Between 1989 and 1998, nearly 2.3 arriving Aussiedler were registered; and, counting from 1950, their number has reached 3.9 million, thus putting them in second place after the Gastarbeiter, who officially numbered 7.3 million as of December 31, 1998. See Bade and Oltmer, *Aussiedler*, pp. 9–51.

11. Ibid.

12. See D. Sabbagh, "L'affirmative action aux États-Unis: Construction juridique et enjeux politiques des dispositifs discrimination raciales" (Ph.D. diss., Institut d'Études Politiques de Paris, 2000).

13. Georges, *L'Immigration en France*, p. 11.

14. Girard and Stoetzel, *Français et immigrés*.

15. S. Thernstrom, "American Ethnic Statistics," in *Immigrants in Two Democracies*, ed. Horowitz and Noiriel, pp. 80–112 (quotation on p. 88).

16. R. Silberman, "French Immigration Statistics," in *Immigrants in Two Democracies*, ed. Horowitz and Noiriel, pp. 112–23.

17. Recencement General de la population de 1982, *Les étrangers* (Paris: La documentation Française sous l'égide du ministère des Affaires Sociales et de la Solidarité Nationale, 1992).

18. Report published by INED, INSEE, supported by the DPM (Direction Populations Migrations) and the FAS (Fonds d'Action Sociale).

19. Tribalat, *Faire France*.

20. Le Bras, *Le démon des origines*.

21. Ibid., p. 194

22. The expression introduces the concept of *Heimat*, "home," to specify their local belonging, unlike those who come from somewhere else. The sociologist Barbara Dietz uses this term in her article "Jugendlische Aussiedler in Deutschland: Risiken und Chancen der Integration," in *Aussiedler*, ed. Bade and Oltmer, pp. 153–76. It is also picked up by President Johannes Rau in his speech to the Haus der Kulturen der Welt of May 12, 2000.

23. *Daten und Fakten zur Ausländersituation*, July 1992 (Mitteilungen der Beauftragten der Bundesregierung für die Belange der Ausländer).

24. Bade and Oltmer, *Aussiedler*.

25. Isaacs, *Idols of the Tribe*, pp. 71–93.

26. The title of an article by Radtke, "Lob der Gleich Gültigkeit."

27. Costa-Lascoux, *De l'immigré au citoyen*, p. 10.

28. Gleason, "Pluralism and Assimilation."

29. Actually, the debate on Americanism began before World War I. See Horace M. Kallen's essay "Democracy vs. the Melting Pot," published in *The Nation* and reprinted in his *Culture and Democracy*; see also the meaning of Americanism in the same book.

30. Gordon, *Assimilation in American Life*.

31. Glazer, "Is Assimilation Dead?"

32. Alba and Nee, "Rethinking Assimilation Theory"; see also Gans, "Toward a Reconciliation."

33. Costa-Lascoux, *De l'immigré au citoyen*, pp. 10–11.

34. Gaspard, "Assimilation, insertion, intégration."

35. J.-C. Barrault, *De l'Islam en général et du monde en particulier* (Paris: Éditions Le Pré aux Clercs, 1991).

36. D. Lüderwaldt, "Integration (politisch-programmatisch)," in *Handwörterbuch Ausländerarbeit*, ed. G. Auernheimer (Basel: Weinheim, 1984), pp. 177–79, quoted by Treibel, *Migration in modernen Gesellschaften*.

37. His ambitions and intentions are developed in a book he wrote in 1992: Cohn-Bendit and Schmidt, *Heimat Babylon*.

38. Y. Lequin, "L'étrangeté française," in *La Mosaïque France*, p. 372.

39. Taguieff, *La force des préjugés*, p. 125.

CHAPTER 2
REPRESENTATION OF POLITICAL TRADITIONS

1. B. Anderson, *Imagined Communities*.

2. See Schnapper, *La communauté des citoyens*.

3. For the construction of models, see Brubaker, *Citizenship and Nationhood*; Dumont, *France-Allemagne et retour*; and Schnapper, *La France de l'intégration*.

4. Pierre Nora, *Les lieux de mémoire* (Paris: Gallimard, 1987).

5. In reference to Eugen Weber's classic book *Peasants into Frenchmen*.

6. S. Rokkan, "The Formation of the Nation-State in Western Europe," in *Building States and Nations*, ed. S. N. Eisenstadt and S. Rokkan (London: Sage Publications, 1973).

7. Schnapper, *La France de l'intégration*, p. 100.

8. J. G. Fichte, *Addresses to the German Nation*, ed. George Armstrong Kelly (New York: Harper & Row, 1968), p. 89.

9. Brubaker, *Citizenship and Nationhood*, p. 9.

10. All quotations are taken from Schlesinger Jr., *The Disuniting of America*, pp. 12, 32–33.

11. Beaune, *Naissance de la nation France*, p. 344.

12. Gordon, *Assimilation in American Life*, p. 135.

13. See B. Badie and P. Birnbaum, *Sociologie de l'État* (Paris: Grasset, 1979);

G. Wilson, "L'État américain: Images et réalités," and D. Lacorne, "Aux origines du fédéralisme américain: Impossibilité de l'État," pp. 38–53, in Toinet, *L'État en Amérique*, pp. 21–38.

14. Marienstras, *Nous, le peuple*.

15. In reference to Hobsbawm and Ranger, *The Invention of Tradition*.

16. J.-P. Azéma and M. Winock, *La Troisième République* (Paris: Hachette-Calmann-Lévy, 1991), pp. 160–67.

17. H. Müller, "De l'*Aufklärung* à Weimar: Mouvement des idées et mutations politiques," in *L'État de l'Allemagne*, by A.-M. LeGloannec (Paris: La découverte, 1995), pp. 33–37.

18. Dumont, *France-Allemagne*.

19. Von Thadden, "Allemagne, France."

20. Nipperdey, *Réflexions sur l'histoire allemande*, pp. 222–45.

21. See M.-F. Toinet, "L'empire des Dieux," *Le nouveau politis* (November–December 1993): pp. 67–72.

22. Nicolet, *L'idée républicaine en France*.

23. Ibid.

24. I will develop the head scarf issue in chapters 5 and 7.

25. For more details, see Déloye, *École et citoyenneté*, especially chap. 5.

26. Quoted by Azéma and Winock, *La Troisiéme République*, p. 166.

27. This implies that instruction in the private school is controlled by the state and these contracts do not apply to the private and denominational schools in Alsace-Lorraine, a region under the influence of German jurisdiction, which enjoys the religious concordat. See Jerôme Tremeau, France, in Table Ronde: "L'École, la religion et la Constitution," *Annuaire internationale de justice constitutionnelle* 12 (1996): 244–66.

28. Dann, *Nation und Nationalismus*, p. 136.

29. Von Krockow, *Les Allemands du XXe siècle*, p. 14.

30. P. Rosanvallon, *L'État en France de 1798 à nos jours* (Paris: Éditions du Seuil, 1990).

31. For France, see Lequin, *La Mosaïque France*; Noiriel, *Le creuset français*; and Tribalat, *Cent ans d'immigration*. For Germany, the most important historical works are by K. Bade; and see Herbert, *Geschichte der Ausländerbeschäftigung*.

32. For different phases of the immigration of ethnic Germans to Germany, see Münz and Ulrich, "Germany and Its Immigrants."

33. Ibid.

34. Bade, *op. cit.*

35. G. Noiriel, *The French Melting Pot: Immigration, Citizenship, and National Identity*, translated by Geoffroy de Laforcasle (Minneapolis: University of Minnesota Press, 1996).

36. See "The Battle of Numbers" in ch. 1.

37. See Ralph Schor on public opinion concerning foreigners, mainly Italians between the two world wars: *L'opinion française et les étrangers, 1919–1939* (Paris: Publications de la Sorbonne, 1985)

38. Marienstras, *Nous, le peuple*, p. 263.

39. See S. Huntington, *American Politics: The Promise of Disharmony* (Cambridge, Mass: Harvard University Press, 1981).

40. Lieberson, *A Piece of the Pie.*

41. Higham, *Strangers in the Land.*

42. See Henry Rousso, *Le syndrome de Vichy* (Paris: Éditions du Seuil, 1987); Noiriel, *Le creuset français.*

43. Brubaker, *Citizenship and Nationhood.*

44. Jean Mathorez, *Étranger en France sous l'Ancien Régime*, 2 vols. (Paris: Librairie ancienne Éduard Champion Ed., 1919–21).

45. *Être français aujourd'hui et demain*, report of the Commission de la nationalité, presented by M. Marceau Long, chairman, to the prime minister, La documentation Française, coll. "10/18," 1988, f. 2, p. 27.

46. A. Lebon, *Migrations et nationalité en France en 1998* (Paris: La documentation Française, 1999).

47. P. Weil, *Rapport sur l'immigration et la nationalité française* (Paris: La documentation Française, 1998).

48. Lebon, *Migrations.*

49. Schmidt and Weick, "Intégration sociale des étrangers en Allemagne." See also Münz and Ulrich, "Germany and Its Immigrants."

50. Brubaker, *Citizenship and Nationhood.* For a more complete reference, see R. M. Smith, *Civic Ideals.*

51. See Sabbagh, "L'affirmative action."

52. Hobsbawm and Ranger, *The Invention of Tradition*, p. 263.

CHAPTER 3
THE TERRITORIES OF IDENTITY

1. Tocqueville, *Democracy in America*, p. 316.

2. Girard and Stoetzel, *Français et immigrés*, p. 39.

3. Mesnil, "Quelques opinions et attitudes.".

4. *Jahrbuch der Öffentlichen Meinung*, 1968–73.

5. Noiriel, *Le creuset français*, and Tribalat, *Faire France.*

6. *L'État de l'opinion*, annual report of SOFRES, 1991.

7. *Être français aujourd'hui et demain.*

8. Dubet, "Les figures de la ville et la banlieue."

9. Le Galès, Oberti, and Rampal, "Le vote Front national."

10. Yet, specific contracts commit public authorities and HLM enterprises to respect a "quota" limiting the percentage of foreigners in the new ones; see Weil, *La France et ses étrangers*, p. 249.

11. H. Reimann, quoted by Treibel, *Migration in modernen Gesellschaften.*

12. According to the statistics of December 3, 1990, the Turks (including the Kurds) represent 37 percent of the foreign population in northern Westphalia, 30 percent of that of Bade-Würtenberg, and 27 percent of that of Bavaria (*Statistisches Bundesamt*).

13. *Statistisches Landesamt Einwohnerregister*, June 30, 1992.

14. For an analysis of violence in the city, see S. Body-Gendrot, *The Social Control of Cities? A Comparative Perspective* (London: Blackwell, 2000).

15. See H. Gans, *The Urban Villagers* (New York: Free Press, 1962).

16. See P. Echinard and É. Temime, *Histoire des Migrations à Marseille* (Aix en Provence: Edisud, 1989).

17. A. Touraine, "Face à l'exclusion," *Esprit* (February 1991): 5–13.

18. W. J. Wilson, *The Truly Disadvantaged: The Inner City, the Underclass, and Public Policy* (Chicago: University of Chicago Press, 1987). See also K. McFate, R. Lawson, and W. J. Wilson, eds., *Poverty, Inequality, and the Future of Social Policy: Western States in the World Order* (New York: Russell Sage Foundation, 1995).

19. Farin and Seidel-Pielen, *Krieg in den Städten.*

20. E. Anderson, *Street Wise.*

21. G. Balandier, *L'éloge du mouvement* (Paris: Fayard, 1992), p. 199.

22. *Intégrer les quartiers difficiles* (Paris: OECD 1998), p. 82.

23. See Le Galès, "Politique de la ville."

24. Y. Lequin, "Métissages imprudents?" in *La Mosaïque France*, p. 403.

25. Puskeppeleit and Thränhardt, *Vom betreuten Ausländer.*

26. N. Glazer, *Affirmative Discrimination: Ethnic Inequality and Public Policy* (New York: Basic Books, 1987).

27. P. Rosanvallon, *The New Social Question* (Princeton: Princeton University Press, 2000).

28. S. Boulot and D. Boyzon-Fradet, *Les immigrés et l'école, une course d'obstacles: Lectures et chiffres, 1973–1987* (Paris: L'Harmattan, coll. "CIEMI," 1988).

29. This testimony is reported by Weil, *La France et ses étrangers*, p. 263.

30. Discussion in the National Assembly, September 29, 1981, p. 1357.

31. Yahiel, "Le FAS."

32. Statute of December 21, 1958, signed by General de Gaulle, cited in ibid., pp. 107–13.

33. *Médiations dans la ville*, research financed by the Ministry of Health, Social Affairs of the City, the Management of Populations and Migrations, the interministerial delegation to the city, and the Fund of Social Action.

34. Welch-Guerra, "La rénovation urbaine à Berlin."

35. The street is called Orient Strasse by Turks.

CHAPTER 4
THE INVENTION OF THE CULTURAL

1. Alba and Nee, "Rethinking Assimilation Theory," pp. 826–75.

2. Interview with the chair of Nana Beur in France, 1990. The activists of the Association of Women in Berlin formulated a similar thought.

3. M. Hamoumou, *Et ils devenus harkis* (Paris: Fayard, 1993), p. 304.

4. Hérvieu-Léger, *La religion pour mémoire*, p. 178.

5. Balandier, *Le désordre*, p. 36.

6. Ponty, *Polonais méconnus.*

7. Hervieu-Léger, *La religion pour mémoire*, p. 129.

8. My research on Islamic associations in Île-de-France shows that seven Islamic associations out of sixty-six declare that they know the law of 1905, and two have simply heard of it; see Diop and Kastoryano, "Le mouvement associatif."

9. In fact, the law of 1905 that marks the separation of church and state is what gives every religious institution in France legal status.

10. Interview with the secretary-general of the Friends of Islam (1991), which is based in Saint-Denis.

11. Eighty-four percent of the Muslims associate Islam with peace, 64 percent with progress, 62 percent with tolerance, and 61 percent with the protection of women; however, 60 percent of the French see Islam as meaning violence, 66 percent as meaning regression, 71 percent as meaning fanaticism, and 76 percent as meaning the submission of women. See *L'Islam en France*, Poll IFOP, *Le Monde*, RTL, *La Vie*, November 1989.

12. Bosnians (19,904), Moroccans (80,278), Tunisians (28,075), Algerians (14,373), and Egyptians (12,605) are the other major Muslim populations; since the reunification, they have been joined by some African nationalities, whose number was high in the East ("Ausländer am 31-12-1992," in *Deutschland nach der Staatsangehörigkeit*).

13. Kastoryano, "Définir les frontières de l'identité."

14. T. S. Halman, "Islam in Turkey," in *Change and the Muslim World*, by P. Stoddard, D. C. Cutnell, and M. W. Sullivan (Syracuse, N.Y.: Syracuse University Press, 1981), p. 156.

15. S. Mardin, "Din sosyolojisi açisindan islam," (Islam from the point of view of sociology of religion), in *Din ve ideoloji* (Religion and ideology) (Istanbul, 1983), p. 61.

16. The results of the big investigation of the INED and INSEE, published in 1995, emphasize this attitude of community withdrawal of the Turks in France in comparison with other Muslim immigrants; see Tribalat, *Insertion et mobilité géographique*.

17. *Milliyet*, March 10, 1994.

18. Gans, "Symbolic Ethnicity."

CHAPTER 5
THE POLITICIZATION OF IDENTITIES IN FRANCE

1. See Omi and Winant, *Racial Formation in the United States*; Webster, *The Racialization of America*.

2. N. Negrouche, "L'échec des associations franco-maghrébines issues de l'immigration (1980–1990)," *Esprit* (January 1992): 41–52.

3. The idea of cultural intermediaries in the framework of immigration was developed by Thierry Fabre, who emphasized their role in the synthesis of cultural identities and their function of mediation between public authorities and immigrants (*Migrations et société* 4, nos. 22–23 (July–October 1992).

4. See C. Young, *Politics of Cultural Pluralism*; D. D. Latin, "Hegemony and Religious Conflict: British Imperial Control and Political Cleavages in Yorubaland," in *Bringing the State Back In*, ed. Evans, Rueschemeyer, and Skocpol, pp. 285–317; J. F. Bayard, *L'État en Afrique* (Paris: Fayard, 1988), esp. the chapter titled "La pénombre de l'ethnicité."

5. Fuchs, *The American Kaleidoscope*, p. 338.

6. Hobsbawm and Tanger, *The Invention of Tradition*.

7. J. S. Coleman argues that an internal division within a community reinforces the bonds instead of dissolving them, despite divergent views and objectives. See *Individual Interests and Collective Action*.

8. See Kepel, *À l'ouest d'Allah*, particularly pp. 246–52.

9. See *Le Monde*, May 24, 2000. It is worth mentioning that the Alsace and Moselle are two regions in France that were German territory in 1905, at the time of the separation of church and state. Consequently, they apply the system of concordat that goes back to 1801 and gives another status to the church (similar to the German case, where the municipality pays for restorations, for example). In the rest of French territory, the law of 1905 marks a definitive separation between state and church.

10. See Y. Deloye, *École et citoyenneté. L'individualisme républicain de Jules Ferry à Vichy: Controverses* (Paris: Presses de FNSP, 1994).

11. I am grateful to Anne Golup, director of research of the FAS, for this information and relevant documentation.

12. *Les relais féminins de l'immigration africaine en Île-de-France et en Haute-Normandie*, report for the FAS by Sonia Fayman and Micheline Keil, June 1994. See also C. Delcroix, *Médiatrices dans les quartiers fragilisés: Le lien* (Paris: La documentation Française, 1997).

13. S. Fayman and M. Keil, report for the FAS, June 1994.

14. Broadcast of Michèle Cotta, RTL, November 2, 1994.

CHAPTER 6
THE POLITICIZATION OF IDENTITIES IN GERMANY

1. In this chapter, I refer to "Turks," sometimes to "Turkish nationals" or "those from Turkey," according to the context in which they appear: "Turks" in a national framework, "Turkish nationals" in a legal and juridical context, and "those from Turkey" with respect to ethnic and religious differences in Turkey that raise a problem of identification in the country. Of course, in the interviews reported here, the choice of terms is up to the interlocutor.

2. I have borrowed the terminology from the classic work of Francis, *Ethnos und Demos*.

3. See François, *Protestants et catholiques en Allemagne*, p. 239.

4. Ibid., p. 15.

5. T. Schmidt, "Le Christ, garant de la cohésion sociale? Polémique autour d'un arrêt de Karlsruhe," *Courrier international*, no. 252, August 31–September 6, 1995 (reprinted from the *Wochenpost*, Berlin).

6. For the report of the discussions that took place between the chamber and the senate, see L. Capéran, *Histoire contemporaine de la laïcité française: La révolution scolaire* (Paris: Librairie Marcel Rivière & Cie., 1960), pp. 81–137.

7. *Frankfurter Allgemeine Zeitung*, August 12, 1995, p. 1.

8. *Der Spiegel*, no. 45, November 6, 1989.

9. Discussion of the foundation of a private school by the Islam Kolleg l.v. Extract of the protocol of the Committee for the School, February 28, 1990.

10. Conversation with Hans-Thomä Venske, in charge of foreigners for the Evangelical Church in Berlin (April 1993); and see Venske, *Islam und Integration*.

11. This concerns only divisions within a national group. Bosnian organizations, as well as those of Africa, belong to the federation representing all the Muslim populations living in Germany.

12. Interview, Berlin, May 1990.

13. Özcan, *Türkische Immigrantenorganisationen*, p. 23.

14. The Party of Prosperity is an organization that has found a basis among the immigrants and is outlawed in Turkey because of its anti-Kemalist ideology and discourse.

15. F. Sen, *Bonn-Ankara Hatti* (The Bonn-Ankara line) (Cologne: Önal Verlag, 1993), p. 25.

16. Interview, Essen, April 1993.

17. Bielefeld, "L'État-nation inachevé."

19. See P. Gleason, "Minorities (Almost) All: The Minority Concept in American Social Thought," *American Quarterly* 43, no. 3 (September 1991): 324–93.

19. H. Giordon, "Droit des minorités, droit linguistiques, droits de l'homme," in *Les minorités en Europe: Droits linguistiques et droits de l'homme*, ed. H. Giordan (Paris: Éditions Kimé, 1992), pp. 9–39.

20. Peter Katzenstein emphasizes the importance of such institutions in German political decisions and refers to the German state as a "semi-sovereign state."

21. Interview, April 1993.

22. For the definition of *minority* in the framework of Turkey, see Kastoryano, "Intégration politique par l'exterieur."

23. Puskeppeleit and Thränhardt, *Vom betreuten Ausländer*, pp. 106–16.

CHAPTER 7
THE NEGOTIATION OF IDENTITIES

1. IFOP Poll, *Le Monde*, RTL, *La Vie, L'Islam en France*, November 20, 1989.

2. Robert D. Putnam, "Bowling Alone: America's Declining Social Capital," *Journal of Democracy* 1, no. 6 (January 1995): 65–78.

3. Leca, "Nationalité et citoyenneté."

4. Soysal, *Limits of Citizenship*.

5. Also according to J. Habermas's typology. See "Citizenship and National Identity: Some Reflections on the Future of Europe," in *Theorizing Citizenship*, ed. Beiner, pp. 255–83.

6. For citizenship as a sense of belonging and citizenship as commitment, see J. Leca, "Individualisme et citoyenneté," in *Sur l'individualisme*, ed. Birnbaum and Leca, pp. 159–213.

7. R. Solé, *Le Monde*, Friday, June 23, 1989.

8. According to an official statement of the France-Plus association, it sponsored the candidacy of 527 persons, 55 percent of whom appeared on the slate of the Socialist Party, 45 percent on the rightist slates (CDS–Union for French Democracy). Candidates were also urged to join the slate of the extreme Left, the French Communist Party, and the environmentalists.

9. See L. Yalçin-Heckmann, "The Perils of Ethnic Associational Life in Europe: Turkish Migrants in Germany and France," in *Politics of Multiculturalism*, ed. Modood and Werbner.

10. Report of G. Paris and T. Romieu, *La participation des communautés étrangeres à la gestion des municipalités*, course taught by Rémy Leveau, Paris, IEP, April 1989.

11. F. Dazi and R. Leveau, "L'intégration par le politique, le vote des 'Beurs,' " *Études* (September 1988).

12. A. Lebon, *Regards sur l'immigration et la présence étrangère en France* (Paris: La documentation Française, 1990), p. 23; and *Situation de l'immigration: La présence étrangère en France, 1993–1994* (Paris: La documentation Française, 1994), pp. 32–34.

13. For statistical information with commentary, see the annual reports of A. Lebon, *Immigration et présence étrangère en France* (Ministère de l'emploi et de la solidarité—direction de la population et des migrations) (Paris: La documentation Française).

14. *Daten und Fakten zur Ausländersituation* (Bonn: Beauftragte der Bundesregierung für die Belange der Ausländer, July 1992).

15. Note that until 1989 this concerned only West Berlin, and since then, the unified city. *Statistisches Landesamt in Bericht zur Integrations und Ausländerpolitik*, Senat von Berlin, Miteinander Leben in Berlin, Die Ausländerbeauftragte des Senats, March 1994.

16. See Schmidt and Weick, "Intégration sociale." And see Münz and Ulrich, "Germany and Its immigrants."

17. Decision 91/290 DC, status of Corsica (May 9, 1991). According to that decision, the term "Corsican people," as a component of the French people, is contrary to the constitution, which recognizes only the French people, composed of "every French citizen without distinction of origin, race, religion" (art. 2).

18. Lochak, "Les minorités dans le droit public français."

19. Harry Goulbourne develops the concept of "communal option," which he analyzes as a reaction of ethnic minorities confronting the majority and the universal values it defends. Goulbourne, *Ethnicity and Nationalism*, p. 41.

20. "La France vue de l'intérieur: Entretien avec Pierre Joxe," *Débat*, no. 61 (September–October 1990): 15.

21. Interview with A. Boyer, minister of religion, in Ministry of the Interior, *Actes*, April 1992.

22. Lochak, "Les minorités," pp. 111–84.

23. See P. Cohen Albert, *The Modernization of French Jewry: Consistory and Community in the Nineteenth Century* (Waltham, Mass.: Brandeis University Press, 1977).

24. Weil, *Mission d'étude*.

25. "Migrations New Sheet," Brussels, December 1991; quoted in *The Economic and Political Impact of Turkish Migration in Germany*, by Zentrum für Türkeistudien, Essen, March 1993.

26. Statistics of the Union of Turkish Entrepreneurs of Berlin. And see Zentrum für Türkeistudien, *Konsumgewohnheiten und wirtschaftliche Situation des türkischen Bevölkerung in der Bundesrepublik Deutschland*, Essen, September 1992.

27. Article reprinted in *Le courrier international*, no. 152, September 1993.

28. Dahrendorf, *The Modern Social Conflict*, p. 34.

29. F. Sen, "L'intégration des Turcs en RFA et ses limites," *Migrations et société* (May–August 1990).

30. F. Sen and Y. Karakaşoğlu, *F. Almanya'da yaşayan Türklerin ve diğer yabancilarin seçme ve seçilme hakki, partiler ve çifte vatandaşlik üzerine görüşleri* (Opinion of Turks and other foreigners on the right to vote, the parties, and dual nationality in the Federal Republic of Germany), Zentrum für Türkeistudien, Essen, September 1994.

CHAPTER 8
THE EUROPEAN UNION: NEW SPACE FOR NEGOTIATING IDENTITIES

1. Sudre, *Droit international et européen*, p. 91.

2. The tables about political decisions at the national or community level, especially, show "cooperation for the development of Third World countries" first (78 percent in December 1991 and December 1992), while knowing that the questions asked in the polls of *Eurobaromètre*, an official publication of the European institutions, aim at Union. *Eurobaromètre* 38 (December 1992): 40.

3. B. de Witte, "The European Community and its Minorities," in *Peoples and Minorities in International Law*, ed C. Brölmann et al. (The Hague: Kluwer Academic Publishers, 1993), pp. 167–85.

4. Statement of François Mitterrand, quoted by Louis-Edmond Petit in the preface to V. Berger, *Jurisprudence de la Cour européenne des droits de l'homme*, 4th ed. (Paris: Sirey, 1994).

5. Among the twelve member states, the rates for Germany are 46 percent for and 20 percent against; and for France, 45 percent for and 30 percent against (*Eurobaromètre* 38 [December 1992]: 82).

6. See Sudre, *Droit international*, pp. 153–58.

7. Art. 29, para. 1 of the Declaration of the Rights of Man, quoted in ibid., p. 154.

8. *Le Monde*, March 21, 1995.

9. Art. 2 of the proposed convention of 1991, quoted by Sudre, *Droit international*, p. 156.

10. In the table of the fourteen subjects of Maastricht, cooperation on immigration is fourth, with 72 percent for and 17 percent against in 1992, and third in 1993, with 79 percent for and 14 percent against. Moreover, 59 percent of those questioned would agree to a common immigration policy (with 36 percent against) and 59 percent agree to a common policy of political asylum (with 33 percent against). *Eurobaromètre* 38 (December 1992): 32 and 40; and 39 (June 1993): 34.

11. R. Barre et al., "L'Union européenne: De l'espace à la puissance," *Le Monde*, October 29, 1993.

12. Morin, *Penser l'Europe*.

13. Leca, "Après Maastricht."

14. *Eurobaromètre* (July 1994), p. vi.

15. Jacques Chirac demanded that the Council of Ministers see "its rein-

forced role," for it is "the only case that draws its legitimacy from the sovereignty of the states." *Le Monde*, March 17, 1995.

16. *Le Monde*, June 17, 1993, p. 7.

17. Extract from the *Bulletin d'information sur le droit d'asile* of the Information and Documentation Center of the Embassy of the Federal Republic of Germany, June 1993.

18. Sources: *SOPEMI-OCDE, Eurostat, INED.*

19. In 1990, 29 percent of the individuals surveyed wanted to curb the rights of immigrants. In 1992 that rate had risen to 34 percent. Similarly, in 1991 60 percent would have accepted immigrants from the Mediterranean with restrictions, and in 1993 only 46 percent of the population agreed. *Eurobaromètre* 38 (December 1992).

20. C. Neveu, "Citoyenneté ou racisme en Europe: Exception et complémentarité britanniques," *Revue européenne des migrations internationales* 10, no. 1 (1994): 95–109.

21. Leca, "Après Maastricht."

22. R. Leveau, *Le sabre et le turban* (Paris: Éditions François Bourin, 1993), particularly the last chapter.

23. Kepel, *Les banlieues de l'Islam.*

24. M. Diop, "Structuration d'un réseau: La Jamaat-Tabligh (société pour la propagation de la foi)," *Revue europeéenne des migrations internationales* 10, no. 1 (1994): 145–57.

25. Quoted by Leveau, "Éléments de réflexion sur l'Islam en Europe."

26. J.-M. Ferry, "Pertinence du postnational," *Esprit*, no. 11 (November 1991): 80–94.

27. J. Habermas, "Citoyenneté et identité nationale," in *L'Europe au soir du siècle*, ed. Lenoble and Dewandre, pp. 17–39.

28. Soysal, *Limits of Citizenship*, p. 143.

29. In France the strongest reactions come from the Spaniards and Portuguese, and in Germany from the Greeks. Absent from the forum, they also have developed networks parallel to the forum, like the CAIE (Council of Immigrant Associations in Europe), a multinational association since it was created, emanating from the Council of Immigrant Associations in France (CAIF). See P. Ireland, "Facing the True 'Fortress Europe': Immigrants and Politics in the EC," *Journal of Common Market Studies* 29, no. 5 (September 1991): 457–81.

30. Touraine, *Qu'est-ce que la démocratie?* pp. 102–3.

31. J. Habermas, "Citizenship and National Identity in Europe: Some Reflections on the Future of Europe," in Beiner, *Theorizing Citizenship.*

CONCLUSION

1. Touraine, *Qu'est-ce que la démocratie?*

2. See J. Scott, *Only Paradoxes to Offer* (Cambridge, Mass.: Harvard University Press, 1996).

3. Taylor, "Les institutions dans la vie nationale."

4. T. H. Marshall, "Citizenship and Social Class," in *Class, Citizenship, and Social Development: Essays by T. H. Marshall* (Chicago: University of Chicago Press, 1977), pp. 71–257.

Bibliography

Adler, F. "New Racism vs Old Anti-Racism in France." *Telos*, no. 90 (winter 1991–92): 148–56.

Alba, R. D. *Ethnic Identity: The Transformation of White America.* New Haven: Yale University Press, 1990.

Alba, R. D., and V. Nee. "Rethinking Assimilation Theory for a New Area of Immigration." *International Migration Review* 31, no. 4 (winter 1997): 826–75.

Aleinikoff, T. A., and D. Klusmeyer, eds. *From Migrants to Citizens: Membership in a Changing World.* Washington, D.C.: Brookings Institution Press, 2000.

Almond, G., and V. Sidney. *Civic Culture Revisited.* Newbury Park, Calif.: Sage Publications, 1989.

Alund, A., and C. U. Schierup. *Paradoxes of Multiculturalism.* Aldershot: Avebury, 1991.

Amersfoort, V. van. "'Minority' as a Sociological Concept." *Ethnic and Racial Studies* 2, no. 1 (April 1978): 218–34.

Amersfoort, H. van, and B. Surie. "Reluctant Hosts: Immigration into Dutch society, 1970–1985." *Ethnic and Racial Studies* 10, no. 2 (April 1987): 169–85.

Amselle, J.-L. *Logiques métisses: Anthropologie de l'identité en Afrique et ailleurs.* Paris: Payot, 1990.

———. *Vers un multiculturalisme français: L'empire de la coutume.* Paris: Aubier, 1996.

Anderson, B. *Imagined Communities: Reflections on the Origin and Spread of Nationalism.* London: Verso, 1983.

Anderson, E. *Street Wise: Race, Class, and Change in an Urban Community.* Chicago: University of Chicago Press, 1990.

Antunes, G. Gaitz. "Ethnicity and Participation: A Study of Mexican-Americans, Blacks, and Whites." *American Journal of Sociology* 80, no. 5:1192–1211.

Arditti, S. "Labour Migration and the Single European Market: A Synthetic and Prospective Note." *International Sociology* 5, no. 4 (December 1990): 461–74.

Aron, R. *Dimensions de la conscience historique.* Paris: Plon, 1961.

Augé, M. "Culture et imaginaire: La question de l'identité." *Revue de l'Institut de Sociologie* 3–4 (1988).

Bachmann, C., and L. Basier. *Mises en images d'une banlieue ordinaire: Stigmatisations urbaines et stratégies de communications.* Paris: Syros, 1989.

Bachmann, C., and N. Leguennec. *Violences urbaines: Ascension et chute des classes moyennes à travers cinquante ans de politique de la ville.* Paris: Albin Michel, 1996.

Bade, K. J. "Politik in der Einwanderungssituation: Migration—Integration—Minderheiten." In *Deutsche im Ausland—Fremde in Deutschland—Migration in Geschichte und Gegenwart*, edited by K. J. Bade. Munich: Verlag C. H. Beck, 1992.

———. "Trends and Issues of Historical Migration Research in the Federal Republic of Germany." *Migration* 6 (1989): 7–28.

———, ed. *Auswanderer, Wanderarbeiter, Gastarebeiter: Bevölkerung, Arbeitsmarkt und Wanderung in Deutschland seit der Mitte des 19. Jahrhunderts.* Vols. 1 and 2. Ostfilden: Scripta Mercaturae Verlag, 1984.

———. *Population, Labour, and Migration in 19th- and 20th-Century Germany.* New York: Berg, 1987.

Bade, K. J., and M. Weiner. *Migration Past, Migration Future: Germany and the United States.* Providence: Berghahn Books, 1997.

Bade, K. J., and J. Oltmer, eds. *Aussiedler: Deutsche Einwanderer aus Osteuropa.* IMIS-Schriften 8. Osnabrück: Universitätsverlag Rasch, 1999.

Baechler, J. "Dépérissement de la nation?" *Commentaire*, no. 41 (spring 1988): 104–13.

———. "Droits de l'homme ou droits du citoyen?" *Commentaire* 10, no. 39 (autumn 1987): 499–508.

Baker, D., and G. Lenhardt. *Nationalismus und Arbeitsmarktintegration in der BRD.* 1991.

Baker, D. P., et al. "Effects of Immigrant Workers on Educational Stratification in Germany." *Sociology of Education* 58 (October 1985): 213–27.

Balandier, G. *Anthropologie politique.* Paris: PUF, 1984.

———. *Le désordre: L'éloge du mouvement.* Paris: Fayard, 1992.

Balibar, E. "Sujets ou citoyens." *Les temps modernes*, no. 452–54 (1984): 1726–53.

Balibar, E., and I. Wallerstein., eds. *Race, Nation, and Class: Ambiguous Identities.* London: Verso, 1991.

Balme, R., A. Faure, and A. Mabileau, eds. *Les nouvelles politiques locales: Dynamiques de l'action publique.* Paris: Presses de Sciences-Po, 1999.

Banks, J. A., and G. Gay. "Ethnicity in Contemporary American Society: Toward the Development of a Typology." *Ethnicity* 5 (1978): 238–51.

Banton, M. "Ethnic Bargaining." In *Ethnicity, Politics, and Development*, edited by D. L. Thompson and D. Ronen. Boulder, Colo.: Lynne Rienner Publishers, 1986.

Bauböck, R. *Transnational Citizenship: Membership and Rights in International Migration.* Aldershot: Edward Elgar Publishing, 1995.

———, ed. *From Aliens to Citizens: Redefining the Legal Status of Immigrants.* Aldershot: Avebury, 1994.

Bauböck, R., A. Heller, and A. Zolberg, eds. *The Challenge of Diversity: Integration and Pluralism in Societies of Immigration.* Aldershot: Avebury, 1996.

Baumgartner, F. R. *Conflict and Rhetoric in French Policy Making.* Pittsburgh: Pittsburgh University Press, 1989.

Baumgartner, F. R., and J. L. Walker. "Educational Policymaking and the Interest Group Structure in France and the United States." *Comparative Politics* 21, no. 3 (April 1989): 273–88.

Bayart, J.-F. "L'énonciation du politique." *Revue française de sciences politiques* 35, no. 3 (June 1985): 343–73.

———. *L'illusion identitaire*. Paris: Fayard, 1996.

Beaune, C. *Naissance de la nation France*. Paris: Gallimard, 1985.

Beiner, R., ed. *Theorizing Citizenship*. Albany: State University of New York Press, 1995.

Bendix, R. *Nation-Building and Citizenship*. 2d ed. Berkeley: University of California Press, 1977.

Benhabib, S., ed. *Democracy and Difference: Contesting the Boundaries of the Political*. Princeton: Princeton University Press, 1996.

Berezin, M. "Fissured Terrain: Methodological Approaches and Research Styles in Culture and Politics." In *The Sociology of Culture: Emerging Theoretical Perspectives*, edited by Diana Crane. Oxford: Blackwell, 1994.

Berger, S., ed. *Organizing Interest in Western Europe*. Cambridge: Cambridge University Press, 1981.

Bernstein, I. *Dictatorship of Virtue: Multiculturalism and the Battle for America's Future*. New York: Knopf, 1994.

Berque, J. *L'immigration à l'École républicaine*. Rapport au Ministère de l'Education Nationale. Paris: La documentation Française, 1985.

Bielefeld, U. "L'État-nation inachevé: Xénophobie, racisme et violence en Allemagne à la fin du 20ème siècle." *Allemagne An V* (December 1994–January 1995).

———. *Inländische Ausländer: Zum gesellschaftlichen Bewusstsein türkischer Jugendlicher in der Bundesrepublik*. Frankfurt am Main: Campus, 1988.

Birnbaum, P. "Du multiculturalisme au nationalisme." *La pensée politique* 3 (1995): 129–39.

———. *La France aux Français: Histoire des haines nationalistes*. Paris: Fayard, 1993.

Birnbaum, P., and J. Leca, eds. *Sur l'individualisme*. Paris: Presses de la FNSP, 1986.

Bloch-Lainé, F. *Associations et développement local*. Part 1: *Les tendances*. Paris: Librairie Générale de droit et de jurisprudence, coll. Décentralisation et développement local, 1988.

Blondiaux, L., G. Marcou, and F. Rangeon. *La démocratie locale: Représentation, participation et espace public*. Paris: PUF, 1999.

Body-Gendrot, S. *The Social Control of Cities?: A Comparative Perspective*. Malden, Mass.: Blackwell, 2000.

———. *Ville et violence: L'irruption de nouveaux acteurs*. Paris: PUF, 1993.

Bonnafous, S. *L'immigration prise aux mots: Les immigrés dans la presse au tournant des années 1980*. Paris: Éditions Kimé, 1991.

Bourdieu, P., ed. *La misère du monde*. Paris: Éditions du Seuil, 1993.

Bourdieu, P., and J. S. Coleman, eds. *Social Theory for a Changing Society*. New York: Westview Press, 1991.

Bourricaud, F. "Qu'est-ce qu'un citoyen aujourd'hui?" *Commentaire* 10, no. 39 (fall 1987): 519–23.

Bovenkerk, F., R. Miles, and G. Verbunt. "Comparative Studies of Migration and Exclusion on the Grounds of 'Race' and Ethnic Background in Western

Europe: A Critical Appraisal." *International Migration Review* 25, no. 2 (summer 1991): 375–91.

———. "Racism, Migration, and the State in Western Europe: A Case for Comparative Analysis." *International Sociology* 5, no. 4 (December 1990): 475–90.

Bowen, J., and R. Peterson. *Critical Comparisons in Politics and Culture*. Cambridge: Cambridge University Press, 1999.

Brass, P. R. "Elite Groups, Symbol Manipulation, and Ethnic Identity among the Muslims of South Asia." In *Political Identity in South Asia*, edited by D. Taylor and M. Yapp. London: Curzon, 1979.

———. "Ethnicity and Nationality Formation." *Ethnicity* 3, no. 3 (September 1976): 225–41.

———, ed. *Ethnic Groups and the State*. London: Croom Helm, 1985.

Brisebarre, A.-M. *La fête du mouton: Un sacrifice musulman dans l'espace urbain*. Paris: CNRS Éditions, 1998.

Brubaker, W. R. *Citizenship and Nationhood in France and Germany*. Cambridge, Mass.: Harvard University Press, 1992.

Brumlik, M., and C. Leggewie. "Konturen der Einwanderungsgesellschaft: Nationale Identität, Multikulturalismus und 'Civil Society.'" In *Deutsche im Ausland, Fremde in Deutschland,- Migration in Geschichte und Gegenwart*, edited by K. J. Bade. Munich: Verlag C. H. Beck, 1992.

Burgess, E. "The Resurgence of Ethnicity: Myth or Reality?" *Ethnic and Racial Studies* 3, no. 1 (July 1978): 265–85.

Burgess, F. "Quel 'pluralisme culturel' aux Etats-Unis?" *Études* (May 1991): 581–90.

Calhoun, C. J. "The Radicalism of Tradition: Community Strength or Venerable Disguise and Borrowed Language?" *American Journal of Sociology* 88, no. 5 (March 1983): 886–914.

Campani, G., and M. Catani. "Les réseaux associatifs italiens en France et les jeunes." *Revue européenne des migrations internationales* 1, no. 2 (1985): 143–61.

Castles, S., and M. J. Miller. *The Age of Migration: International Population Movement in the Modern World*. London: Macmillan, 1993.

Cesari, J. *Être Musulman en France: Associations, militants, mosquées*. Paris: Karthala, 1994.

Chazel, F. "La mobilisation politique: Problèmes et dimensions." *Revue française de sciences politique* 25, no. 3 (1975): 502–17.

Citrin, J., B. Reingold, and D. P. Green. "American Identity and the Politics of Ethnic Change." *Journal of Politics* 52, no. 4 (November 1990): 1124–54.

Coakley, J. "The Resolution of Ethnic Conflict: Towards a Typology." *International Political Science Review* 4, no. 13 (October 1992): 343–449.

Cohen, I. J. "On Hechter's Interpretation of Weber." *American Journal of Sociology* 81, no. 5 (March 1976): 1160–68.

Cohen, J. L. "Strategy or Identity: New Theoretical Paradigms and Contemporary Social Movements." *Social Research* 52, no. 4 (winter 1985): 663–716.

Cohen, R. "Ethnicity: Problem and Focus in Anthropology." *Annual Review of Anthropology* 7 (1978): 379–403.

Cohen, S. M. "Participation of Blacks, Puerto Ricans, and Whites in Voluntary Associations: A Test of Current Theories." *Social Forces* 56, no. 4 (June 1978): 1053–71.

Cohn-Bendit, D., and T. Schmidt. *Heimat Babylon: Das Wagnis der Multikulturellen Demokratie*. Hamburg: Hoffman und Campe, 1992.

Coleman, J. S. *Individual Interests and Collective Action: Selected Essays*. Cambridge: Cambridge University Press, 1986.

Connolly, W. E. *Identity Difference: Democratic Negotiations of Political Paradox*. Ithaca: Cornell University Press, 1991.

Connor, W. *Ethnonationalism: The Quest for Understanding*. Princeton: Princeton University Press, 1994.

———. "A Nation Is a Nation, Is a State, Is an Ethnic Group, Is a. . . ." *Ethnic and Racial Studies* 1, no. 4 (October 1978): 377–400.

———, ed. *Mexican-Americans in Comparative Perspective*. Washington, D.C.: Urban Institute Press, 1985.

Costa-Lascoux, J. *De l'immigré au citoyen*. Paris: La documentation Française, 1989.

Dagger, R. *Civic Virtues: Rights, Citizenship, and Republican Liberalism*. New York: Oxford University Press, 1997.

Dahl, R. A. *Dilemmas of Pluralist Democracy: Autonomy vs. Control*. New Haven: Yale University Press, 1982.

Dahrendorf, R. *The Modern Social Conflict: An Essay on the Politics of Liberty*. Berkeley: University of California Press, 1990.

Dalton, R. *Politics in West Germany*. Glenview, Ill.: Scott Foresman, 1989.

Dann, O. *Nation und Nationalismus in Deutschland, 1770–1990*. Munich: Verlag C. H. Beck, 1993.

Dazi, F., and R. Leveau. "L'intégration par la politique: Le vote des Beurs." *Études* (September 1988).

Déloye, Y. *École et citoyenneté: L'individualisme républicain des Jules Ferry à Vichy: Controverses*. Paris: Presses de Sciences-Po, 1994.

Diop, M. "Regards croisés." *Hommes & Migrations*, no. 1135 (September 1990): 34–38.

Diop, M., and R. Kastoryano. "Le mouvement associatif islamique en Île de France." *Revue européenne des migrations internationales* 7, no. 3 (1991): 91–117.

Dittrich, E. J., and F. O. Radtke, eds. "Einleitung der Beitrag der Wissenschaften zur Konstruktion ethnischer Minderheiten." In *Ethnizität: Wissenschaft und Minderheiten*. Opladen: Westdeutscher Verlag, 1990.

Dohse, K. *Ausländische Arbeiter und bürgerlicher Staat: Genese und Funktion von staat. Ausländerpolitik und Ausländerrecht. Vom Kaiserreich bis zur Bundesrepublik Deutschland*. Königstein/Ts., 1981.

Donegani, J.-M., and M. Sadoun. *La démocratie imparfaite*. Paris: Gallimard, 1988.

Dubet, F. "Les figures de la ville et la banlieue." *Sociologie du travail*, no. 2 (1995): 127–51.

———. *Immigration, qu'en savons-nous? Un bilan des connaissances*. Paris: La découverte, 1989.

Dubet, F., and D. Lapeyronnie. *Les quartiers d'exil*. Paris: Éditions du Seuil, 1992.

Duchesne, S. *Citoyenneté à la française*. Paris: Presses de Sciences-Po, 1997.

Dumont, L. *France-Allemagne aller retour*. Paris: Gallimard, 1991.

Dunn, J. *Contemporary Crisis of the Nation-State*. Oxford: Blackwell, 1995.

Duroselle, J.-B. *L'Invasion: Les migrations humaines, chance ou fatalité?* Paris: Plon, 1992.

Eder, K. "The 'New Social Movements': Moral Crusades, Political Pressure Groups, or Social Movements?" *Social Research* 52, no. 4 (winter 1985): 869–90.

Eisenberg, B. "Blacks in American Politics." In *America's Ethnic Politics*, edited by Joseph S. Roucek and Bernard Eisenberg, 113–32. Westport, Conn.: Greenwood Press, 1982.

Eisenstadt, S. N. "L'analyse anthropologique des sociétés complexes." *Cahiers internationaux de sociologie* 60 (1976): 5–41.

———. "Analysis of Patterns of Immigration and Absorption of Immigrants." *Population Studies* 7, no. 2 (November 1953): 167–80.

Esser, H. "Ethnische Differenzierung und moderne Gesellschaft." *Zeitschrift für Soziologie* 17, no. 4 (June 1988): 235–48.

Etzioni, A. "Social Science as a Multicultural Canon." *Society* 29, no. 1 (November–December 1991): 14–18.

Evans, P. B., D. Rueschemeyer, and T. Skocpol. *Bringing the State Back In*. New York: Cambridge University Press, 1985.

Farin, K., and E. Seidel-Pielen. *Krieg in den Städten: Jugendgangs in Deutschland*. Berlin: Rothbuch Verlag, 1991.

Faul, E. "Is Germany Becoming a Multiracial State?" *German Comments* (April 1992): 26–34.

Favell, A. *Philosophies of Integration*. London: Macmillan,1998.

Feldblum, M. *Reconstructing Citizenship: The Politics of Nationality Reform and Immigration in Contemporary France*. New York: State University of New York Press, 1999.

Feuer, L. S. "From Pluralism to Multiculturalism." *Society* 29, no. 1 (November–December 1991): 19–22.

Fijalkowski, J. "Nationale Identität versus multikulturelle Gesellschaft." In *Die Bundesrepublik in den achtziger Jahren*, edited by W. Süss, 236–50. Opladen: Leske und Budrich, 1991.

———. "Les obstacles à la citoyenneté: Immigration et naturalisation en république fédérale d'Allemagne." *Revue européenne des migrations internationales* 5, no. 1 (1989): 33–47.

———. "Solidarités intra-communautaires et formations d'associations au sein de la population étrangère d'Allemagne." *Revue européenne des migrations internationales* 10, no. 1 (1994): 33–59.

Fitzgerald, K. *The Face of the Nation: Immigration, the State, and the National Identity*. Stanford: Stanford University Press, 1996.

Francis, E. *Ethnos und Demos: Soziologische Beiträge zur Volkstheorie*. Berlin: Dunker & Humboldt, 1965.

François, E. *Protestants et catholiques en Allemagne: Identités et pluralisme, Augsbourg 1648–1806*. Paris: Albin Michel, 1993.

Fraser, J. "Community, the Private, and Individual." *Sociological Review* 35, no. 4 (November 1987): 795–818.

Freeman, G. " Modes of Immigration Politics in Liberal Democratic States." *International Migration Review* 29, no. 4 (1995): 881–902.

Fuchs, L. H. *The American Kaleidoscope: Race, Ethnicity, and the Civic Culture*. Hanover, N.H.: Wesleyan University Press, 1990.

Funcke, L. "Gesellschaftliche Einheit durch politische Mitsprache." In *Facetten des Fremden: Europa zwischen Nationalismus und Integration*, edited by M. Haerdter et al., 32–36. Berlin: Argon Verlag, 1992.

Gans, H. "Symbolic Ethnicity: The Future of Ethnic Groups and Cultures in America." *Ethnic and Racial Studies* 2, no.1 (January 1979): 1–21.

———. "Toward a Reconciliation of 'Assimilation' and 'Pluralism': The Interplay of Acculturation and Ethnic Retention." *International Migration Review* (1997): 875–93.

Gaspard, F. "Assimilation, insertion, intégration: Les mots pour devenir Français." *Hommes et migrations*, no. 1154 (May 1992): 14–23.

Gauchet, M. *La religion dans la démocratie: Parcours de la laïcité*. Paris: Gallimard, 1998.

Geertz, C. "The Integrative Revolution." In *Old Societies and New States: The Quest for Modernity in Asia and Africa*, edited by C. Geertz, 105–57. New York: Free Press; London: Collier-Macmillan, 1963.

———. *The Interpretation of Cultures*. New York: Basic Books, 1973.

Georges, P. *L'immigration en France: Faits et problèmes*. Paris: A. Colin, 1986.

Girard, A., and J. Stoetzel. *Français et immigrés: L'attitude française, l'adaptation des Italiens et des Polonais*. Paris: PUF, 1953.

Girardet, R. *L'idée nationale en France de 1871 à 1962*. Paris: Pluriel, 1979.

Gitlin, T. *The Twilight of Common Dreams: Why America Is Wracked by Culture Wars*. New York: Henry Holt, 1995.

Glazer, N. "Beyond the Melting Pot Twenty Years After." *Journal of American Ethnic History*, no. 1 (fall 1981): 43–55.

———. "Is Assimilation Dead?" *The Annals of the American Academy of Social and Political Sciences* 30, no. 5 (1993): 122–36.

———. "The Political Distinctiveness of the Mexican-Americans." In *Mexican-Americans in Comparative Perspective*, edited by W. Connor, 205–24. Washington, D.C.: Urban Institute Press, 1985.

———. *We Are All Multiculturalists Now*. Cambridge, Mass.: Harvard University Press, 1995.

Gleason, P. "Pluralism and Assimilation: A Conceptual History." In *Linguistic Minorities, Policies, and Pluralism*, edited by J. Edwards, 221–57. London: Academic Press 1984.

Gordon, M. M. *Assimilation in American Life*. New York: Oxford University Press, 1964.

Goulbourne, H. *Ethnicity and Nationalism in Post Imperial Britain*. London: Cambridge University Press, 1991.

Granovetter, M. S. "The Strength of Weak Ties." *American Journal of Sociology* 78, no. 6 (1973): 1360–80.

Greeley, A. M. "Political Participation among Ethnic Groups in the United States: A Preliminary Reconnaissance." *American Journal of Sociology* 80, no. 1 (1974): 170–204.

Green, N. *Du sentier à la 7e^{me} Avenue: La confection et les immigrés, Paris–New York 1880–1980*. Paris: Éditions du Seuil, 1997.

———. "L'immigration en France et aux Etats-Unis: Historiographie comparée." *Vingtième siècle: Revue d'histoire*, no. 29 (January–March 1991): 67–83.

Green, V. "Old Ethnic Stereotypes and the New Ethnic Studies." *Ethnicity* 5 (1978): 328–50.

Grillo, R. D.. *Pluralism and the Politics of Difference: State, Culture, and Ethnicity in Comparative Perspective*. Oxford: Clarendon Press; New York: Oxford University Press, 1998.

Guillaume, G. *Collectivités territoriales et associations*. Paris: Economica, 1987 (Coll. "Collectivités territoriales." Série: Centre de formation des personnels communaux).

Guiraudon, V. *Les politiques d'immigration en Europe: Allemagne, France, Pays-Bas*. Paris: L'Harmattan, 2000.

———. "The Reaffirmation of the Republican Model of Integration: Ten Years of Identity Politics in France." *French Politics and Society* 14, no. 2 (1996).

Gutmann, A., ed. *Multiculturalism*. Princeton: Princeton University Press, 1994.

Habermas, J. *Écrits politiques: Culture, droit, histoire*. Paris: Les éditions du Cerf, 1990.

———. *L'espace public*. Paris: Payot, 1993.

———. *L'intégration républicaine: Essais de théorie politique*. Translated by Rainer Rothlitz. Paris: Fayard, 1998.

Hacker, A. *Two Nations: Black and White, Separate, Hostile, Unequal*. New York: Charles Scribner's Sons, 1992.

Hall, S. "Culture, Community, Nation." *Cultural Studies* 7, no. 3 (1993).

Hall, S., and D. Held. "Citizens and Citizenship." In *New Times: The Changing Face of Politics in the 1990s*, edited by S. Hall and D. Held. London: Lawrence & Wishard, 1989.

Hammar, T. *Democracy and the Nation State: Aliens, Denizens, and Citizens in a World of International Migration*. Aldershot: Avebury, 1990.

———, ed. *European Immigration Policy: A Comparative Study*. Cambridge: Cambridge University Press, 1985.

Hannan, M. T. "The Dynamics of Ethnic Boundaries in Modern States." In *National Development and the World System: Educational, Economic, and Political Change*, edited by J. W. Meyer and M. T. Hannan, 253–75. Chicago: University of Chicago Press, 1979.

Hargreaves, A. *Immigration, "Race," and Ethnicity in Contemporary France*. London: Routledge, 1995.

Hartmann, M. "Ausländer in Ostdeutschland." *Deutschland Archiv* 11, no. 24 (November 1991): 1137–40.

Hassner, P. "Vers un multiculturalism pluriel?" *Esprit*, no. 187 (1992): 102–13.

Hechter, M. "Ethnicity and Industrialization: On the Proliferation of the Cultural Division of Labor." *Ethnicity* 3, no. 3 (September 1976): 214–24.

———. "Theories of Ethnic Relations." In *The Primordial Challenge: Ethnicity in the Contemporary World*, edited by J. F. Stack Jr., 13–24. Westport, Conn.: Greenwood Press, 1986.

———. "Towards a Theory of Ethnic Change." *Politics and Society* 2, no. 1 (fall 1971): 21–45.

Heckmann, F. "Ethnicity, Nation-State, and Political Problems of Ethnic Minorities." Paper presented to the seminar Les Populations Musulmanes en Europe, Poitiers, November 7–9, 1991, Observatoire du Changement Social en Europe Occidentale.

Herbert, U. *Geschichte der Ausländerbeschäftigung in Deutschland, 1880 bis 1980: Saisonarbeiter, Zwangsarbeiter, Gastarbeiter.* Berlin: Verlag J.H.W. Dietz Nachf, 1986.

Hérvieu-Léger, D. *La religion pour mémoire.* Paris: Éditions du Cerf, 1993.

Higham, J. "Current Trends in the Study of Ethnicity in the United States." *Journal of American Ethnic History* 2 (fall 1982): 5–15.

———. "Integrating America: The Problem of Assimilation in the Nineteenth Century." *Journal of American Ethnic History* 1 (fall 1981): 7–25.

———. *Strangers in the Land: Patterns of American Nativism, 1860–1925.* New York: Atheneum, 1963.

Hirschman, C. "America's Melting Pot Reconsidered." *American Review of Sociology*, no. 9 (1983): 397–423.

Hobsbawm, E. "Whose Fault-Line Is It Anyway?" *Anthropology Today* (February 1992).

Hobsbawm, E., and T. Ranger, eds. *The Invention of Tradition.* New York: Cambridge University Press, 1983.

Hochschild, J. *Facing Up to the American Dream: Race, Class, and the Soul of the Nation.* Princeton: Princeton University Press, 1995.

Hoffmann, L. *Die unvollendete Republik: Zwischen Einwanderungsland und deutschem Nationalstaat.* Köln, 1992.

Hoffmann-Nowotny, H. J. "European Migration after World War II." In *Human Migration: Patterns and Policies*, edited by W. H. McNeill and R. S. Adams, 85–105. Bloomington: Indiana University Press, 1978.

Hollifield, J. F. *Immigrants, Markets, and States: The Political Economy of Postwar Europe.* Cambridge, Mass.: Harvard University Press, 1992.

———. *L'immigration et l'État-nation à la recherche d'un modèle national.* Paris: L'Harmattan, 1997.

Hollinger, D. *Postethnic America: Beyond Multiculturalism.* New York: Basic Books, 1995.

Horowitz, D. "Conflict and Accommodation: Mexican-Americans in the Cosmopolis." In *Mexican-Americans in Comparative Perspective*, edited by W. Connor, 56–103. Washington, D.C.: Urban Institute Press, 1985.

———. "Racial Violence in the United States." In *Ethnic Pluralism and Public Policy: Achieving Equality in the United States and Britain*, edited by N. Glazer and K. Young, with the assistance of C. S. Schelling, 187–211. Lexington, Mass.:Lexington Books, 1983.

———. "Three Dimensions of Ethnic Politics." *World Politics* 23, no. 2 (January 1971): 232–44.

Horowitz, D. L., and G. Noiriel, eds. *Immigrants in Two Democracies: French and American Experiences.* New York: New York University Press, 1992.

Hughes, E. C. "Race Relations and the Sociological Imagination." *American Sociological Review* 28, no. 6 (December 1963): 879–90.

Hull, E. *Without Justice for All: The Constitutional Rights of Aliens.* Westport, Conn.: Greenwood Press, 1985.

Ireland, P. *The Policy Challenge of Ethnic Diversity: Immigrant Politics in France and Switzerland.* Cambridge, Mass.: Harvard University Press, 1994.

Isaacs, H. R. *Idols of the Tribe: Group Identity and Political Change.* Cambridge, Mass.: Harvard University Press, 1989.

Jazouli, A. *Les années banlieues.* Paris: Éditions du Seuil, 1992.

Jenkins, J. C. "Resource Mobilization Theory and the Study of Social Movements." *American Review of Sociology* 9 (1983): 527–53.

Joppke, C. *Immigration and the Nation-State.* Oxford: Oxford University Press, 1999.

———, ed. *Challenge to the Nation-State: Immigration and Citizenship in Western Europe and the United States.* Oxford: Oxford University Press, 1998.

Kallen, H. M. *Culture and Democracy in the United States.* New York: Boni & Liveright, 1924.

———. "Democracy vs the Melting-Pot." *The Nation*, February 18 and 25, 1915.

Kastoryano, R. "Construction de communautés et négociations d'identités: Les Musulmans en France et en Allemagne." In *Cartes d'identité: Comment dit-on "nous" en politique*, edited by D. C. Martin, 229–45. Paris: Presses de la FNSP, 1994.

———. "Définir les frontières de l'identité: Turcs et Musulmans." *Revue française des sciences politiques* 37, no. 6 (December 1987): 833–55.

———. "Les États et les immigrés." *Revue européenne de migrations internationales* 5, no. 1 (1989): 9–22.

———. *Être Turc en France: Réflexions sur familles et communauté.* Paris: L'Harmattan, 1987.

———. Intégration politique par l'extérieur. *Revue française des sciences politiques* 42, no. 5 (October 1992): 786–802.

———. "Mobilisation des migrants en Europe: Du national au transnational." *Revue européenne de migrations internationales* 10, no. 1 (1994): 169–83.

———. "Paris-Berlin: Politiques d'immigration et modes d'intégration des Turcs." In *Les Musulmans dans la société française*, edited by R. Leveau and G. Kepel, 141–69. Paris: Presses de la FNSP, 1988.

Katzenstein, P. *Policy and Politics in West Germany.* Philadelphia: Temple University Press, 1988.

Keane, J. *Civil Society: Old Images, New Visions.* Cambridge: Polity Press, 1998.

Keller, S. "The American Dream of Community: An Unfinished Agenda." *Sociological Forum* 3, no. 2 (1988): 167–83.

Kellor, F. A. "What Is Americanization?" *Yale Review*, no. 2 (1919): 282–99.

Kepel, G. *À l'ouest d'Allah*, Paris: Éditions du Seuil, 1994.

———. *Les banlieues de l'Islam: Naissance d'une religion en France*. Paris: Éditions du Seuil, 1987.

Kerr, D. A. "Religion, State, and Ethnic Identity." In *Religion, State, and Ethnic Groups*, edited by D. A. Kerr. Vol. 2. New York: New York University Press, 1992.

Kessel, D. "Laïcité: Du combat au droit. Entretien." *Le débat*, no. 77 (1993): 95–101.

Keyes, C. F. "The Dialectics of Ethnic Change." In *Ethnic Change*, edited by C. F. Keyes, 4–30. Seattle: University of Washington Press.

Klobus-Edwards, P., J. N. Edwards, and D. L. Klemmack. "Differences in Social Participation: Blacks and Whites." *Social Forces* 56, no. 4 (June 1978): 1035–51.

Knight, U., and W. Kowalsky. *Deutschland nur den Deutschen? Die Ausländerfrage in Deutschland, Frankreich und den USA*. Straube, 1991.

Knoke, D. "Associations and Interest Groups." *Annual Review of Sociology* 12 (1986): 1–21.

———. "Commitment and Detachment in Voluntary Associations." *American Sociological Review* 46 (April 1981): 141–58.

Knoke D., and R. Thomson. "Voluntary Association Membership Trends and the Family Life Cycle." *Social Forces* 56, no. 1:48–65.

Kopmans, R., and P. Statham. "Challenging the Liberal Naton-State? Postnationalism, Multiculturalism, and the Collective Claims Making of Migrants and Ethnic Minorities in Britain and Germany." *American Journal of Sociology* 105, no. 3 (November 1999): 652–97.

Koven, R. "Muslim Immigrants and French Nationalists." *Society* 29, no. 4 (May/June 1992): 25–33.

Kurthen, H., J. Fijalkowski, and G. Wagner, eds. *Immigration, Citizenship, and the Welfare State in Germany and the United States: Immigrant Incorporation*. Stamford, Conn.: Jai Press, 1998.

Kymlicka, W. *Liberalism, Community, and Culture*. New York: Oxford University Press, 1989.

———. *Multicultural Citizenship: A Liberal Theory of Minority Rights*. New York: Oxford University Press, 1995.

———. *The Rights of Minority Cultures*. New York: Oxford University Press, 1995.

Lacorne, D. *L'invention de la République: Le modèle américain*. Paris: Hachette (Pluriel), 1991.

Lal, B. B. "Perspectives on Ethnicity: Old Wine in New Bottles." *Ethnic and Racial Studies* 6, no. 2 (April 1983): 154–73.

Lamont, M. *The Dignity of Working Men: Morality and the Boundaries of Race, Class, and Immigration*. New York: Russell Sage Foundation; Cambridge, Mass.: Harvard University Press, 2000.

Lamont, M., and M. Fournier, eds. *Cultivating Differences: Symbolic Boundaries and the Making of Inequality*. Chicago: University of Chicago Press, 1992.

Lamont, M., and L. Thévenot, eds. *Rethinking Comparative Cultural Sociology Politics and Repertoire of Evaluation in France and the United State.* Cambridge: Cambridge University Press; Paris: Presses de la MSH, 2000.

Lamphere, L. *Structuring Diversity: Ethnographic Perspectives on the New Immigration.* Chicago: University of Chicago Press, 1992.

Lapeyronnie, D. "Assimilation, mobilisation et action collective chez les jeunes de la seconde génération de l'immigration maghrébine." *Revue française de sciences politiques* 28 (1987): 287–317.

———. *L'individu et les minorités: La France et la Grande Bretagne face à leurs immigrés.* Paris: PUF, 1993.

Lash, S., and J. Friedman. *Modernity and Identity.* Oxford: Blackwell, 1991.

Lavau, G. "A propos de trois livres sur l'État." *Revue française de sciences politiques* 30, no. 2 (April 1980): 396–411.

Layton-Henry, Z. *The Political Rights of Migrant Workers in Western Europe.* London: Sage Publications, 1990.

Le Bras, H. *Le démon des origines: Démographie et extrême droite.* Paris: Éditions de l'Aube, 1998.

Leca, J. "Après Maastricht." *Témoin* 1, no. 1 (1993): 29–39.

———. "La démocratie à l'épreuve du pluralisme." *Revue française de sciences politiques* 46, no. 2 (1996).

———. "Individualisme et citoyenneté." In *Sur l'individualisme*, edited by P. Birnbaum and J. Leca. Paris: Presses de la Fondation de Sciences Politiques, 1987.

———. "Nationalité et citoyenneté dans l'Europe des immigrations." In *Logiques d'État et immigration en Europe*, edited by J. Costa-Lascoux and P. Weil. Paris: Éditions Kimé, 1992.

Le Galès, P. "Politique de la ville en France et en Grande-Bretagne: Volontarisme et ambiguïtés de l'État." *Sociologie du travail*, no. 2 (1995): 249–77.

Le Galès, P., M. Oberti, and J.-C. Rampal. "Le vote Front national à Mantes-la-Jolie. Analyse d'une crise locale à retentissement national: Le Val-Fourré." *Hérodote*, nos. 69–70 (2d and 3d semiannual 1993): 31–52.

Lemay, M. C., ed. *The Gatekeepers: Comparative Immigration Policy.* New York: Praeger, 1989.

Lenoble, J., and N. Dewandre, eds. *L'Europe au soir du siècle.* Paris: Éditions du Seuil, coll. Esprit, 1992.

Lequin, Y. *La Mosaïque France.* Paris: Librairie Larousse, 1988.

Leveau, R. "Éléments de réflexion sur l'Islam en Europe." *Revue européenne des migrations internationales* 10, no. 1 (1994): 157–69.

———. "Les partis et l'intégration des Beurs." In *Idéologies, partis politiques et groupes sociaux*, edited by Y. Mény, 247–61. Paris: Presses de la FNSP, 1989.

Leveau, R., and G. Kepel, eds. *Les Musulmans dans la société française.* Paris: Presses de la FNSP, 1988.

Lichbach, M. I., and A. S. Zuckerman, eds. *Comparative Politics: Rationality, Culture, and Structure.* New York: Cambridge University Press, 1997.

Lieberson, S. *A Piece of the Pie: Blacks and White Immigrants since 1880.* Berkeley: University of California Press, 1980.

———. "Unhyphenated Whites in the United States." *Ethnic and Racial Studies* 8, no. 1 (January 1985): 159–80.

Lieberson, S., and M. C. Waters. "Ethnic Groups in Flux: The Changing Ethnic Responses of American Whites." *Annals* 487 (September 1986): 79–91.

——. "The Location of Ethnic and Racial Groups in the United States." *Sociological Forum* 2, no. 4 (1987): 778–810.

Liebman, L. "Anti-Discrimination Law: Groups and the Modern State." In *Ethnic Pluralism and Public Policy: Achieving Equality in the United States and Britain*, edited by N. Glazer and K. Young, with the assistance of C. S. Schelling, 11–31. Lexington, Mass.: Lexington Books, 1983.

Lind, M. *The Next American Nation: The New Nationalism and the Fourth American Revolution*. New York: Free Press, 1995.

Linz, J. J. "From Primordialism to Nationalism." In *New Nationalisms of the Developed West: Toward Explanation*, edited by E. A. Tiryakian and R. Rogowski, 203–53. Boston: Allen & Unwin, 1985.

Lipsky, M. "Protest as a Political Resource." *American Political Science Review* 62 (December 1968): 1144–58.

Lochak, D. "Les ambiguïtés du principe de séparation." *Actes*, no. 79/80 (April 1992): 9–14.

——. *Étrangers de quel droit?* Paris: PUF, 1985.

——. "Les minorités dans le droit public français: Du refus des différences à la gestion des différences." In *Les minorités et leur droit depuis 1789*, 111–84. Paris: L'Harmattan, 1989.

Macridis, R. C. "Interest Groups in Comparative Analysis." *The Journal of Politics* 23, no. 1 (February 1961): 223–38.

Mandel, R. "Turkish Headscarves and the 'Foreigner Problem': Constructing Difference through Emblems of Identity." *New German Critique*, no. 46 (winter 1989): 27–46.

Manent, P. "L'État moderne: Problèmes d'interprétation." *Commentaires*, no. 41 (spring 1988): 328–35.

Manfrass, K. *Türken in der Bundesrepublik, Nordafrikaner in Frankreich: Ausländerproblematik im deutsch-französischen Vergleich*. Bonn: Bouvier, 1991.

Mann, M. "Ruling Class Strategies and Citizenship." *Sociology* 21, no. 3 (August 1987): 339–54.

Marienstras, É. *Nous, le peuple: Les origines du nationalisme américain*. Paris: Gallimard, 1988.

Martin, D. C., ed. *Cartes d'identité: Comment dit-on "nous" en politique?* Paris: Presses de la FNSP, 1994.

Martiniello, M. *Sortir des ghettos culturels*. Paris: Presses de Sciences-Po, 1997.

Martiny, A. "Multikulturelles Zusammenleben in der Bundesrepublik Deutschland." In *Facetten der Fremden: Europa zwischen Nationalismus und Integration*, edited by M. Haerdter et al., 127–42. Berlin: Argon, 1992.

Matthews, F. H. "The Revolt against Americanism: Cultural Pluralism and Cultural Relativism as an Ideology of Liberation." *Canadian Review of American Studies* 1, no. 1 (spring 1970): 4–31.

Mayer, N. "Racisme et xénophobie dans l'Europe des douze." In *La lutte contre le racisme et la xénophobie*. Paris: La documentation Française, 1994.

Meadwell, H. "Cultural and Instrumental Approaches to Ethnic Nationalism." *Ethnic and Racial Studies* 12, no. 3 (July 1989): 309–28.

Melucci, A. "The Symbolic Challenge of Contemporary Movements." *Social Research* 52, no. 4 (winter 1985): 789–816.

Mény, Y. "Les politiques des autorités locales." In *Traité de science politique*, edited by M. Grawitz and J. Leca, 423–66. Vol. 4. Paris: PUF, 1985.

Mesnil, J. "Quelques opinions et attitudes des Français à l'égard des travailleurs africains." *Esprit* 4 (April 1966): 744–57 (special edition: *Les étrangers en France*).

Miller, D. *On Nationality.* New York: Oxford University Press, 1995.

Milza, P. "Un siècle d'immigration étrangère en France." *Vingtième siècle: Revue d'histoire,* no. 7 (1985): 3–18.

Modood, T. "Establishment, Multiculturalism, and British Citizenship." *Political Quarterly* 65, no. 1 (1993).

Modood, T., and P. Werbner, eds. *The Politics of Multiculturalism in the New Europe: Racism, Identity, and Community.* London: Zed Books, 1997.

Moon, J. D. *Constructing Community: Moral Pluralism and Tragic Conflicts.* Princeton: Princeton University Press, 1993.

Morin, E. *Penser l'Europe.* Paris: Éditions du Seuil, 1988.

Münz, R., W. Siefert, and R. Ulrich. *Zuwanderung nach Deutschland: Strukturen, Wirkungen, Perspektiven.* Frankfurt am Main: Campus, 1997.

Münz, R., and R. Ulrich. "Germany and Its Immigrants: A Socio-Demographic Analysis." *Journal of Ethnic and Migration Studies* 24, no. 1 (January 1998): 25–56.

Münz, R., and M. Weiner, eds. *Migrants, Refugees, and Foreign Policy: U.S. and German Policies toward Countries of Origin.* Providence: Berghahn Books, 1997.

Muxel, A. "Les attitudes socio-politiques des jeunes issus de l'immigration maghrébine en région parisienne." *Revue française de sciences politiques* 38, no. 6 (1988): 925–39.

Myrdal, G. *An American Dilemma: The Negro Problem and Modern Democracy.* New York: Harper & Row, 1944.

Nanton, P. "National Frameworks and the Implementation of Local Policies: Is a European Model of Integration Identifiable? *Policy and Politics* 19, no. 3 (1991): 191–97.

Nassehi, A. "Zum Funktionswandel von Ethnizität im Prozess gesellschaftlicher Modernisierung: Ein Beitrag zur Theorie funktionaler Differenzierung." *Soziale Welt* 3, no. 90:261–82.

Neveu, C. ed. *Espace public et engagement politique: Enjeux et logiques de la citoyenneté locale.* Paris: L'Harmattan, 1999.

Nicolet, C. *L'idée républicaine en France (1789–1924).* Paris: Gallimard, coll. "Tell," 1995.

Nipperdey, T. *Réflexions sur l'histoire allemande.* Paris: Gallimard, 1992.

Noiriel, G. *Le creuset français: Histoire de l'immigration XIXe et XXe siècle.* Paris: Éditions du Seuil, 1988.

Oberndörfer, D. *Die offene Republik: Zur Zukunft Deutschlands und Europas.* Freiburg: Herder Spektrum, 1991.

Offe, C. "New Social Movements: Challenging the Boundaries of Institutional Politics." *Social Research* 52, no. 4 (winter 1985): 817–68.

Oldfield, A. "Citizenship: An Unnatural Practice?" *Political Quarterly* 61, no. 2 (April–June 1990): 177–87.

Olzak, S. "Analysis of Events in the Study of Collective Action." *Annual Review of Sociology* 15 (1989): 119–41.

Omi, M., and H. Winant. *Racial Formation in the United States: From the 1960s to the 1980s.* New York: Routledge & Kegan Paul, 1986.

Opp, K.-D. "Community Integration and Incentives for Political Protest." *International Social Movement Research* 1 (1988): 83–101.

Özcan, E. *Türkische Immigrantenorganisationen in der Bundesrepublik Deutschland.* Berlin-West: Hitit Verlag, 1989.

Özdemir, C. *Ich bin Inländer: Ein anatolischer Schwabe im Bundestag.* Munich: Premium, 1997.

Parekh, B. "The Concept of National Identity." *New Community* 21, no. 2 (1995).

———. "Discourses on National Identity." *Political Studies* 42, no. 3 (1994).

Perotti, A. "Pour une politique d'immigration." *Études* (September 1992): 191–202.

Phillips, A. *Democracy and Difference.* Philadelphia: Pennsylvania University Press, 1993.

———. *The Politics of Presence: Issues in Democracy and Group Representation.* Oxford: Calderon Press, 1995.

Pickus, N.M.J., ed. *Immigration and Citizesnhip in the Twenty-first Century.* Boston: Rowman and Littlefield, 1998.

Ponty, J. *Polonais méconnus: Histoire des travailleurs immigrés en France dans l'entre-deux-guerres.* Paris: Éditions de la Sorbonne, 1988.

Portes, A., and R. G. Rumbaut. *Immigrant America: A Portrait.* Berkeley: University of California Press, 1990.

Portes, A., and M. Zhou. "The New Second Generation: Segmented Assimilation and Its Variants." *Annals*, no. 530 (1993): 74–96.

Puskeppeleit, J., and D. Thränhardt. *Vom betreuten Ausländer zum gleichberechtigten Bürger.* Freiburg: Lambertus, 1990.

Radtke, F. O. "Lob der Gleich Gültigkeit: Zur Konstruktion des Fremden im Diskurs des Multikulturalismus." In *Das Eigene und das Fremde*, edited by U. Bielefeld, 79–96. Hamburg: Junius, 1991.

———. "Multikulturelle: Das Gesellschaftsdesign der 90er Jahre?" *Informationsdienst zur Ausländerarbeit* 4, no. 90 (1990): 27–34.

———. "Sozialangst und reaktiver Nationalismus in West-Europa: Probleme der Entethnisierung der Politik: Ein Rückblick auf das Jahr 1988." *Informationsdienst zur Ausländerarbeit*, no. 1 (1989): 65–71.

Rawls, J. *Political Liberalism.* New York: Columbia University Press, 1993.

Raynaud, D. "De la tyrannie de la majorité à la tyrannie des minorités." *Le débat*, no. 69 (1992): 50–59.

Raz, J. "Multiculturalism: A Liberal Perspective." *Dissent* (winter 1994): 67–79.

Rex, J. *Ethnic Identity and Ethnic Mobilization in Britain.* Monographs in Ethnic Relations, no. 5, Centre for Research in Ethnic Realtions, Warwick, 1991.

Rex, J., D. Joly, and C. Wilpert. *Immigrant Associations in Europe.* Studies in European Migration. Aldershot: Gower, 1987.

Reynaud, E. "Groupes secondaires et solidarité organique: Qui exerce le contrôle social?" *L'année sociologique* 33 (1983): 181–94.

———. "Identités collectives et changement social: Les cultures collectives comme dynamique d'action." *Sociologie du travail*, no. 2 (1982).

Reynaud, J.-D. *Les règles du jeu: Régulation sociale et action collective.* Paris: A. Colin, 1989.

Rogers, R. *Guests Come to Stay: The Effects of European Labor Migration on Sending and Receiving Countries.* Boulder, Colo.: Westview Press, 1985.

Rokkan, S., and C. Tilly, eds. *The Formation of National States in Western Europe.* Princeton: Princeton University Press, 1974.

Roman, J., ed. *Ville, exclusion et citoyenneté.* Paris: Éditions Esprit, 1992.

Rosanvallon, P. *L'État en France, de 1798 à nos jours.* Paris: Éditions du Seuil, 1990.

———. *La nouvelle question sociale: Repenser l'État-Providence.* Paris: Éditions du Seuil, 1995.

———. The New Social Question (trans. Barbara Harshav). Princeton: Princeton University Press, 2000.

Rouland, N., and H. Giordon, eds. *Les minorités en Europe: Droits linguistiques et droits de l'homme.* Paris: Éditions Kimé, 1992.

Rufin, J.-C. "Minorités, nationalités, États." *Politique étrangère*, no. 3 (fall 1991): 629–42.

Safran, W. "The French State and Ethnic Minority Cultures: Policy Dimensions and Problems." In *Ethnoterritorial Politics, Policy, and the Western World*, edited by J. R. Rudolph Jr. and R. J. Thompson, 115–57. Boulder, Colo: Lynne Rienner Publishers, 1989.

———. "State, Nation, National Identity, and Citizenship: France as a Test Case." *International Political Science Review* 12, no. 3 (1991): 219–38.

Sayad, A. *Immigration et paradoxes de l'altérité.* Brussels: De Boeck, 1991.

Schain, M. "Ordinary Politics: Immigrants, Direct Action, and the Political Process in France." *French Politics and Society* 12, no. 2–3 (1994): 65–83.

Schlesinger, A. M., Jr. *The Disuniting of America: Reflections on a Multicultural Society.* New York: W. W. Norton, 1992.

Schmidt, P., and S. Weick. "Intégration sociale des étrangers en Allemagne." *Revue de l'OFCE*, no. 69 (April 1999): 267–76.

Schnapper, D. *La communauté des citoyens.* Paris: Gallimard, 1994.

———. *La France de l'intégration: Sociologie de la nation en 1990.* Paris: Gallimard, 1991.

Schor, R. *L'opinion française et les étrangers, 1919–1939.* Paris: Publications de la Sorbonne, 1985.

Schuck, P. H., and R. M. Smith. *Citizenship without Consent: Illegal Aliens in the American Polity.* New Haven: Yale University Press, 1985.

Schultze, G. "Première et deuxième générations de migrants turcs en RFA: Mobilité professionnelle et son incidence sur le processus d'intégration." Paper presented at Strasbourg, February 2, 1991.

Segrestin, D. "Les communautés pertinentes de l'action collective: Canevas pour l'étude des fondements sociaux des conflits du travail en France." *Revue française de sociologie* 21 (1980): 171–203.

Seligman, A. B. *The Idea of Civil Society.* New York: Free Press, 1992.

————. *The Problem of Trust.* Princeton: Princeton University Press, 1997.

Silverman, M. *Deconstructing the Nation: Immigration, Racism, and Citizenship in Modern France.* New York: Routledge, 1992.

Skinner, Q. "The State." In *Political Innovation and Conceptual Change*, edited by T. Ball, J. Farr, and R. L. Hansin. Cambridge: Cambridge University Press, 1989.

Skocpol, T. *States and Social Revolutions: A Comparative Analysis of France, Russia, and China.* New York: Cambridge University Press, 1979.

Skocpol, T., and E. Amenta. "States and Social Policies." *American Sociological Review*, no. 12 (1986): 131–57.

Smith, A. D. "Ethnic Myths and Ethnic Revivals." *Archives européennes de sociologie* 25, no. 2 (1984): 283–305.

————. "National Identity and the Idea of European Unity." *International Affairs* 68 (1992): 55–76.

————. "The Origins of Nations." *Ethnic and Racial Studies* 12, no. 3 (July 1989): 340–67.

Smith, J. "Communities, Associations, and the Supply of Collective Goods." *American Journal of Sociology* 2 (1982): 291–308.

Smith, R. M. *Civic Ideals: Conflicting Visions of Citizenship in U.S. History.* New Haven: Yale University Press, 1997.

Smith, T. L. "Religion and Ethnicity in America." *American Historical Review* 83, no. 5 (December 1978): 1155–85.

Sowell, T. "A World View of Cultural Diversity." *Society* 29, no. 1 (November/December 1991): 37–44.

Soysal, Y. *Limits of Citizenship: Migrants and Postnational Membership in Europe.* Chicago: University of Chicago Press, 1994.

Spinner, J. *The Boundaries of Citizenship: Race, Ethnicity, and Nationality in the Liberal State.* Baltimore: Johns Hopkins University Press, 1994.

Stack, J. F., Jr. "Ethnic Mobilization in World Politics: The Primordial Perspective." In *The Primordial Challenge: Ethnicity in the Contemporary World*, edited by J. F. Stack Jr., 1–12. Westport, Conn.: Greenwood Press, 1986.

Sudre, F. *Droit international et européen des droits de l'homme.* Paris: PUF, 1995.

Swidler, A. "Culture in Action: Symbols and Strategies." *American Sociological Review* 51 (April 1986): 273–86.

Taguieff, P. A. *La force des préjugés: Essai sur le racisme et ses doubles.* Paris: La découverte, 1988.

————. "Nationalisme et réactions fondamentalistes en France." *Vingtième siècle: Revue d'histoire* (January–March 1990): 49–73.

————, ed. *Face au racisme.* 2 vols. Paris: La découverte, 1991.

Tarrow, S. "National Politics and Collective Action: Recent Theory and Research in Western Europe and the United States." *American Review of Sociology* 14 (1988): 421–40.

Taylor, C. "Les institutions dans la vie nationale." In *Rapprocher les solitudes: Écrits sur le fédéralisme et le nationalisme au Canada*, edited by G. Laforest, 135–53. Sainte-Foy: Presses de l'Université de Laval, 1992).

————. *Multiculturalism and the "Politics of Recognition": An Essay.* Princeton: Princeton University Press, 1992.

Thompson, R. J., and J. R.Rudolph Jr. "Ethnic Politics and Public Policy in Western Societies: A Framework for Comparative Analysis." In *Ethnicity, Politics, and Development*, edited by D. L. Thompson and D. Ronen, 25–64. Boulder, Colo.: Lynne Rienner Publishers, 1986.

Tilly, C. "Migration in Modern European History." In *Human Migration Patterns and Policies*, edited by W. H. McNeill and R. S. Adams, 48–69. Bloomington: Indiana University Press, 1978.

———. "Reflections on the History of European State-Making." In *The Formation of National States in Western Europe*, edited by C. Tilly, 3–83. Princeton: Princeton University Press, 1975.

———. "Transplanted Networks." In *Immigration Reconsidered: History, Sociology, and Politics*, edited by V. Yans-McLaughlin, 79–95. New York: Oxford University Press, 1990.

Tocqueville, A. de. *Democracy in America*. Edited by J. P. Mayer and Max Lerner. Translated by George Lawrence. New York: Harper & Row, 1966.

Todd, E. *Le destin des immigrés: Assimilation et ségrégation dans les démocraties occidentales*. Paris: Éditions du Seuil, 1994.

Todorov, T. *Nous et les autres: La réflexion française sur la diversité humaine*. Paris: Éditions du Seuil, 1989.

Toinet, M.-F., ed. *L'État en Amérique*. Paris: Presses de la FNSP, 1989.

Touraine, A. *Qu'est-ce que la démocratie?* Paris: Fayard, 1994.

Treibel, A. *Engagement und Distanzierung in der westddeutschen Ausländerforschung: Eine untersuchung ihrer soziologischen Beiträge*. Stuttgart: F. Enke Verlag, 1988.

———. *Migration in modernen Gesellschaften soziale folgen von Einwanderung und Gastarbeit, grundlagentexte Soziologie*. Weinheim: Juventa Verlag, 1990.

Tribalat, M. *Cent ans d'immigration en France*. Paris: PUF, 1989.

———. *Faire France: Une grande enquête sur les immigrés et leurs enfants*. Paris: La découverte, 1995.

———, ed. *Insertion et mobilité géographique*. Report INED, INSEE, March 1995.

Tripier, M. *L'immigration dans la classe ouvrière en France*. Paris: L'Harmattan, 1990.

Tully, J. *Strange Multiplicity: Constitutionalism in an Age of Diversity*. Cambridge: Cambridge University Press, 1995.

Turner, B. S. "Outline of a Theory of Citizenship." *Sociology*, no. 24 (1990): 189–217.

———. "Personhood and Citizenship." *Theory, Culture, and Society* 3 (1986): 1–16.

Valensi, L. "La tour de Babel: Groupes et relations ethniques au Moyen-Orient et en Afrique du Nord." *Annales ESC*, no. 4 (July–August 1986): 817–38.

Venske, H.-T. *Islam und Integration: Zur Bedeutung des Islam im Prozess der Integration türkischer Arbeiterfamilien in der Gesellschaft der Bundesrepublik*. Hamburg, 1981.

Von Krockow, C. *Les Allemands du XXe siècle, 1890–1990: Histoire d'une identité*. Paris: Hachette, 1990.

Von Thadden, R. "Allemagne, France: Comparaisons." *Le genre humain* (February 1989): 62–72. Special issue: *Émigrer, immigrer.*

———. *Nicht Vaterland, nicht Fremde: Essays zu Geschichte und Gegenwart.* Munich: C. H. Beck, 1989.

Wacquant, L. "Banlieues françaises et ghetto américain: De l'amalgame à la comparaison." *French Politics and Society* 10, no. 4 (1992).

Walklerstein, I. "The Construction of Peoplehood: Racism, Nationalism, Ethnicity." In *Sociological Forum* 2, no. 2 (1987): 373–88.

Walzer, M. "The Civil Society Argument." In *Dimensions of Radical Democracy: Pluralism, Citizenship, and Community*, edited by C. Mouffe. London: Verso, 1992.

———. *On Toleration.* New Haven: Yale University Press, 1997.

———. *What It Means to Be an American: Essays on the American Experience.* New York: Marsilio, 1994.

Waters, M. *Ethnic Options: Choosing Identities in America.* Berkeley: University of California Press, 1990.

Waters, M. C., and V. Leiter. "The Intergenerational Transmission of Race Identity in the 1980 Census." Paper presented at the American Sociological Annual Meeting, August 1989.

Weber, E. *From Peasants into Frenchmen: Modernization of Rural France, 1870–1914.* Stanford: Stanford University Press, 1979.

Webster,Y. O. *The Racialization of America.* New York: St. Martin's Press, 1992.

Weil, P. *La France et ses étrangers: L'aventure d'une politique d'immigration, 1938–1991.* Paris: Calmann-Lévy, 1991.

———. *Mission d'étude de la législation de la nationalité et de l'immigration.* Paris: La documentation Française, 1997.

Weil, P., and R. Hansen, eds. *Nationalité et citoyenneté en Europe.* Paris: La découverte, 1999.

Weiner, M. "Labor Migrations as Incipient Diasporas." In *Modern Diasporas in International Politics*, edited by G. Sheffer, 47–74. London: Croom Helm, 1986.

Welch-Guerra, M. "La rénovation urbaine à Berlin depuis 1989: La grande transformation." *La recherche sur la ville en Allemagne*, 77–79. Actes des journées franco-allemandes du PIR Villes, March 28–29, 1994. Paris: CNRS éditions.

White, N. R. "Ethnicity, Culture, and Cultural Pluralism." *ERS* 1, no. 2 (April 1978): 139–53.

Wievorka, M., ed. *La société fragmentée: Le multiculturalisme en débat.* Paris: La découverte, 1996.

Withol de Wenden, C. *Les immigrés et la politique.* Paris: Presses de la FNSP, 1988.

Yahiel, M. "Le FAS: Questions de principe." *Revue européenne des migrations internationales* 4, nos. 1 and 2 (1988).

Yancey, W. L., E. P. Ericksen, and R. N. Juliani. "Emergent Ethnicity: A Review and Reformulation." *American Sociological Review* 41, no. 3 (June 1976): 391–403.

Yans-McLaughlin, V., ed. *Immigration Reconsidered: History, Sociology, and Politics*. New York: Oxford University Press, 1990.

Yinger, J. M. "Ethnicity." *Annual Review of Sociology* 11:151–80.

Young, C. *The Politics of Cultural Pluralism*. Madison: University of Wisconsin Press, 1976.

Young, I. M. *Justice and the Politics of Difference*. Princeton: Princeton University Press, 1990.

Zolberg, A. R. "Beyond the Nation-State: Comparative Politics in Global Perspective." In *Beyond Progress and Development: Macro-Political and Macro-Societal Change*, edited by J. Berting and W. Blockmans, 42–69. Aldershot: Gower Publishing Company, 1987.

Zolberg, A., and Long Litt Woon. "Why Islam Is like Spanish: Cultural Incorporation in Europe and the United States." *Politics and Society* 27, no. 1 (1999): 5–38.

Index